Natural Histories

Natural Histories
Stories from the Tennessee Valley

Stephen Lyn Bales

With a Foreword by
Sam Venable

Outdoor Tennessee Series • Jim Casada, Series Editor

The University of Tennessee Press / Knoxville

The Outdoor Tennessee Series covers a wide range of topics of interest to the general reader, including titles on the flora and fauna, the varied recreational activities, and the rich history of outdoor Tennessee. With a keen appreciation of the importance of protecting our state's natural resources and beauty, the University of Tennessee Press intends the series to emphasize environmental awareness and conservation.

All illustrations are by the author.

This book is printed on acid-free paper.

Bales, Stephen Lyn.
Natural histories : stories from the Tennessee Valley / Stephen Lyn Bales; with a foreword by Sam Venable. — 1st ed.
    p. cm. — (Outdoor Tennessee series)
Includes index.
ISBN-13: 978-1-57233-561-5 (pbk. : alk. paper)
ISBN-10: 1-57233-561-0 (pbk. : alk. paper)
1. Natural history—Tennessee River Valley.
2. Seasons—Tennessee River Valley.
I. Title.

QH104.5.T46B35 2007
508.768—dc22   2006024474

To Lindalee,
whose love of possibilities makes all things possible

The deep, boundless forest surrounded the banks on either side, growing close down into the water, with its long branches, twisted roots, and graceful drooping foliage mirrored in the blue expanse o'ver which it cast rich deep shadows, and broken here and there by a streak of light, the flash of an arrowy-darting fish, or the dip of a swooping swallow. . . .

How different, thought I, as I sat smoking a cigar on the stern of the boat, watching the rainbows forming in the spray of the wheel, and the forming and vanishing of beautiful vistas where the river came to a point in the perspective, shifting and changing each moment as every stroke of the paddles altered the point of view of the living panorama before my eyes—how different this cool, quiet, delightful scene, of mountain and hill, and wood and limped water—this picture of wondrous beauty, far away in the wilds of Tennessee—this romantic river of the wilderness. . . .

Here was a dark wood; there a rustling canebrake rising sharp up from the water-line; here a little merry islet, a dense cluster of bushes and trees, so thick that you could see nothing but a mass of green leaves rising up pyramidally, tier above tier, in most picturesque fashion; there a green meadow or a waving field of young wheat—but these were rare; mostly the forest scenery in endless variety: a heron perched on the bleached and ragged branch of a dead tree; a flock of wild ducks floating on the water, or, startled by the puffing steamer, flying circling around with wild screams; the delicious flower fragrance of the wild grapes wafted through the cool evening air; such were the charms of the fair Tennessee. . . .

For miles above where the Connasauga, which deserves its beautiful name, comes out from the dark hills and forests, and mingles its waters with the broad blue Tennessee, the scenery is one continual fairy dream.

R. Lacy
"The Land of the Cherokee," 1851

Contents

Foreword

As their very name suggests, ironies tend to show up in the strangest places.

This observation never proved more true than on an April mid-morning in 2006, just as I was about to cross gurgling Bull Run Creek in rural Union County, Tennessee, en route to my truck after an unsuccessful hunt for wild turkeys.

"Unsuccessful" in the context of bagged game, you understand.

By every other measure, it had been a positively spectacular day. After a week of cloudy, damp, foggy conditions, the weather had turned gorgeous. The highland scenery I savored all morning—from a forest floor carpeted in trillium and bloodroot to the crowns of oaks dripping in catkin—might well have been lifted straight from the cover of a Cabela's catalog. The warm air hung heavy with the perfume of spring soil and the symphony of birdsong. Even the turkeys themselves had been cooperative enough to gobble temptingly, virtually on command. Then they gave me the slip. As usual.

But by now, the brilliant sunshine filtering through the thin canopy felt more like August than April. When I finally worked myself downhill to the banks of the creek, the long johns that had been so comfortable before daybreak were drenched with sweat. Just before rock-hopping across, I stopped for a moment and, for perhaps the dozenth time in the last ten minutes, removed my hunting cap to wipe my brow.

Just then, something caught my eye: the trunk of a streamside tree, its base uniformly ringed by beavers. Cap still in the grasp of two fingers, I knelt long enough to stroke the tip of another finger across the smooth indentations. And I couldn't help but chuckle at the bonnets-and-beavers connection.

You see, I'd just been reading the chapter about beavers in Lyn Bales's *Natural Histories: Stories from the Tennessee Valley*, specifically the part about how changes in men's hat fashions down through the centuries had sent this magnificent animal plunging toward the brink of extinction—and, happily, back to abundance once more. Of course, the camouflaged, baseball-style cap I was holding was a far cry from a stovepipe top hat of the seventeenth century, a rounded bowler from the nineteenth century, or a snappy fedora from the mid-twentieth.

Nonetheless, the symbolism wasn't lost on me. When those other styles of hats had been the fashion rage, beavers paid a heavy price—for it was their pelts that supplied the raw materials.

That's one of the beauties of Bales's narrative. Here is not only a trained naturalist and keen observer of the abundant flora and fauna of the Tennessee Valley region, but also a skilled writer who weaves into his stories the ever-changing, and yet never-changing, interplay these same plants and animals have shared with human beings, past and present.

Libraries brim with books about wildlife and the environmental stewardship necessary for its welfare. Just looking across my office right now, I count more than 150 volumes in one bookcase alone. Their subjects range from waterfowl to grouse, bass to trout, woodcock to doves, and dozens in between. Each, in its own way, stresses the need for suitable habitat if the particular animal is expected to survive, let alone flourish.

But rarely does any single text paint the proverbial "big picture" any better than *Natural Histories.* Reading Bales's book, I'm reminded of Aldo Leopold's classic work, *A Sand County Almanac,* which set the standard for illustrating the interrelationship between all living things on this planet.

Impact one, and you impact all the others. It's a natural law as old as time. Alas, it's also a law that continues to be broken, invariably with dire consequences.

Consider Bales's fascinating chapter on the American toad (which, by the way, provides a comical, colorful diversion into the root of the word "toady"; I won't spoil it for you with details here).

"In the southeastern United States, forty-six species of amphibians are currently listed as being 'imperiled,' a term now being used to mean endangered, threatened, or in need of monitoring," he writes. "Of these, thirty-nine are salamanders, and seven are frogs. It appears that the region is not experiencing the dramatic population declines that are happening in the rest of the world, but herpetologists are quick to point out that that may be the result of a lack of historical data, which makes it difficult to establish a baseline for comparison. Most will also say that amphibian habitat in the area is rapidly being destroyed, fragmented, or degraded in some way. Amphibians have not garnered the attention or research funding that game animals like wild turkey, white-tailed deer, or even many sport fishes have received. Some might even argue that salamanders, frogs, and toads are not that important in the overall scheme of things, and that if we lose a few, so what? It's as though there are two lists: one for animals that have an economic value and one for those that do not. Yet, many of the creatures that would find themselves on the latter list are part of the food chain that supports the glamorous ones on the former."

Again he reiterates the theme, this time in his treatise on freshwater mussels: "Because of human interference through water pollution, dam construction, erosion, channelization, fertilizer run-off, coal slurry spills, and commercial harvesting, populations of mussels have dropped sharply in the past 150 years. Any drop in biodiversity is a concern because it can create a domino effect, and few can predict which domino might be the last to fall. Famed Harvard professor E. O. Wilson is often asked: 'If enough species are extinguished, will the ecosystems collapse? And will the extinction of most other species follow soon afterward?' Wilson responds, 'The only answer anyone can give is: possibly. By the time we find out, however, it might be too late. One planet, one experiment.' Or in my case, one valley."

To quote an auto-repair advertising slogan of yesteryear: "You can pay me now or pay me later." Be not deceived or lulled into a false sense of security. At some time, the bill will most assuredly come due. More than likely with a substantial rate of interest.

Yes, there are some very somber portions of this book, most dealing with calamitous social and ecological havoc wreaked by the arrival of Europeans to this continent, starting with Hernando de Soto in 1540. In addition to introducing a variety of deadly new diseases to the so-called "new" world, de Soto and his explorers systematically and brutally plundered their way through the territory.

Bales also uses the plight of the Cherokees to set the historic stage for many of his essays, particularly the Indians' intimate role with the natural resources of this area. As any student of American history will attest, this role largely ended with the genocidal, forced removal of these people—under the authority of the United States government, no less—in 1838–39. Bales's chapter on river cane, a plant of vital importance to the natives, delves deeply into this tragedy. If you can read his account of the infamous Trail of Tears and not feel an abiding sense of grief, anger, and injustice, ice water flows through your veins.

Bales's unique feel for history shows up in other ways. His chapter on Osage orange includes a riveting episode of how this thorny tree played an integral role in the bloody and decisive Battle of Franklin during the Civil War. On a much more pleasant note, he makes a historic journey birdwatchers everywhere should appreciate: on December 1, 2002, precisely one century after the first Christmas Bird Count in Knoxville, he retraces the steps of the city's first avian census taker and compares inventories.

There's plenty of pure entertainment to be found in these pages. Until I read this book, I'd never heard of Grey Owl, "a backwoodsman, fur trapper, wilderness guide, and park ranger in Alberta and Saskatchewan, Canada." In the 1930s, Grey Owl's poignant writing and passionate oratory made him one of the nation's most heralded and prominent spokesman for environmental awareness. Indeed, Grey Owl performed a significant role in shaking the American psyche and planting the first seeds of ecological concern.

This is a book to be read for enjoyment as well as instruction. With Bales as your guide, you will taste flavorful pawpaws in September, listen to whip-poor-wills and chuck-will's-widows in May, marvel at how chickadees in January regulate their body temperatures to cope with frigid conditions, watch the explosion of a year-class of cicadas in mid-summer, and share his joy at the first sighting of a homegrown bald eagle.

Not only do his words come alive with description; his drawings do, too. In a rare combination of talents, Lyn Bales is a gifted illustrator as well as author. Each chapter begins with one of his sketches, demonstrating the plant or animal being featured.

"It is said that Thoreau carried two notebooks with him as he walked around his beloved New England," Bales observes in one entry. "One notebook was to record things he saw in nature, and the other for poetry he was inspired to write. There were times when he encountered something that thrilled him so that he wouldn't know which notebook to record it in. In other words, nature itself is sheer poetry. Therein lies the conundrum for the nature writer. Do you write with your head or your heart, or try to balance precariously somewhere in between the two?"

Not a problem here. Lyn Bales strikes a perfect balance every time.

Sam Venable
Columnist, *Knoxville News Sentinel*

Acknowledgments

Special thanks to Scot Danforth, the editor who saw the merit of this project, and to my parents, Helen and Russ, and sister, Darlene, who have always seen the merit in me.

This book would not exist without Lindalee, who proofread the work and was there for the entire process, seeing me through the highs and the lows.

Books are not easy creatures to wrestle into this world. They are surprisingly evanescent and can easily be slowed to a wisp and twinkle away. Luckily for me there were people who helped keep the adventure alive through their positive support. Because of this and a host of other reasons, I would be remiss not to sincerely thank Pam Petko-Seus and Paul James for their kindness and genuine reassurance, as well as Mary Thom Adams, Vickie Henderson, Sam Venable, and Dr. Guy Smoak for cheering me along.

Portions of this book have appeared in other forms in the *farragutpress, Hellbender Press,* and *West Side Story;* special thanks to the editors of those publications—Dan Barile, Thomas Fraser, and Rikki Hall—for their continuing support.

Books are not created in a vacuum. In addition to Scot, I'd like to thank the staff of UT Press—Jennifer Siler, Gene Adair, Kelly Gray, Cheryl Carson, and Tom Post—for helping this book along.

I also want to thank the board of Ijams Nature Center and its staff—Peg, Todd, Ed, Misty, Patti, Marielle, Ben, Kara, Kelley, Sean, Alison, Louise—and all of the many, many people who took the time along the way to talk to me and answer my questions. I admire people who dedicate their lives to honorable causes.

I should also acknowledge the importance of Henry David Thoreau, Loren Eiseley, David Attenborough, Ken Burns, James Burke, and, of course, Annie Dillard, who opened the door and showed me that art and science are unequivocally linked; both embody humankind's most noble aspirations.

Introduction

There comes a time in everyone's young life when he or she realizes that the world is wide indeed. Growing up in Gatlinburg, Tennessee, in the shadows of towering Mt. LeConte, mountains were all I had known until I became old enough to gaze out of the back window of our '49 Ford Coupe. On family trips to the big city, we'd pass through Sevierville and head west along Chapman Highway, U.S. 441. North of Chilhowee Mountain, in Seymour, I noticed that the terrain begins to open up as the highlands give way to rolling fields and grassy pastures. Passing through the tip of Blount County, we'd enter Knox County from the south, zipping past a dizzying array of small businesses, fruit stands, and used car lots that clung to the highway like ants to sugar water—establishments like French's Market, the white and windowless Farmer Dan's, and the Sleepy Hungry Tired and Sunset motels. Closer to the city I'd see the Ol' Smoky Tourist Court, the much-beloved Young High School, Babe Maloy's Drive In, and the Hill Top Market just before Cas Walker's, the brick building of Kern's Bakery, and a three-story-tall RC Cola sign with a giant smiling face that rocked back and forth, showing its obvious approval of the popular soft drink. The wonderfully kitschy billboard was amazing, but it, like most commercial signage, had the permanence of early morning mist. The pop culture cola advertisement sat opposite Baptist Hospital, and it was there, where Old Maryville Pike intersects Chapman Highway, that we'd cross the Henley Bridge over the Tennessee River. At the time it was the biggest body of water I had ever seen. Today I live less than a mile from that great river, and like so many before me, I now call the valley my home.

From a loftier vantage point the Tennessee Valley is unmistakable. It carves through the mountainous terrain diagonally: northeast to southwest. To the east lie the rugged Appalachian Highlands, to the west the elevated and flattened Cumberland Plateau. The expanse is a continuation of Virginia's Shenandoah Valley that fades to the south into Alabama's gulf coastal plain. In East Tennessee the broad valley, wider to the north, is roughly forty-five miles across and two hundred miles long, but the gash through the southeastern mountains is not clean—it's ragged, as though routed by a chainsaw.

Geologists call the province "valley and ridge," for within the broad lowlands of the Tennessee Valley are numerous long, parallel ridges giving the valley the look of a plowed field. I live on one of these raised furrows: Chapman Ridge, just south of downtown Knoxville and the University of Tennessee. The valley's ridges are products of weathering, made up of erosion-resistant rock like sandstone and siltstone, while the valley floor itself is primarily shale and limestone, softer rock that has been dissolved away over time. The valley's limestone bedrock crumbles to yield sweet, alkaline soil—perfect for growing cedars, grasses, pastures, and fields.

Because the valley is centrally located, it's the northern-most limit of some tropical plants and the southern-most of some northern ones. During the last ice age, glacial ice never reached this far south, but the colder climate that spawned them forced northern trees, like the eastern hemlocks that grow near my driveway, to retreat south. In Shady Valley, in the northeastern part of the state, naturally occurring cranberry and sphagnum bogs can still be found today pushed south by the advancing ice sheets. Tropical trees like pawpaws and South American animals such as opossums moved north as the climate warmed.

Similarly, the valley is the summer nesting ground for many birds such as whip-poor-wills and cuckoos that spend their winters far to the south and the winter vacation retreats for northern species such as sapsuckers and hermit thrushes that spend their summers farther to the north.

The combined waterways of the Southeast lead all global temperate regions in total aquatic diversity, which is believed to be second only to the tropical Amazon River Basin. The World Wildlife Fund and Nature Conservancy report that the Tennessee River and Cumberland River basins have the highest number of fish, crayfish, and mussel species and the highest number of endemic species in North America, making it one of the most diverse river systems in the world. (The Cumberland flows into the Ohio River just north of the Land Between the Lakes in Kentucky.) The state of Tennessee has more than 315 species of fish, while 500 species can be found in the Southeast. The Tennessee River system has about 210 species of fish and hundreds of varieties of freshwater mussels, crayfish and aquatic insects. As Pat Rakes of Conservation Fisheries points out, "A single pool or reach in Little River in the Tennessee Valley can have more species of fish than several combined river watersheds, spanning multiple states in the American West."

While the last ice age was still in place, the first humans entered the valley roughly fifteen thousand years ago. They were nomadic hunters whose presence, a former campsite near Chattanooga, was first documented at a site called LeCroy. The Tennessee Valley they camped in was a very different place than the one we know today. Over the next several millennia other early Native Americans moved into the Southeast. They gave up their nomadic lifestyle and settled down to grow corn, beans, and squash. Eventually they organized themselves into territories called chiefdoms. A high chief reigned over each province, and great mounds were built at the heart of the towns the rulers called home. This way of life existed for thousands of years until it disintegrated after Spanish conqueror Hernando de Soto and his army marched though the Southeast in the mid-1500s. After the death, disease, and destruction caused by the Spaniards, the indigenous people slowly re-formed into the Cherokees, Creeks, Seminoles, Chickasaws, and Choctaws of the eighteenth and nineteenth centuries. The plants and animals they found around them were an integral part of their everyday lives. They made canoes from tulip tree and homes from river cane.

Seeking a stronger alliance with the Overhill Towns of the Cherokee, the British Colony of South Carolina built Fort Loudoun near the town of Chota during the winter of 1756–57. It was the first planned trans-Appalachian fort built by the English in East Tennessee. The relationship soon soured, and the garrison was forced to withdraw in August 1760. But that didn't stop the "new" Americans—trappers and traders followed by settlers of European ancestry—from pouring into the valley.

To the newly arriving pioneers, the territory beyond the Appalachians was the rugged, unknown West. Pioneers who moved there were known as "westerners." Traveling down from Pennsylvania, the restless Scotch-Irish progressed southwest through the Shenandoah Valley. The early settlers looked for cedars, sycamores, and river cane. The cedars were a sign of sweet pasture-loving soil, the sycamores an indication of good water, and the cane served as silage for their livestock. The settlers built homes from tulip trees and hunted wild turkey and deer. In 1769 they settled along the Watauga River near today's Elizabethton. These pioneers thought they were in the British colony of Virginia, only to learn two years later that their home was part of North Carolina instead. They sought protection and were denied, probably because their wilderness home was too remote to be governed. To establish law and order, the group formed their own government known as the Watauga Association, and the Wataugans became the first group of American-born settlers to create a free and independent community. The association was short-lived. After the American Revolution they became the "Lost State of Franklin," and finally the growing cluster of communities fell under the protection of the new state of Tennessee.

To sate the growing appetite for more land, the U.S. government rounded up the last of the native Cherokee and marched them at gunpoint from the valley in 1838. Thousands died. This shameful episode of American history is today known as the "Trail of Tears."

The sixteenth state took its name from the great river that flows through its boundaries, not once but twice. The first pass through the state—which includes the upper Tennessee River and its tributaries (the French Board, Holston, Clinch, Pigeon, Powell, Little Tennessee, Nolichucky, and Hiwassee rivers)—is the heart of the Tennessee Valley. Communities have formed along the shorelines of these rivers for thousands of years: first came the Native Americans, then the European newcomers.

It's the interaction between these peoples and the plants and animals they found in the valley that is the heart of this book. Call it the collision of human and natural history, for the advent of people has caused the greatest change to the valley's environment since the last ice age. Passenger pigeons and Carolina parakeets are no longer found in the skies over the valley, while European starlings and house sparrows are commonplace. For a time, turkeys, beavers, and eagles had all but disappeared, but with a little help they have returned, while bison and wolves are still missing. The latter have been replaced naturally by a burgeoning population of eastern coyotes.

Arguably, the Tennessee Valley Authority has been the boldest mover and shaker. The agency's construction of dams brought jobs and abundant electricity to the poor valley. It also changed the raging river into a series of controlled reservoirs that have been called the "Great Lakes of the South." In the process, several plants and animals have declined or been lost, while birds such as great blue herons, ospreys, and cliff swallows nest in places they've never been before.

There's an ebb and flow at play here, part of it natural and part human-related, but suffice it to say our influence has not always been negative. Working on this book, I've met many people who have dedicated their lives to restoring a balance to the biodiversity—variety of life—historically found here. Scientists know that the greater the variety, the healthier the environment.

It's this rich variety found in the Tennessee Valley that serves as the grist for the millstone of this project. This is not a natural history of the valley but rather a collection of natural histories of individual plants and animals. All the stories in this volume begin, end, or pass through the valley. As a writer, I simply followed the thread wherever it led. Interwoven, the threads form a tapestry. Surprisingly, the individual strands often took me not only through the greatest stories of East Tennessee history but through the great human stories of America as well.

Winter

Carolina Chickadee

Parus carolinensis

To the attentive eye, each moment of the year has its own beauty and in the same field, it beholds, every hour, a picture which was never seen before, and which shall never be seen again.

Ralph Waldo Emerson
Nature, 1836

The new year dawned pallid—no wonderland. A heavy gray sky hugged Chapman Ridge and the entire river valley like a sodden blanket. If the sun was still in its rightful place, you'd never know. Printmakers Currier and Ives would have found little to ballyhoo. But then again, things are not always as they seem.

A mixed flock of woodland birds chatted through: six chickadees, three titmice, a pair of kinglets, a nuthatch, and a downy woodpecker or two. The chickadees and titmice served as kingpins, keeping the group together by their constant vocalizations. Winter is a time for hunkering down, huddling up, and pooling one's resources, but chickadees rarely seem to give into the season. During the bleakest, coldest days of winter, their effervescence is often the perkiest part of any given day. As they lead their flock mates through the woods beyond our home, it's impossible not to notice their vitality. No wonder they're the ringleaders; their vigor is contagious. There are advantages in being part of a group; more foragers looking for food is a plus. Safety is another boon, with more eyes to watch the neighborhood tabby or the lurking Cooper's hawk, a bird-killer that hunts like a feline, with quiet stealth.

Later in the year, as the seasons warm in early spring, this group cooperation will vanish as the flocks break up and individual mated pairs establish nesting sites within the woods, but for now it's one for all and all for one.

The mixed winter flock of small birds is loosely formed, its dynamics constantly shifting. The flock changes as individual chickadees called "floaters" drift in and out of the mix. These birds are opportunists, looking to break into the group's dominance hierarchy and take the place of an established bird—and perhaps its mate—should the senior member be killed. Within each flock, each bird postures to improve its position in the pecking order. Pair formation is also an important part of the social structure. Studies of black-capped chickadees reveal that a floater that pairs with a dominant mate improves its position profoundly. Openings created by the death of a low-ranked individual usually go unfilled. For an unmatched floater it's better to drift in and out of different flocks, waiting for an opening in the higher ranks. Why is this? Researcher Susan Smith speculates that there's no guarantee that a low-ranked pair will get to nest locally; they may be driven out of the neighborhood by high-ranked pairs when breeding season starts. So, it's better for the unmated floater to keep its options open and wait for the inevitable opening among the higher ranked birds. All it has to do is drift from flock to flock and seize the moment—*carpe diem.* This leads me to another speculation. Because floaters have a wider range, moving from flock to flock, wouldn't they get a better sense of a broader area, information that would serve them well if they are able to move quickly into the high ranks?

It's generally believed that chickadees mate for life, which means until one of the mated pair dies, something that happens often. As a general rule, in the world of birds, 50 percent of the population of most species die each year. To overcome this high mortality, birds have to produce copious offspring. A typical pair of chickadees will raise a family of five each year; but a clutch of as many as eight is possible, and at times they'll generate two broods during nesting season. It's an arduous life but necessary. Few chickadees live longer than five years.

Depending on the territory and availability of food, a mixed winter flock can have anywhere between two and eighteen chickadees, although six to ten is the norm. There may be more than one flock in a given location, and the separate flocks may merge at times to work together. If the mixed flock contains several nuthatches, kinglets, and woodpeckers, the actual number of chickadees may be smaller. Suburban neighborhoods with lots of bird feeders tend to have larger flocks. If food sources become scarce, chickadees higher in the pecking order will drive away the lower-ranked birds.

Chickadees are small songbirds of woodlands and suburbia—just a handful of feathers held together by an intense will to live. I recall a Carolina chickadee that smashed into a window at a family Thanksgiving several years ago. Alarmed, eight-year-old Leigh-Anna and I rushed to it. Picking it up, we held it as it twitched, apparently dying, its head askew; then it trembled, righted itself, blinked, and flew away. Its death rattle had not yet come.

Bird expert and author David Allen Sibley lists the weight of a chickadee at 0.37 ounce (about the same as two U.S. quarters). It would take forty-three Carolina chickadees to make a pound, fewer if they're soaking wet. With little body fat and a high metabolism, these tiny dynamos search for food almost unceasingly.

A chickadee's daytime temperature rises to about 108 degrees, but on a cold night in January they can lower it to around 86 degrees using controlled hypothermia. This ability to go into a nightly torpor is called "noctivation," and it saves valuable energy. During this downtime, if they're startled, they can still fly but only feebly.

At first light they're searching again for new food sites or tidbits they've cached since fall. The autumnal chickadee has to grow a new brain, or at least part of one. Studies show that a chickadee's hippocampus fluctuates in size with the seasons. In the fall it enlarges as the bird changes from purely a forager to a hunter-gatherer. The increased hippocampus helps the bird remember where it hoards its foodstuffs. As the seasons cool, chickadees change from eating mostly insects to a more mixed diet. Seed collecting becomes important. They also begin to hide most of the food they find—a seed here and a dead moth there. They'll cram their piecemeal larder under bits of lichen, loose bark, or sprigs of verdant pine needles. Each piece of food is separately stashed and memorized. Surprisingly, they seem to have the ability to remember just where they've stored hundreds, perhaps thousands, of food-bits. It's called "scatter hoarding"—spreading the wealth—a strategy that works even though up to 20 percent of the chickadee's hoarded food may be lost to foraging squirrels and nuthatches that hear what naturalist Robert Michael Pyle calls "serendipity's whisper."

There are currently seven chickadee species listed in North America. Two have limited ranges: the Mexican chickadee is the southernmost, while the hardy gray-headed chickadee, once known as the Siberian tit, is a subarctic species found only in northern Alaska and Canada. The black-capped and Carolina chickadees are the most common species. The two are closely related and virtually identical in appearance. Yet, side-by-side, you'd notice that the Carolina is slightly smaller and somewhat drabber and that it has a shorter tail. Their breeding songs are also noticeably different: the black-capped has a whistled three-note song, *fee bee-be*, while the Carolina's song is a four-note *fee-bee fee-bay*.

Both species have wide ranges: the black-capped is found in the northern half of the United States, extending into Canada; the Carolina is found in the Southeast. Both occur in East Tennessee, but while the black-capped chickadee lives only in the higher elevations of the Appalachians, the Carolina chickadee is found at lower elevations and far and wide throughout the Tennessee Valley. Despite their close proximity, the breeding ranges of the two species don't really overlap, and it is believed that they rarely interbreed.

Chickadees are highly social. On February 9, 1854, Henry David Thoreau recorded the following in his journal:

> I do not hear Therien's axe far of late. The moment I came on his chopping-ground, the chickadees flew to me, as if glad to see me. They are a peculiarly honest and sociable little bird. I saw them go to his pail repeatedly and peck his bread and butter. They came and went a dozen times while I stood there. He said that a great flock of them came round him the other day while he was eating his dinner and lit on his clothes 'just like flies.' One roosted on his finger, and another pecked a piece of bread in his hand. They are considerable company for the woodchopper.

A consummate observer, Thoreau is best known for his book about his two years living alone on Walden Pond. But his most formidable work is a handwritten journal he kept from 1837 to 1862. He missed few details around his Concord, Massachusetts, home, and he often wrote of the lively chickadees. On January 12, 1860, this country's seminal nature writer recorded:

> As I stand by the hemlocks, I am greeted by the lively and unusually prolonged *tche de de de de de* of a little flock of chickadees. The snow has ceased falling, the sun comes out, and it is warm and still, and this flock of chickadees, little birds that perchance were born in their midst, feeling the influences of this genial season, have begun to flit amid the snow-covered fans of the hemlocks, jarring down the snow—for there are hardly bare twigs enough for them to rest on—or they plume themselves in some snug recess on the sunny side of the tree, only pausing to utter their *tche de de de*.

There's a curious irony at work here: Thoreau, the transcendental loner, caught up in the chattering lives of the gregarious chickadees, like a bystander quietly watching the festivities of an impromptu party. Yet, this is more than just reticent voyeurism. All nature writers share the secret. It's impossible not to feel totally alive and "in the moment" when witnessing such scenes in nature. You want to shout with joy or, at least, wax poetic: "I, too, am alive!" Even on the coldest day, a chickadee's energy is infectious. The tableau the master of Walden is describing—chickadees foraging through snow—is one of the great winter dramas. I've watched it dozens of times, bundled and pink-cheeked, always wondering: how do these little sprites survive this harsh season?

Part of what helps them endure may be the use of their own semi-language. Yes, language. The *tche de de de* Thoreau refers to is the often-uttered, highly variable call made by the elfin songbirds. Chickadees, in fact, get their name from the call they make: *chick-a-dee-dee-dee,* although Thoreau the scientist would have been delighted to learn that there is more to the phrase than a sing-along name. *Chick-a-dee-dee-dee* calls vary. They have hidden nuance. According to Todd Freeberg, assistant professor of psychology at the University of Tennessee, a highly social animal needs a complex system of communication. As the group size increases, social organization and interaction becomes more complicated; human beings are a perfect example. Freeberg first became interested in chickadee communication in Indiana in the early 1990s when he read a paper by Jack Hailman and Millicent Fieken. The account reported on the chickadee's communication skills. Skeptical, Freeberg began his own investigation of chickadee calls, first in Indiana and later in Tennessee. In addition to noting behavior, he made audio recordings and produced visual representations (called sonograms) of the calls, looking for hidden syntax.

Buried within the chick-a-dee-dee-dees, his Indiana recordings found four note types he labeled A, B, C, and D. The high-frequency A notes "virtually always" came first, and the lower-frequency D notes, if they occurred, "virtually always" came last. If Bs occurred, they followed the higher As, and Cs, if present, preceded the D-note coda. To most human ears the calls happen so quickly they're gibberish. Yet, Freeberg and his colleague Jeffrey Lucas deciphered a subtle meaning. The presence of a C note seemed to coincide with the discovery of a new food source—a call-to-action, as if to say "hey troops, heads up. I found some food." The flock rallies and moves in to investigate. It's teamwork like this that helps the mixed flock survive winter.

"Isn't it interesting," remarked biologist Pam Petko-Seus, "that a chickadee would alert other chickadees to available food? You'd think it would want to keep it all to itself."

"It's an example of reciprocal altruism," answered Freeberg. "A sort of *quid pro quo.*" I'll show you where food is today, if you return the favor tomorrow. This also brings to mind the theories presented by famed Harvard biologist E. O. Wilson. His controversial 1975 book, *Sociobiology: the New Synthesis,* explored the origins and benefits of social behavior and the unselfish act of altruism. How does group behavior benefit individual chickadees and the likelihood that their genes are passed on to future descendents? Although Wilson's work primarily focuses on social insects—ants, termites, bees—it could apply to groups of all kinds. "How well does that group survive vis-à-vis other groups and vis-à-vis solitary individuals of the same species, and how well does that group produce its own kind?" asks Wilson. "For group [natural] selection to happen, all you need is one gene that would cause individuals to come together, and for some of them to be willing to be subordinated and become workers." Could there possibly be a bit of DNA that codes for altruism? But doesn't that fly in the face of survival of the fittest; dog eat dog; reproduce *your* genes or pass from this earth?

Follow-up studies conducted in Tennessee at Norris Dam State Park, the University of Tennessee Forest Resources Research and Education Center near Oak Ridge, and Ijams Nature Center in south Knoxville seem to suggest that the communication within the chickadee's call is even more complicated. Eight note types have now been isolated, which may be the components of the little bird's rudimentary language. Their avian lexicon may help the tiny social birds warn one another of predators, keep track of the number of birds in the flock, and communicate location and whether or not they are in flight or getting ready to be, as if to say, "I'm here now, but I'm getting ready to move on." All of this would serve a highly mobile flock well.

One secondary study conducted by UT graduate student Ellen Mahurin suggests that the Tennessee chickadees produce more D notes than C notes when a new food source is discovered. This contradicts Freeberg's earlier Indiana study, but it may be just a geographic variation or dialect difference between the two populations. Thoreau would have been captivated. One wonders: could his Walden birds have chattered to my Chapman Ridge troop?

Research conducted by Chris Templeton of the University of Washington in Seattle also suggests that black-capped chickadees have "one of the most sophisticated means of communication discovered in animals." His study indicates that if a chickadee detects a predator in the vicinity of its flock, it adds extra *dee* notes to the end of its *chick-a-dee-dee* call; the more dangerous the perceived threat, the more *dee* notes it adds. In this case, however, size matters. Smaller, more maneuverable predators illicit more *dees* than large birds of prey that would in truth have a hard time catching the sprightly chickadee's flock mates. Small predators like pygmy owls sometimes garner as many as twenty-three extra *dees* at the end of alerted chickadee's call.

There is an even more ominous cloud than winter hanging over this mixed flock, a plague that even teamwork cannot overcome. The newly imported West Nile virus has rapidly spread across North America, reducing bird populations in its wake. It first appeared in this country in New York in 1999, and by 2002 West Nile had moved to forty-four states and five provinces in Canada.

Birds play a part in the pathogen's modus operandi. They serve as unsuspecting hosts for the virus. Blood-sucking mosquitoes replicate the virus from one bird to the next and can spread the sickness to mammals they also bite. So far, the primary mammals made ill by West Nile are humans, horses, and a small number of squirrels, dogs, and cats.

The illness was first isolated in a feverish adult woman in the West Nile District of Uganda in Africa in 1937, but the virus didn't make the jump across the Atlantic until the late 1990s. By 2005 it had been reported in all forty-eight continental states, throughout Mexico, and in seven provinces in Canada. Since its introduction into this country, more than fifteen thousand people have contracted the illness and five hundred have died. Somewhat lost in the front page headlines is the enormous toll avian populations are suffering, for it's fatal to birds as well. Crows and blue jays are most often mentioned in newspaper accounts, but according to the U.S. Centers for Disease Control and Prevention (CDC), by 2002 West Nile virus had been found in 138 different species. Birds as different as bald eagles and ruby-throated hummingbirds are among those stricken.

Initial losses from the Midwest were alarming. Regions around Chicago were almost completely devoid of crows. In late summer 2002, between eight hundred and one thousand bird-of-prey deaths in Ohio may have been caused by the virus. The two species of raptors that seem to have been most affected were great horned owls and red-tailed hawks. Infected birds act disoriented, unaware of their surroundings. They lose the ability to stand and eat, and eventually they develop tremors and blindness before they die.

By October 2002 researchers wondered about the status of songbirds. As reported online by *Chicago Wilderness Magazine,* a study was initiated by the National Audubon Society and the Bird Conservation Network. Chickadees were chosen because of their known ubiquitous presence. A six-county region around Chicago was searched by seventy-four trained monitors. They found that the black-capped chickadee, the northern look-alike to the southern Carolina chickadee, was "completely extirpated in large areas." Twenty-two separate searches in one 120-square-mile area northwest of the city turned up only two chickadees. There should have been hundreds.

Bird enthusiasts everywhere were obviously alarmed by the apparent disappearance of chickadees in the Chicago area, but was the decline even more widespread than that? In the spring of 2003, David Bonter and Wesley Hochachka of the Cornell Laboratory of Ornithology conducted another study. They looked at the combined census data of two separate bird counts held during the winter 2002–03. The first, Project FeederWatch (PFW), is conducted by thousands of birdwatchers at backyard birdfeeders across the country. The second, the Audubon Christmas Bird Count (CBC), is held every winter at widely dispersed "count circles" fifteen miles in diameter. The advantage of the PFW data is that it's collected at thousands of locations; the disadvantage is that the count has only been going on since 1988 and in many areas even fewer years than that. The CBC data comes from more widespread locations, but the count has been going on for decades.

For the purpose of the study, Bonter and Hochachka combined all sightings of both the black-capped and the Carolina chickadees in the FeederWatch numbers. The data from the winter of 2002-03 was compared to that from the winter before and revealed that indeed chickadee populations had declined at 74 percent of 203 PFW sites in the upper Midwest and Northeast. Since the Christmas Bird Count has been taking place longer, Bonter and Hochachka were able to look at data from several count circles for the past thirty years. The CBC totals confirmed the PFW data and revealed that black-capped chickadees had declined at twenty-six of twenty-eight locations in the same parts of the country.

Surprisingly, though, the CBC data also revealed that the chickadee population had had other declines in the past thirty years. In fact, the 2002–03 decline was at most only the third-largest fluctuation recorded since the early 1970s. It's altogether possible that West Nile virus caused the most recent drop in chickadee numbers, but if that's so, what caused the earlier ones? Are sudden drops in population completely normal? And will the Chicago chickadees recover as they have before? Will surviving pairs produce more young? More clutches? And would they know their population was down? Do the chickadees do a head count during the winter flocking season? A verbal census? Is that information also hidden in their chatter?

At this point, no one knows what the long-term affect of West Nile virus will be on chickadees or other birds. Recent loses may just be a temporary blip on the radar. It may be commonplace for their populations to fluctuate. But, as for me, living in a world without the commonplace *chick-a-dee-dee-dees* is virtually impossible to imagine. One cannot help but wonder what Thoreau would have thought. His affection for the woodland pixies is obvious in his writings, as he noted on October 15, 1859: "The chickadees sing as if at home. They are not traveling singers hired by Barnum. Theirs is an honest, homely, heartfelt melody. Shall not the voice of man express as much content as the note of a bird?"

Thoreau was right to express concern about the voice of man, for when are human beings ever content? We're restless, to put it mildly. Needless to say, as I watch the mixed winter flock of small birds work its way over Chapman Ridge, chattering as they pass, I can't help but be apprehensive about what lies ahead; call it gray winter or cabin fever. That's why the chickadee's melody, honest and homely, is such a needed respite.

Yet, as any good naturalist knows, there's an ebb and flow in the natural world; manmade or otherwise, the pulse is unmistakable. There's fluidity to winter chickadee flocks, perhaps even to whole populations—a rise and fall, hither and thither, always in motion. Nature is an ethereal beast, filled with permutations, never quiescent; it's embarrassingly hard to pin down to anything constant. What is here one year may not be here the next, or vice versa. The valley I live in today is very different from the one that existed three hundred years ago. The dynamics are observable: all you have to do is apply Emerson's "attentive eye," and what lies ahead is truly anyone's guess.

River Cane
Arundinaria gigantea

The whole country was then almost untrod by the foot of the white
man. It was the hunting-ground of the Chickasaws, Creeks, and
Cherokees, and was full of deer, elk, bears, and buffaloes. The rich
uplands, as well as the alluvial bottoms of the rivers, were covered
with cane-brakes, which were almost impervious to man. Whoever
penetrated these regions, did so with knife and hatchet to cut away
the cane, and with rifle and hatchet to oppose the savage beasts
and savage men who swarmed through its deep fastnesses.

M.A.H.
"Historical Traditions of Tennessee," 1852

The European settlers were not the first people to live along the Tennessee River.
Several generations of Native Americans preceded their arrival. They first entered
the Southeast around fifteen thousand years ago—nomadic hunters who over
time essentially walked here from Asia, across a land bridge that formed between
the two continents during the last ice age. They were searching for large—now
extinct—mammals: mammoths, mastodons, ice age bison, and giant sloths, to
name a few. Their existence in the Tennessee Valley, a former camp near Chattanooga, was first documented at a site archaeologists call LeCroy.

Researchers specializing in the Southeastern Indians divide the timeframe
since LeCroy into four distinct cultural periods known as the Paleo-Indian,
Archaic, Woodland, and Mississippian Traditions. These societies eventually
evolved into the tribes that most of us are familiar with today. One of these
tribal groups, the Cherokee, lived in small villages sprinkled along the rivers.

They hunted and fished, grew corn and beans. Like all humans, they raised their children and grieved for their dead, felt disappointment over their failures, and, we can only assume, glowed with pride in their abilities to deal with life's obstacles. These first Tennesseans lived in the valley until they were forcibly removed in 1838.

At its height, the Cherokee Nation included parts of today's Georgia, Alabama, Tennessee, the western Carolinas, and Virginia—roughly forty thousand square miles that included the fertile Tennessee Valley. The word *Cherokee* had no meaning in their language and is probably of foreign origin. They called themselves *Ani'-Yun'wiya*, or the Principal People, and believed that their home was the center of the world.

Historically, the Cherokee were one of the tribes that coalesced into a common group after the collapse of their ancestors' way of life, known by historians as the Mississippian Tradition; it was a culture noted for large chiefdoms and extensive mound building. The Cherokee were a homogenous tribal group living in roughly eighty scattered towns with names like Chota, Toquo, Hiwassee, Tuskegee, and Tellico. There were seven clans that intermingled freely. The Cherokee had a matrilineal kinship system in which people traced their ancestors through their mother's family, not their father's. Everyone belonged to the clan of their mother; their only relatives came from that side of the family. All homes and land, as well as certain other property, were under the control of the matrilineal groups. Children sought guidance and support from their mother's brother more so than from their father, who was, after all, not related by blood to the matrilineal family. Thus, in Cherokee society, women were influential, and there were a few female chiefs. By and large, however, the men made the important tribal decisions and held the political power.

The Cherokee had a common culture, fought common enemies, and spoke three dialects of the same language. The dialects corresponded to three general divisions by location: the Lower Towns along the upper Savannah River in northern Georgia; the Middle or Valley Towns found in the watersheds of the Oconaluftee, Nantahala, and Little Tennessee Rivers in western North Carolina; and the Upper, or Overhill, Towns in East Tennessee. At the time of the first English contact, the Cherokee probably numbered between twenty and twenty-five thousand people.

The Cherokee religion was centered on maintaining harmony and balance. Unhappy marriages were dissolved at the annual Green Corn Ceremony, murder was avenged quickly—an eye for an eye—and owning more material possessions than was necessary to survive was frowned upon. Once you had everything you needed, why would you want anything more?

The Cherokee celebrated friendships at their annual *Atohuma*, or "friends made" festival. The relationships acknowledged were between two people, either of the same or opposite sex. During the celebration, the pair vowed eternal friendship or brotherly love as long as they lived. Also during *Atohuma*, friends who had quarreled during the previous year were reconciled so that no ill feelings lingered to disrupt the group's symmetry.

The Cherokee also didn't exploit nature, for it provided all the raw materials they needed to survive. When a deer was killed, a special ritual was performed to apologize to the dead animal's spirit, with the hunter explaining that his family needed to eat. Killing an animal just for the sport of watching it die was not done.

River cane was one of the most important plants used by these early Tennesseans. The Cherokee called the plant *i-hi*, and although it could be harvested at any time, in the winter cane could be cut without encountering snakes and ticks. (Several species of snake, including timber rattlers and copperheads, like to hunt along the water's edge and were often found in thick stands of cane.) The Cherokees divided their year into the warm season, *gogi*, and the cold season, *gola*. Harvesting during *gola* gave the tribe's craftspeople time to make the objects needed for the upcoming year.

Switch cane, a slender variety that grows in the uplands, was used to make arrow shafts. The historic Cherokee called it *guni*, their word for arrow. An eight-and-a-half-inch section of a cane arrow was found in Greene County in 1956. Charred in a long-ago fire, the artifact has been determined to be two thousand years old. The recovered section was the "fletched" or feathered end that was fitted into the bowstring. Blowguns, used to propel wooden darts tufted with thistledown, were also made from a hollowed-out section of river cane, about eight feet long.

River cane also served as an important building material. The Cherokee villages ranged in size from a dozen to two hundred dwellings. The individual family homes were built from local materials. First, a framework of poles was planted in the ground, one at a time, and bent inward to form a domed roof. The rafter ends were interwoven, over and under, as they were individually installed. A lattice of river cane cut to length and lashed together was attached to the exterior walls. The cane lattice was then plastered with muddy clay, and a roof of thatched grass was added. Inside, beds covered with woven cane mats were made on raised platforms. A fireplace with a large rock hearth was positioned in the center of the house below a hole in the roof that allowed the smoke to escape.

River cane, tied in bundles, was also used to make torches. As far back as five thousand years ago, Native Americans explored local caves looking for rocks and minerals like fine-grained chert. Similar to flint and quartz, chert was flaked into shape to make arrowheads. Surprisingly, Indian miners traveled as deep as three miles into caves in search of the desired rock. Most of these quests would have occurred in total darkness were it not for the river cane torches they burned, evidence of which can still be found on cave walls. Venturing deep into a cave, every so often the miners would pause to rub the lit end of their torches on the wall to expose a more burnable surface. These black smudge marks on cave walls still exist.

Perhaps the most enduring use of river cane was in basketry. The Cherokee made an assortment of basket sizes and shapes, from breadbox to laundry-hamper size. Native artisans in Cherokee, North Carolina, are still practicing the art form, but its historical roots can be traced back many centuries to the Carolinas.

The English naturalist Mark Catesby made his first trip to the New World in 1712, spending seven years in Virginia collecting plants. Back in England, his collection of drawings and reports impressed fellow botanists. The English were eager for information about the colonies. In 1722 Catesby found financial backing to return to America, this time the Carolinas. Catesby's two-volume *Natural History of Carolina, Florida and the Bahama Islands* was completed in 1743 and contained two hundred hand-colored plates depicting the curious plants and animals he discovered in North America. In that book Catesby noted: "The baskets made by the more southern Indians . . . are exceeding neat and strong, and is one of their masterpieces in mechanicks. These are made of cane in different forms and sizes, and beautifully dyed black and red with various figures; many of them are so close wrought that they will hold water, and are frequently used by the Indians for the purposes that bowls and dishes are put to."

River cane, a member of the bamboo family, historically grew in low-lying wetlands, along the creeks and rivers. In some places the plant created dense colonies. The thick stands of cane were common in the Southeast, extending for miles along the river and stream banks. The dense cane stands helped to stabilize shorelines and control erosion, but they were virtually impenetrable. In the late 1700s noted botanist and wanderer William Bartram wrote about the dense stands in the southern states: "The Canes are ten or twelve feet in height, and as thick as an ordinary walking-staff; they grow so close together, there is no penetrating them without previously cutting a road."

John James Audubon also described the thick growth:

> The cane, kind reader, formerly grew spontaneously over the greater portion of the State of Kentucky and other western districts of our Union, as well as in many farther south. Now, however, cultivation, and introduction of cattle and horses, and other circumstances connected with the progress of civilization, have greatly altered the face of the country, and reduced the cane within comparatively small limits. It attains a height of from twelve to thirty feet, and a diameter of from one to two inches, and grows in great patches resembling osierholts in which occur plants of all sizes. The plants frequently grow so close together, and in course of time become so tangled, as to present an almost impenetrable thicket. A portion of ground thus covered with canes is called a cane-brake.

River cane is a woody grass, the tallest native grass in America. It's also the only local grass with hollow stems between its joints. Individual stems can live for as long as ten years. Colonization is accomplished primarily by sending up new growth from horizontal underground stems called rhizomes. Actual seed production is considered sparse and unpredictable. New foliage growth usually occurs from late April through early July, and the long, thin leaves survive until the next spring, making the plants green and vibrant in winter. Flowering occurs from spring through early summer.

The European settlers who displaced the Cherokee relied on river cane to feed their livestock. Cattle munched and ultimately destroyed many of the canebrakes, turning the stream banks into muddy, eroding cow slops. Today, only remnants of these early canebrakes exist. Driving along a country road in January, you can spot them easily. River cane, being evergreen, stands out against the dull grays and browns of winter. The cane is clustered in small patches along stream and riverbanks.

The loss of Southern canebrakes as animal habitat may have been a principal reason for the decline of Bachman's warbler, named in honor of a friend of John J. Audubon, the Reverend John Bachman, who discovered the previously unknown species in 1832. Audubon ultimately painted the bird, giving it the name Bachman's Swamp-warbler. The small songbird, a summer resident of the Southeast, was perhaps never very common. Because of its rarity, little is known of the mysterious passerine other than that it inhabited swamps and lowland forests, nesting in canebrake, fashioning its nests out of cane, Spanish moss, lichen, dried grass, and dead leaves. The last documented sighting occurred in 1961 in South Carolina. Today many believe the colorful yellow, olive-green, and black warbler is probably extinct.

Some 250 years after the arrival of the first Europeans, the environmental importance of river cane is once again coming to the forefront. Historical interest and the need to reestablish healthy riparian zones to control erosion have brought new attention to the once-common grass. Riparian plants grow along stream and riverbanks, holding the soil in place during high water. TVA's Clinch-Powell River Action Team, the U.S. Fish and Wildlife Service, and the U.S. Forest Service have partnered on cane restoration projects in the upper reaches of the Tennessee Valley. In the late 1990s the consortium worked together to transplant existing plants into three sites in Lee and Wise counties in southwest Virginia. As these colonies spread, cane will be harvested from these sites and transplanted at other promising locations. Similar restoration projects using native black willow have been successful throughout the valley.

In the mid-1700s the East began to meet the West in the Tennessee Valley. Humans who had come to the fertile valley from two different directions separated by thousands of years began to encounter one another in the western foothills of the Smokies. Today, the reconstructed Fort Loudoun overlooks Tellico Lake in Monroe County. The original was built during the winter of 1756–57 on seven hundred acres of land given to the British government by the Overhill Cherokee. It was the first planned trans-Appalachian fort built by the English and, for a time, their westernmost in America.

The fort served as a foothold into the region. South Carolina, a British colony, felt threatened by French activities in the Mississippi River Valley and beyond. It desired to create a stronger relationship with the mighty Cherokee Nation, particularly the Overhill towns in the Tennessee Valley. The fortification was named after the commander of all British forces in America, John Campbell, the fourth Earl of Loudoun. The fortress was of a traditional European design: diamond shaped walls with a raised bastion in each corner. The palisades were created with sharpened logs, eighteen feet long, buried three feet into the ground, tilted outward fifteen degrees. Inside the palisades was a cluster of buildings that served as home for the assigned garrison: 90 British regulars and 120 South Carolinian militiamen.

Built on a sloping hill on the land given by the Cherokee, the fort overlooked the Little Tennessee River and the Cherokee village of Tuskegee. Its garrison's mission was to befriend the natives, and for a time all went well. A small cluster of settlers, traders, artisans, blacksmiths, and gunsmiths formed around the site. Supplies and trading goods were brought in overland from Charleston, South Carolina, 450 miles away. Initially, interactions and trade between the two groups were cordial, but relations soon soured. Largely because of French influence and minor conflicts elsewhere, tensions began to build around the area. The old Cherokee emperor Old Hop, who had supported the fort, died. His successor, Standing Turkey, was less receptive to the English and wanted them off their land. In 1760 the Cherokee blockaded Fort Loudoun's garrison, and with no incoming supplies—by the summer they were down to eating their horses—the beleaguered assemblage was ultimately forced to withdraw in August. Captain Paul Demere negotiated the peaceful surrender and lowered the flag, pledging no "fraud" or deceit, and on August 9 the people under his charge left with a Cherokee escort on a 140-mile march to Fort Prince George. All went well on the first day, but after searching the abandoned fort, the Indians discovered that Demere had hidden quantities of powder and ball. Since the captain had agreed to surrender all surplus ammunition, this discovery was deemed a betrayal. The next morning, 700 Cherokee attacked the exposed and weary travelers; they captured, scalped, and mutilated Captain Demere for his subterfuge and took 120 prisoners. The first English presence in the Tennessee Valley had ended.

Today the fort has been painstakingly rebuilt. The scene has changed since the 1700s. Tellico Dam, finished in 1979, has flooded the low-lying floodplain, and the site of Tuskegee is now underwater. In 2002 a new Cherokee winter lodge, a traditional cold-weather dwelling, was built below the fort to represent the village. This lone structure sits at the water's edge. The project used traditional Cherokee materials and methods. The size, shape, and orientation of the lodge were determined by archaeological evidence collected from Tuskegee before the reservoir waters inundated it after the dam was completed.

"Surprisingly, the lodges at Tuskegee were rectangular and not round like many of the Cherokee homes of the period," said Will Kinton, a member of the restoration crew. Kinton, a state park ranger at the historic site, spoke passionately about their project. "We spaced the posts for the walls exactly as they had done," he added. The restoration crew used locust posts, charred on the ends to resist rotting, as the studs to create the walls. The rafters creating the roof were also made of locust.

River cane was used throughout the structure. First, green cane was stripped of foliage, cut to length, and woven through the locust studs. To the latticework of cane, a mixture of clay, sand, and straw was applied by hand. Chief Jones, at the time the principal chief of the Eastern Band of Cherokee, was in the area one day during the lodge's construction in 2002. When the high chief learned of the project, he stopped by to watch as the crew was applying the red clay mixture to the walls. It was dirty, messy work.

"He was wearing a nice dress shirt," said Kinton, "but when he saw what we were doing, he rolled up his sleeves and started to help. It's not every day that the head of a sovereign nation joins your work crew. I sort of felt that the Cherokee were blessing our project." One can only imagine that, for Chief Jones, it must have felt good applying the red clay mud as his ancestors had surely done over three hundred years before.

After the walls were completed, bundles of river cane were lashed to the rafters forming the roof. They were topped with large slabs of tulip tree bark that served as roofing shingles. "On a hot day, the lodge stays surprisingly cool," said Kinton, "and on a cold day, it's warmer than you might think." Openings left at either end, under the eaves, allow smoke to escape from the fire pit in the center of the building. Inside, bunks made of river cane stems were later added.

The newly built lodge stands as a showcase of traditional Cherokee architecture and construction. Standing in the manicured grass between the restored British fort and the Cherokee lodge, you get a sense of the true relationship between the two long-ago powers. The symbolism is clear. The reborn British fortification, wood and stone, spiky and imposing, towers on the hillside over the humble Cherokee structure. The fort's presence is overpowering. Cane arrows and blowguns were truly no match to British muskets and steel. The ouster of the garrison at Fort Loudoun in 1760 was, for the native Cherokee, a minor, short-lived victory, like the removal of a splinter from a festered finger. But the English were not easily deterred; there would be more to come, as reported by the *American Whig Review*:

> On the 7th September, 1794, this formidable army of invasion set out
> for Nickajack; and, although the route had been unexplored, and the
> mountains and the river lay between them and their enemies, they had

counted the cost, fitted out their boats, and had resolved to strike a blow that would teach the lawless Indians a severe lesson.

The troops made a forced march, reached the Tennessee River just after dark on the fourth day, and in thirty minutes had their raw-hide boats afloat in the river, ready to bear over the arms. They immediately began to cross the river, landing a short distance below the town of Nickajack. Most of the men swam over in perfect silence, their arms and clothes being conveyed in the boats, and on rafts rudely constructed of bundles of canes. . . . A young man by the name of Joseph B. Porter, who could not swim at all, tied an armful of dry canes together, and, nothing daunted, plunged into the rapid river, and kicked himself over in safety. . . .

Although Nickajack contained about three hundred warriors, they were so completely surprised that they made but little resistance. . . . The whole town ran with blood. About seventy warriors were slain, and a large number of women and children taken prisoners. . . . In one instance, [Joseph] Brown killed an Indian warrior in a single combat, and carried away his scalp.

After the Louisiana Purchase in 1803 added eight hundred thousand square miles to this country, people began to see the newly acquired Great Plains as unfit for farming, yet suitable for Native Americans. Many asked: why not let all tribes living east of the Mississippi River move west into the "great American desert"? The area would be classified as Indian Territory. President Thomas Jefferson supported the idea but felt that the relocation should be voluntary. And indeed, some Native Americans decided to move to avoid any future conflict, but most did not.

When Tennessee's own Andrew Jackson ran for president twenty-five years later, he promised to forcibly remove all holdouts, and after his election, on May 28, 1830, he signed the Indian Removal Act. The Black Hawk War in Illinois, the second Creek War in Alabama, and the second Seminole War in Florida were all fought to remove various tribes from their land. The collective removal of the Five Civilized Tribes—Choctaws, Creeks, Chickasaws, Seminoles, and Cherokees—is known as the "Trail of Tears." In 1835, the fraudulent Treaty of New Echota, negotiated between the U.S. government and a small group of affluent Cherokees in Georgia, set a deadline for all Cherokees to leave their homes. That deadline was May 23, 1838. The forced removal began in the Tennessee Valley only eighty-one years after Fort Loudoun was built. Even though the tribe had done everything humanly possible to adapt to the white man's culture, the "highly civilized Cherokee Nation" could no longer be tolerated. Two thousand had moved peaceably, but more drastic measures were needed for the estimated fifteen thousand who resisted. The newly elected president, Martin Van Buren, announced: "No State can achieve proper culture, civilization and progress in safety as long as Indians are permitted to remain."

According to the official White House Web site, Van Buren was "only about 5 feet, 6 inches tall, but trim and erect." He "dressed fastidiously. His impeccable appearance belied his amiability and his humble background." You wonder what goes through a person's mind when they are evicting a people from a homeland they had occupied for over ten thousand years. The amiable eighth president sent Brigadier General Winfield Scott, "Old Fuss and Feathers," to Fort Cass in Charleston, Tennessee, in Bradley County to assume command of the army for the Cherokee removal; roughly seven thousand troops were designated to carry out the eviction. Thirteen stockade forts were built along the Tennessee River and other locations to serve as concentration camps.

Scott's army swept through Cherokee lands taking everyone, regardless of age, sex, or social status, as prisoners, marching them at bayonet point to the nearest detention camp. By this time, many Cherokee had successfully integrated themselves into white society. They had large, prosperous plantations, and some had even converted to Christianity. But that mattered little. After their capture, poor whites described as a jubilant rabble quickly moved in to burn crops, seize livestock, and ransack and torch homes. The possessions of the Native Americans were snatched and sold to the highest bidder. Looters dug up Cherokee graves to steal the jewelry they might contain, and the land was parceled out in a government-sanctioned lottery. At the detention centers conditions were inhuman. The lack of proper food and facilities for washing and bathing, along with foul drinking water and poor sanitation, caused disease to spread rapidly. It has been estimated that twenty-five hundred died before the trip west began. It could be said that they were the lucky ones.

On June 16, 1938, Reverend Evan Jones from Tennessee sent a dispatch to the *Baptist Missionary Magazine:*

> The Cherokees are nearly all prisoners. They have been dragged from
> their houses, and encamped at the forts and military posts, all over
> the [Cherokee] nation. In Georgia, especially, multitudes were allowed

no time to take any thing with them except the clothes they had on. Well-furnished houses were left a prey to plunderers, who, like hungry wolves, follow in the trail of the captors. These wretches rifle the houses and strip the helpless, unoffending owners of all they have on earth. Females who have been habituated to comforts and comparative affluence are driven on foot before the bayonets of brutal men. Their feelings are mortified by the blasphemous vociferations of these heartless creatures. It is a painful sight. The property of many has been taken and sold before their eyes for almost nothing—the sellers and buyers, in many cases, having combined to cheat the poor Indians.

Many years later a Georgia militiaman wrote: "I fought through the Civil War and have seen men shot to pieces and slaughtered by the thousands, but the Cherokee removal was the cruelest work I ever knew."

The Cherokee were sent to the new Indian Territory in present-day Oklahoma either by water or by one of three overland routes along existing roads and trails. The unpredictable Tennessee River was the first major obstacle. The summer of 1838 was hot and dry. A drought gripped the Tennessee Valley. The first group, sixteen hundred captives from Georgia, was sent to Ross's Landing to board boats. Another two thousand Cherokee captives spent that summer with little food or water in a camp at the site, awaiting their own fate. The landing, named after Cherokee high chief and businessman John Ross, was located at the present-day site of Chattanooga. Ross, known as *Cooweescoowee,* or "White Bird," by his followers, was seven-eighths white, educated, and highly respected in both worlds. He made trip after trip to Washington, D.C., to speak to Congress and to meet with supporters who hoped to stop or at least slow the removal. Henry Wise, U.S. representative from Virginia, opined that the Cherokee "were more advanced in civilization" than the rest of the Georgians, whom he regarded as riffraff. Daniel Webster defended the Native Americans repeatedly in the U.S. Senate; his words were highly regarded but lightly heeded. In the end, Chief John Ross himself was taken captive and marched west with his people.

In the time of the Cherokee, Blythe's Ferry in Meigs County marked the northwestern boundary of their ancestral lands. During the summer of 1838, an estimated nine to ten thousand detainees were gathered there to wait their turn to ford the river. Departure was delayed for many because of a lack of water along the route, and they were forced to wait up to two months for their turn. The rains finally came in late September, and since the detainees had only been allowed to keep what they were wearing when captured, they had to survive in sloppy, wet clothing. The roads and trails became muddy, rutted quagmires. By November the first group had already reached the Mississippi River while others still waited to cross the Tennessee. The late start meant that they had to endure a particularly harsh winter. Men, women, and children who had never in their lives lived outside in the elements were forced to travel by foot, many without shoes and with little more than blankets to keep themselves warm. The elderly, sick, and dying rode in wagons.

It was a long trek to what would eventually become Oklahoma; those who died along the way were placed in quickly dug graves. At virtually every stop-over, fourteen or fifteen who had died during the day were buried in what must have become a nightly ritual. Quatie, the full-bloodied Cherokee wife of Chief John Ross, died of pneumonia, having given up her blanket to a sickly child. She had made it as far as Little Rock. The child ultimately survived. Ross, the leader of his people, watched as his wife's lifeless body was laid to rest in a tiny grave dug in the frozen ground. He had little time to mourn at the site.

As Edward King records in *Scribner's Monthly* in 1874, "Depleted and worn down by every imaginable privation, more than four thousand of the unfortunates died on their long march of six hundred miles to their new homes west of the Mississippi,—forming a ghastly sacrifice to commemorate the white man's greed." This unspeakable act was carried out with the full consent and blessing of the U.S. president and a majority in Congress. Unnoticed, the tears of the marchers fell to the mud between their feet. They grieved the loss of their sisters, brothers, wives, and mothers, as they themselves grew weaker and more distraught. Jurisprudence and common decency simply looked the other way.

On a raw January morning 165 years later, I stood on the water's edge at Blythe's Ferry gazing across the river. It was bitterly cold, perhaps a lot like that winter of 1838–39. A biting wind blew in from the west, chapping my exposed face. Snow was forecast for later in the week. The remains of a campfire and broken beer bottles littered the shoreline. At this spot on the river the east shore is rocky; large limestone boulders garnished with spindly red cedars dominate the hilly location. A new Cherokee Removal Memorial Park to commemorate the dark episode is under construction; a park pavilion on the bluff among the cedars overlooks the river.

At times like these, you pause to listen to the murmur filtering through the trees. It had been over a century and a half since the last of the valley's original inhabitants had spent their waning days in their homeland. At the site, they had slept in guarded camps, not knowing what the next day would bring. In the end, as the drought of 1838 gave way to autumn and the late season rains, the last of the natives gathered their precious few belongings and turned west to ford the river beginning what was later called *nu-no-du-na-tlo-hi-lu,* literally "the trail where they cried." The Cherokee way of life—river cane, locust posts, and clay mud lodges—had come to an end in the Tennessee Valley.

Beaver

Castor canadensis

Of all the beasts he learned the language,
Learned their names and all their secrets,
How the beavers built their lodges,
Where the squirrels hid their acorns,
How the reindeer ran so swiftly,
Why the rabbit was so timid.

Henry Wadsworth Longfellow
The Song of Hiawatha, 1855

Safe and warm, inside a lodge built by their parents, Tennessee Valley beaver kits are born in late winter and early spring—February through April. Their parents are among the few monogamous mammals, and the youngsters are born with both their fathers and older siblings present. For the next two years, they will be a part of a close-knit family that remains together through the seasons. After a gestation of over three months, the litter of two to four join the yearlings from last year's litter and their parents in creating a colony that will defend its territory from other encroaching beavers. The family may have as many as eight members.

Weighing roughly one pound each and fully furred at birth, the kits are able to walk and even go into the water the first day, although their fur isn't initially water-repellent like that of their parents and older siblings. Nature writers refrain from using the words "cute" or "adorable" to describe young mammals, but with their distinctive paddle-shaped tails and pudgy faces, young beavers are just that. Perhaps precocious is a better choice, although the meaning is hardly the same.

Like other mammals, beaver mothers feed milk to their young, but both parents groom and bathe them. The kits nurse during the day and sleep at night, when their mothers are outside the lodge. Primarily vegetarian, once the kits are weaned, they begin to eat leaves brought to them by their parents until they're old enough to eat tree bark, one of the beaver's principal foods. After about four weeks, the kits' anal glands begin to produce the grease that the young beavers use to coat their fur, making it repel water. After a second month, the young begin to venture from the lodge with the rest of the family.

The largest rodents in North America, beavers are excellent swimmers and can remain underwater for up to fifteen minutes. Four-year-old beavers attain a weight of between thirty and forty-four pounds, and for the rest of their lives their weight will fluctuate with the seasons, dropping in the winter and rising during the warmer months, when more vegetation is available. The winter diet consists mostly of the sweet inner bark of trees and branches; during the warmer months they eat a lot of grasses, herbs, fruits, and aquatic plants.

Besides the long, flat, paddle-shaped tail, a beaver's most prominent feature is its large front teeth—incisors strong enough to fell trees. These teeth are long and rootless, curving far back in the skull. They grow throughout the animal's life, having a hard layer of enamel backed by a much softer one of dentine. Because this back layer wears away much faster, the teeth always retain a sharp chisel edge. A beaver's back feet are webbed, which makes swimming easier. Its front feet are dexterous like human hands. Frontiersman Grey Owl referred to the mammals as "beaver-people." In 1935 he wrote about their "hands" and other humanlike qualities:

> They could pick up very small objects with them, manipulate sticks and stones, strike, push, and heave with them and they had a very firm grasp which it was difficult to disengage. When peeling a stick they used them both to twist the stem with supple wrist movements, while the teeth rapidly whittled off the succulent bark as it went by, much after the fashion of a lathe.
>
> This creature comported itself as a person, of a kind, and she busied herself at tasks that I could, without loss of dignity, have occupied myself at: she made camp, procured and carried in supplies, could lay plans and carry them out and stood robustly and resolutely on her own hind legs, metaphorically and actually, and had an independence of spirit that measured up well with my own, seeming to look on me as a contemporary, accepting me as an equal and no more. I could in no way see where I was the loser from this association, and would not, if I could, have asserted my superiority, save as was sometimes necessary to avert willful destruction.

As Grey Owl observed, beavers put their time to good use. They are the most dynamic developers in nature. Other than humankind, beavers are the only animals that can move into an area; cut trees; clear land; build tunnels, canals, and pathways; create structures—dams, lodges—and totally alter the parcel to suit their purposes, essentially taking a slow-moving wooded stream and changing it into a pond with surrounding wetland. In time, as the pond fills with silt, the cleared space becomes a grassy meadow. Consequently, a host of other plants and animals follow the beaver into the newly re-formed and open habitat.

In addition to being expert developers, beavers are master loggers capable of felling up to 216 trees a year. A single beaver can topple a small tree, but it may take two to tackle a large one. Beaver lodges and dams are constructed to last for years, built from small trees, branches, vegetation, mud, bones, and rocks. They may also include wire, beer bottles, cans, roofing paper, burlap, and any other human throwaway item. They're tenacious fixer-uppers and will repair leaks in dams soon after they occur. Sections of trees are floated in from as far away as a half mile up- or downstream to the construction site. Paths are created and obstacles removed to bring in material overland. In the end, the complete beaver habitat may be the cumulative effort of several generations; the young kits and yearlings learn their construction techniques from their parents.

It is generally believed that in aboriginal America beavers lived in all sections, along the tributaries of all the rivers. An early published account estimated that there were perhaps 400 million beavers living in North America prior to the late 1600s. Because they are nocturnal and excellent swimmers in water, they encountered few predators if they remained in their element. That changed when the Europeans came.

Early naturalist John Lawson wrote in *A New Voyage to Carolina:*

> Bevers are very numerous in Carolina, there being abundance of their Dams in all Parts of the Country, where I have travel'd. They are the most industrious and greatest Artificers (in building their Dams and Houses) of any four-footed Creatures in the World. Their Food is chiefly the Barks of Trees and Shrubs, viz. Sassafras, Ash, Sweet-Gum, and several others. If you take them young, they become very tame and Domestick, but are very mischievous in spoiling Orchards, by breaking the Trees, and blocking up your Doors in the Night, with the Sticks and Wood they bring thither. If they eat any thing that is salt, it kills them. Their Flesh is a sweet Food; especially, their Tail, which is held very dainty. Their Fore-Feet are open, like a Dog's; their Hind-Feet webb'd like a Water-Fowl's. The Skins are good Furs for several Uses, which every one knows. The

Leather is very thick; I have known Shooes made thereof in Carolina, which lasted well. It makes the best Hedgers Mittens that can be used.

The plume hunters of the late 1800s who killed so many birds for the millinery trade were not the first to wreak havoc in the name of fine headwear. In 1638 King Charles II of England issued a decree that called for the killing of all European beavers. Why? His proclamation went on to command that all beaver furs should be collected and used in the manufacture of men's hats. At the time, no fashionable man would be seen in public without a proper hat, one made from beaver felt, which was impervious to water. In short order, all the beavers in Europe and most of Asia were eliminated. This made American beavers worth top dollar, and their furs became legal tender. It's reported that in 1659, Thomas Mayhew sold most of Nantucket Island off the coast of Massachusetts for thirty English pounds and two beaver hats. In 1624 the Dutch, in their first full season of settlement in New York, shipped fifteen hundred beaver pelts back to fashion-conscious Europeans. The broad-brimmed, tall hats were all the rage and would remain so for over two hundred years. The stylish "top hat" was introduced in the 1780s, and it became part of the daily attire for any well-dressed man on either side of the Atlantic. Although American trappers and fur traders collected a variety of furs—deer, otter, fox, mink, and bear—beaver fur was black gold, and it became the driving force behind colonial development.

Actual money or currency had no place in the fur trade. It was a barter system where goods were exchanged for other items. The French and other parties had deemed a top beaver pelt as the unit by which all other goods were measured. Before a trade could commence, the trade partners had to establish an acceptable exchange rate. Two otter skins were worth one beaver, and brass kettles could be swapped pound for pound for beaver furs. A marten skin could be set at half a beaver's; it was up to the trading partners to haggle over the particulars. In the 1640s the Jesuit priest Paul Le Jeune, a Canadian missionary, wrote: "He mocks the Europeans who are passioned for the skin of this animal. My Indian host told me one day, showing me a very handy knife: the English do not think right; they give us 20 knives like this one for one beaver skin."

Trading companies were organized to monopolize commerce with the Indians. The most famous, Hudson's Bay Company (HBC), is the oldest corporation still in existence today. Its acronym, HBC, has often been referred to as standing for "here before Christ." Founded with a Royal Charter from King Charles II on May 2, 1670, it was a cooperative effort between two adventurous French traders, Pierre-Esprit Radisson and Médard des Groseilliers, and a group of businessmen in Boston. The Hudson's Bay Company controlled the fur or Indian trade throughout most of British-controlled North America for several centuries. Trapping was unregulated, and the Hudson's Bay Company alone sold over three million beaver pelts in a twenty-five-year period in the late 1800s.

Trade companies like HBC and its chief rival, North West Company (NWC), also set up a unit of value. The best furs were called "Made-Beaver," or MB for short. The same standard was then used at all their outposts. A musket was worth eleven MBs, a wool blanket worth seven, and a pistol was valued at four. A single MB could purchase two pounds of sugar, two hatchets, twelve dozen buttons, or one pair of breeches. The traders and trappers affiliated with these companies were the first Europeans to venture into many remote areas, and the first to set up trading posts and forge relationships with Native American communities.

Curiously, the best beaver furs had some wear on them. A beaver has two layers of fur: an outer coat of coarse guard hair, roughly two inches long, and a soft inner coat of underhair, one inch thick, called fur-wool. It was this thick underfur that was processed to make beaver felt. In the manufacture of hats, the outer layer of guard hair had to be removed; if this had already occurred, the process was speeded up. The guard hairs generally dropped off a beaver hide worn as a garment by a Native American for a season, so these made the best, or MB, furs. Hatmakers referred to beaver pelts as being either "coat" or "parchment." The coat pelts, the ones that had been worn by Indians as winter garments, were missing the guard hairs. Parchment pelts were furs that still retained their layer of guard hairs, which had to be removed, and up until the late seventeenth century, only the Russians had an easy way of doing it. So all parchment pelts had to be sent to Russia for this important step, which increased the manufacturing cost and delayed production.

The process of making a beaver hat was lengthy and included over thirty procedures. Turning the underfur into the necessary felt required a complex process of combing, beating, and drying. In one step called carroting, the pelt was treated with nitrate of mercury. Hatmakers, who were constantly breathing the poisonous mercury vapors, often developed uncontrollable nervous twitches and difficulty talking or thinking. Consequently, the term "mad as a hatter" found its way into the vernacular of the day. In another step called planking, the pelt was immersed over and over in a solution of sulfuric acid, beer grounds, and wine sediments and then flattened with a rolling pin or squeezed between two planks. Planking reduced the thickness of the pelt by half. To stiffen the hat, the inside was painted with gum Arabic, Flaunder's glue, and common gum. After this step, a quality top hat could support the weight of a two-hundred-pound man. Because of the special properties of its underfur, a beaver pelt worked better than hides from other animals. It also held its shape longer and made the best-quality hats. Cheaper hats, like the ones worn by soldiers, were made from a combination of beaver, rabbit, and horse hair.

Traders desiring the best beaver pelts ventured deeper inland. This new wave of commerce inflamed old rivalries and led to the French and Iroquois Wars, also known as the "Beaver Wars"; these were an intermittent series of bloody conflicts in eastern North America that pitted the Iroquois Confederacy and their Dutch allies against the Algonquin tribes and their French allies. The Iroquois Confederacy, or the League of Peace and Power, was founded by prophet and shaman Deganawidah, "The Great Peacemaker," and Hiawatha (made famous by Longfellow) in the late 1500s. It was composed of the Five Nations: Seneca, Onondaga, Oneida, Cayuga, and the powerful Mohawk. The Iroquois actually called themselves the Haudenosaunee. "Iroquois," a word they shunned, is a derogatory term that comes from the French. It's a rough rendering of the word the Huron used for their Mohawk enemies, and it means "black snakes."

As an alliance, the Haudenosaunee was a formidable group. At stake in the Beaver Wars was the right to be the principal middleman in the fur trade, and tensions were fueled by the growing scarcity of beavers on lands controlled by the five confederacy nations. With the introduction of firearms, beavers were disappearing at a faster rate. By 1640 they were all but gone from the Hudson Valley. The Beaver Wars were marked by extreme brutality and ultimately led to the expansion of Iroquois territory, which for them was a necessity if they were going to stay in the fur trade. As a result, the Algonquin-speaking Shawnee were driven out of the Ohio country, and the Lakota were pushed west of the Mississippi River into the Great Plains. The Haudenosaunee ultimately controlled all of the northern lands from New York to the Mississippi River. The French and Iroquois Wars ended when the Dutch gave up the fight and the French decided to switch sides, wanting to align themselves with the stronger Iroquois, whom they would need in their growing competition with the English.

As the beavers disappeared from one area, the traders ventured farther into unknown territory. In the summer of 1673, two Englishmen, James Needham and Gabriel Arthur, were sent on an exploration foray by Abraham Wood, a plantation owner in Virginia. Needham and Arthur traveled across the Alleghenies from Appomattox Falls to the Cherokee villages on the Little Tennessee River. They were surprised to discover that the Cherokee already had sixty muskets and an assortment of brass kettles and pots. The natives spoke of white people with whiskers and big clothes living downriver, men who traded for beaver furs.

Other traders were soon to follow Needham and Arthur along three principal routes, all very difficult. The English either ventured south from Virginia or inland from Charleston by way of northern Georgia. The French followed the Tennessee River upstream from the west. It's been estimated that between the years 1690 and 1750, after a single season of enterprise, industrious trappers and traders left the Tennessee Valley with skins and furs that brought $1,600 or $1,700 in the outside world, a princely sum in those days.

It's easy to imagine a lone trader leading a line of horses loaded with manufactured goods, clanging and clattering his way into the valley. His was a life of isolation. His mission of commerce took weeks, but with him came a change in a way of life. What he kindled was a desire for merchandise. What he created were inland markets. The Cherokee who had never coveted material belongings very quickly became infatuated with European goods. They were very willing trade partners. The desire to own a mirror, a pair of scissors, or a musket began to change the culture. Breaking or losing a needle made the owner want another. Having a flintlock created a need for powder and ball. The bow and arrow soon became a child's weapon. Women stopped crafting woven baskets and began to tan hides to trade for brass pots.

Unscrupulous traders also dealt in rum, for they knew that if they gave an Indian alcohol before the negotiations began, they could work a better deal and increase their profit. Native Americans had no real experience with alcohol; some say they had no built-up genetic tolerance. It hit them hard, but it can also be said that turning their society into one of mass consumers disrupted them even more, for they began to empty the valley of furs and hides to pay for their trinkets. An independent people became dependent on the wares brought to them over the mountains. It was a never-ending cycle, one the traders exploited with an increasing variety of goods.

Initially, the Cherokee traded for practical items—tools, pots, muskets, and knives—like the other tribes. Yet more than any other tribe, they developed a penchant for brightly colored fabrics and clothes—striped shirts and silver earrings. The Cherokee had always prized self-adornment; they were a highly decorative people who took pride in their appearance. It was not uncommon for a warrior to trade for a pocket mirror in order to look at himself in his new attire. The English government encouraged traders to open generous lines of credit. For the first time the owner of a new ruffled shirt might find himself in debt to pay for it. Proud of their new dress, the Cherokee would order even more magnificent suits of red baize and rich scarlet trimmed with silver tassels. The English knew that the Native Americans would eventually be rendered dependent on the goods that only they could supply. At first the goods were paid for with furs and deerskins, but in time, if the debts grew large enough, the Cherokee would be forced to give up portions of their land.

The beaver furs of the South were not as thick and luxuriant as those taken in the North, so trade soon moved on to deerskins and slaves. The tribes of the Southeast fought constantly with each other. Often they took captives, but these spoils of war were rarely forced into real servitude. Instead, they either eventually escaped or became part of their captors' tribe. However, once the natives learned they could trade their captives to the English for anything of desire, a lively slave trade sprang up. It was short-lived, however, for the black slaves brought from Africa proved to be more desirable to southern plantation owners than the Indian captives. The Africans were better workers because if they happened to escape they had no way to get back home.

As far as trading is concerned, the French and the English had become the major players, vying for control of the eastern half of the continent. The French claimed Canada and the entire Mississippi River from the Great Lakes to New Orleans, while the English held the Atlantic coastal states east of the Appalachian Mountains. Each wanted to expand their sphere of influence and began to see the Tennessee River as a way to fulfill their goals. The English claimed all of the land that stretched west from their colonies, and the French claimed all of the lands that drained into the interior rivers they had explored. The two claims overlapped west of the Appalachians, and it was the potential of local Indian trade in this region they both desired. The two European rivals fought a series of four conflicts collectively called the French and Indian Wars, but it was really the French against the English. Indians fought for both sides, and both the French and English had the help of the regular military from their home countries, which were also engaged in the Seven Years' Wars across the Atlantic. The bloodshed in North America was an expansion of the larger war underway in Europe. On this side of the Atlantic, the seven-year war lasted nine years: 1754–63. Like many conflicts, it was muddled and got out of hand. Wars are like kudzu: they spread in ways and into places the combatants don't expect at the outset. They're messy. Initially, because of their well-established trade relations, the Cherokee sided with the English. But when the trade slowed because the goods were needed in the war effort, the Cherokee were quick to strike up a deal with the French. Ultimately, this proved disastrous but not before the Cherokee, on behalf of the French, laid siege and routed the British garrison at Fort Loudoun on the Little Tennessee River. Great Britain ultimately won the war and with the victory gained control of Canada and all the other territory claimed by France except for two tiny islands—Saint Pierre and Miquelon—south of Newfoundland, which the French used as unfortified fishing stations. The war now over, the Cherokee had to bargain for a return of favorable trade with the English.

One of the most intriguing stories about trade with the Cherokee appeared in *Harper's New Monthly* magazine in 1870 and was later picked up and amplified in 1885 in a book by George Foster. As the account goes, it was customary for a trader to arrange a marriage of convenience and take a Cherokee wife because women held power and the trader fell under her legal status and protection. In addition to respectability, the Cherokee wife provided for him and kept him housed, cared for, and well fed. In the spring of 1768, one such trader, a Dutch or German peddler named George Gist, traveled north through the mountains of Georgia. He only made one or two trips, trading his wares for furs, and was never seen again. He left behind his pregnant wife, who gave birth to a son named Se-quo-yah. It's reported that the author of the *Harper's* article, William A. Phillips, knew the family of Sequoyah and even had one of his sons in his regiment during the Civil War. Phillips reports that, as a boy, Sequoyah learned from his mother to be a good judge of furs and that he would accompany the hunters on trips and select the best hides for her to trade with the French or English. Crippled from birth or injured in a hunting accident (accounts vary), Sequoyah walked with a limp, and his name may come from the Cherokee word Sikwo-yi, meaning "pig's foot."

Today, the Phillips account of Sequoyah's actual father is a matter of dispute. Other sources, including an 1835 transcription and stories collected by the prominent nineteenth-century anthropologist James Mooney, say that his father was actually a young Virginia trader named Nathaniel Gist, who crossed the mountains into the Tennessee Valley as early as 1753. The "German peddler" story may have been advanced by Nathaniel's prominent family to protect their good name, since Nathaniel was the son of Christopher Gist, a scout of George Washington.

Despite the mystery surrounding his paternity, Sequoyah went on to become far more influential than any scout of Washington. As a young boy, he spent his early years with his mother Wut-the of the Paint Clan in the Cherokee village of Tuskegee on the Little Tennessee River. (It's traditionally accepted that Sequoyah and his mother were abandoned by his white father.) Bright and creative, Sequoyah had an inventive bent and grew up to become a silversmith but is more famous for a creation that had a much greater impact on his people: an alphabet that converted the Cherokee language into written form. It took him twelve years to finish his alphabet, or syllabary, which is made up of eighty-five characters that represent syllables or spoken sounds. Since all other alphabets are considered group or cultural efforts, Sequoyah is believed to be the only known individual in five thousand years of recorded history to have created a written language single-handedly, and he did it without first being literate in some other language. In essence he started from scratch, and his source material, spoken Cherokee, is considered to be the most structurally complex language in North America. Within a year of its completion, 1821, thousands of Cherokees became literate—a remarkable achievement. A weekly newspaper called the *Cherokee Phoenix* was soon to follow, and it continued regular publication until 1834, when Georgia guardsmen confiscated the specially designed printing press.

By the late 1800s, beavers got something of a reprieve. They had to because there were very few of them left. In 1896, S. N. Rhoads reported that, in Tennessee, "It is not likely that any beavers now exist in the eastern half of the State." This was also true for most parts of the country, but luckily men's fashion turned in another direction. The beaver-felt top hat that had been popular for over two hundred years gave way to bowlers, known as derbies in this country. Bowlers were originally created by an Englishman, James Cook, in 1850. Designed as a halfway point between the tall top hats worn by the upper class and the casual, soft felt hats worn by the lower classes, the derby became enormously popular on both sides of the Atlantic and remained so after the turn of the century. The rounded bowlers were made primarily from wool felt, not beaver.

The creation of a system of national parks around the turn of the century gave beavers some isolated safe havens around the country where they could collect to lick their wounds. But beaver conservation efforts really began in the 1930s, and as with many other species, it took a champion to come to their aid. In this case, rescue came in the guise of a self-professed Ojibwa (pronounced O-JIB-wa, anglicized to Chippewa)—a gaunt, enigmatic Canadian, quiet and unassuming, who pulled himself from his wilderness home to write articles and books and to travel about giving lectures on beavers and the importance of maintaining wild places. His name was Wa-sha-quon-asin, or Grey Owl, and he had been a backwoodsman, fur trapper, wilderness guide, and park ranger in Alberta and Saskatchewan, Canada. His 1934 book, *Pilgrims of the Wild*, and the 1935 *Sajo and the Beaver People* detailed his backcountry life with beavers. Grey Owl himself had had an epiphany: his heart and mind made a life-changing, 180-degree turn. After killing beavers for years, he slowly began to notice, both literally and metaphorically, their dying whimpers. Their displays of emotions, particularly affection, along with their communication skills, mischievousness, and family structure, made them seem almost human and eventually cracked his matter-of-fact complacency and rough demeanor. His revelation came after he was forced to adopt two young kits left orphaned by his own hand. "From a purely economic viewpoint," he wrote, "I had long been opposed to the whole-sale slaughter now going forward, which was indeed almost at an end for want of victims. But this was different. These beasts had feelings and could express them very well; they could talk, they had affection, they knew what it was to be happy, to be lonely—why, they were little people!"

Grey Owl's writing and public appearances were widely popular and raised awareness of the plight of these much-persecuted mammals. He spoke with a clear voice from the page or podium, and for the first time many people began to understand what was at stake. "He deplored the way men of his time looked upon wild animals, first at their commercial value and only later at their useful role in maintaining a rich and varied environment," wrote Victor Scheffer in 1971. Grey Owl created his own beaver sanctuary largely because one hundred thousand square miles of Ontario had become beaver-less. His transformation made public by his own proclamation made him one of the earliest proponents of environmental sensitivity. *Pilgrims of the Wild* looks sorrowfully at the van-ishing wilderness and a way of life that was rapidly disappearing. The author was also an excellent example of the concept "you are who you say you are," for the buckskin-clad and weathered Grey Owl began his life in Hastings, England, as Archibald Belaney.

Born on September 18, 1888, the young Belaney showed an early interest in nature. It is said that as a boy he dreamed of being an Indian. In 1906, he immi-grated to Canada, became a student of the Native American lifestyle, married an Ojibwa woman, and, in time, took the name Grey Owl, sloughing off all the trappings of his former European life. He lived for years as a native of the vast Canadian backwoods. In 1915, with World War I—also known as the "war to end all wars," or what the French called *la der des der,* "the last of the last"—rag-ing in Europe, he enlisted and was sent to France. Wounded in the foot, he spent time in a British infirmary before being sent back to Canada with an honorable discharge and a small disability pension. His war experience taught him the "utter futility of civilization."

At the urging of his second Native American wife, Anahareo, he started to concentrate on his writing and conservation issues. In 1931 Grey Owl's first of several magazine articles was published; four books came later. By this time his roughhewn Indian persona was honed to perfection. A photograph of Grey Owl taken in 1936 shows a stoic man with dark, piercing eyes, long hair, and chis-eled, lantern jaw. He toured and lectured wearing full Native American regalia, and no one, not even his publisher, knew the secret of his British heritage. Grey Owl told stories of the beavers living near their home and of ones they had domesticated. He toured England in 1935 and again in 1937 and even visited his hometown of Hastings. Two of his aunts recognized him but remained silent. On his later trip he met King George VI and his family, which included the future queen, Princess Elizabeth. His lectures in England routinely drew several thousand people. Ironically, he became quite a celebrity in his home country.

Grey Owl has been described as sensitive and withdrawn, but through his writings and convictions he was forced into the spotlight of lecture halls. The more famous he became, the more "Indian" the general public expected him to be. The ruse became harder and harder to sustain. Ultimately, his travels, noto-riety, and perhaps even the weight of maintaining his assumed identity weak-ened him. He gave his last lecture in Regina, Saskatchewan, on March 29, 1938, after which he returned to Beaver Lodge, his cabin on Ajawaan Lake. Grey Owl died of pneumonia fifteen days later. He was only forty-nine years old. The truth about his English identity surfaced soon after his death, but his legacy endured and people began to look upon the environment and the beaver's role in it more sympathetically. The furry, industrious rodents were seen as something more than just a harvestable commodity and their utter destruction as senseless. Trapping in most locations stopped, in some cases because there were simply no beavers left to snare. Many governments responded, and beaver trapping was closed for many years while the beaver population started to recover, helped, at least in part, by wildlife agencies that reintroduced beavers into areas where they had formerly lived.

Finally, nearly twenty-five years after Grey Owl's death, President John F. Kennedy did the water-loving mammal a tremendous favor. Before Kennedy moved into the Oval Office—and into the national spotlight—practically all men still wore hats, mostly fedoras, a design that had been popular since the 1930s. And the best fedoras were still being made from beaver underfur. If you look at old photos, pre-1960, fedoras were as common as cigarettes. Kennedy himself often wore a hat—that is, until he became president. On January 20, 1961, he wore the traditional formal top hat to his presidential inauguration and promptly took it off. Rarely was he ever seen in a hat again. He was a young, handsome president with a bushy head of hair. Why cover it? To follow his lead, men all across the country stopped wearing hats; they became passé. In the matter of only a few years, fedoras basically disappeared. Finally, after over three hundred years, hats made from beaver fur were no longer in vogue, and the paddle-tailed rodents could quietly go back to doing what they do best—making other beavers. Their population has been steadily growing ever since.

Although they had formerly been widespread in the lower elevations along slow-moving streams, no beavers lived inside the Great Smoky Mountains National Park for the first several decades of its existence. In 1966 they reappeared on the North Carolina side in Swain County. Today their national population mirrors the Smokies: they are rebounding in many locations. In some places their population has recovered enough that some trapping occurs. Each state has its own set of regulations concerning beaver trapping, but the regulations vary tremendously. In Arkansas it's legal to trap nuisance beavers that are causing damage to property; in Mississippi they're classified as predators and can be trapped year-round; and in Tennessee, in certain counties, they can be trapped year-round, with no limit to the number that can be taken. Animal-rights advocates are concerned that such terms as "pest," "nuisance," and "predator," when applied to certain species across the country, are employed too loosely and that killing methods used on trapped animals are largely unregulated. In some states they have worked to ban or limit certain kinds of traps and trapping practices, especially those methods deemed too cruel. As the beaver population continues to grow and as developed areas expand, animal-control methods will fall under greater scrutiny. It's inevitable.

For many centuries beavers represented the unbridled frontier. As trappers sat around campfires, they told stories of territory just over the next ridge where the animals existed in huge numbers; all they had to do was get there to claim the black gold that awaited, unmolested and ready for the taking. As Grey Owl lamented, for a long, long time, beavers "*were* the wilderness." But as wild places disappeared, the beaver were expatriated, slaughtered not for food but for the fur on their back. Their dens, lodges, and dams remained as ghost towns, bleaching gray in the sun.

What about today? Most people are surprised to learn that if the water is deep enough in rivers or lakes, beavers don't need to build dams or lodges. Instead, they construct underground burrows along shorelines. These burrows are from ten to thirty feet in length, with their entrances located underwater. The tunnels themselves run uphill to a chamber or room above the water line. Consequently, as the amphibious mammal's population rebounds, many urban areas built on lakes or deep impounded rivers are beginning to see beavers, once the absolute symbol of virgin wilderness, appear in their waters. In the late 1990s beavers moved into the Tidal Basin between the Jefferson Memorial and Washington Monument in the nation's capital. We can only assume that Thomas Jefferson would have been enormously pleased to see the beavers in the basin, but they got into trouble when they started gnawing down the famous cherry trees near the third president's shrine. They were quickly live-trapped and moved far away, which wouldn't have been the first time a well-meaning soul was evicted from the District of Columbia.

The notion of urban beavers may be a foreign one, but in downtown Chattanooga they can be seen on Maclellan Island, an eighteen-acre sanctuary owned by the Chattanooga Audubon Society near Hunter Museum and the Museum for Decorative Arts. I have also seen them swimming along the river beside Volunteer Landing in downtown Knoxville, near the mouth of First Creek and the anchorage of the Star of Knoxville riverboat. Along the Neyland Drive Greenway that follows the river past the University of Tennessee, trees are often debarked close to the ground. One fifteen-foot-tall sycamore, planted by the city to shade the greenway, was completely removed. For the beaver, it was just its form of urban renewal.

To describe Dr. Marcella Cranford as petite is an injustice; it doesn't take into account her remarkable spirit. She's one of those people who radiates more than you see before you; in other words, her being far exceeds her corporeal form. The truth is, you simply cannot take in and care for injured and orphaned animals and not be blessed with copious compassion. Marcella is a doctor of veterinary medicine and licensed wildlife rehabilitator, but she elects to spend most of her time driving around East Tennessee doing educational programs about wildlife for students. She's a champion of predators and routinely speaks about their necessary role in the environment. "We're talking bats, we're talking snakes, we're talking wolves," she once quipped in reference to all those things we're taught to fear. When asked to describe herself, she simply says, "I'm an educator"—a teacher-on-wheels who routinely travels with an opossum, a screech-owl, and a twenty-three-year-old red-tailed hawk to places like Camp Wesley Woods and the Great Smoky Mountains Institute at Tremont. She knows that such programs leave impressions, and someday these young people will be in charge. If you want to effect change, speak to the kids. They need a balanced picture—a better understanding of these animals, a part of nature they might otherwise learn to hate, fear, and even destroy.

Many people simply know Marcella as the "Wolf Lady," for she has worked with the American gray wolf for over thirty years. Its detractors often vilify the much-maligned predator, but Marcella has yet to receive as much as a scratch from one of the wild canines. At times she's had as many as eight adopted wolves she has taken in, but currently her pack is down to two: brothers, one gray named Tsali and one black named Navarre. She's had both for eight years, and each thinks he's the alpha male of the group, a designation they debate often.

Marcella's interest in wolves began in the late 1970s when she spent two years in Nova Scotia at the Canid Research Center, after which she took in her first two young wolves, which had been removed from their pack by another researcher. Wolves are portrayed as being ferocious, with eyes that glow bright red in the dark. As children, we're read stories and literally taught from infancy that these are the kind of animals that would eat our grandmothers. But wolves are really quite shy, even skittish. "There is not one documented case in U.S. history of an attack on humans by a wolf," Marcella reports.

On my October visit, we stood outside her wolf enclosure as she pointed out some of the differences between wolves and dogs. "Notice the stance," she said. "A wolf stands with its front two paws actually touching. Cherokees called them 'two paws,' because at times they only left two tracks. Dogs stand with their front legs wide apart." Tsali and Navarre paced back and forth nervously, looking at me with suspicion because they did not know me. The fact that I was with Marcella gave me license to be there; as to my intentions, they were unsure. But my motivations were elsewhere. Standing outside the wolf enclosure, I simply gazed at two of the most beautiful and timid creatures I had ever seen. "Oh, you think they look good now," said Marcella, "wait until they get their full winter coats."

The true reason for my visit to Marcella's log home built in the woods was another mammal. I was there to talk about beavers, and although they are not predators like wolves, there is a parallel: both have been persecuted in this country. The aquatic rodents were slaughtered as a commodity, wolves because they were considered vermin. Neither justification is valid.

Weeks earlier I had met the Wolf Lady at the nature center, and the topic of beavers had entered the flow of conversation. "Yes, I know where there is an active beaver lodge," she had answered to one of my queries. "It's very near a restaurant that serves the best cobbler you've ever eaten."

"Cobbler?" I replied. "You must take me there." How could I pass up a chance at a beaver lodge and a favored dessert?

It was a pleasant autumn day when I picked up Marcella. The cobbler served by the Back Porch Restaurant was as she had presented: sublime. She had peach, and I had my perennial favorite, blackberry, which was as good as the dark, luscious dish my late grandmother Pearl used to make. We both opted to forgo the scoop of vanilla ice cream, wanting to experience the crusty concoction in its purest form. We left the crowded eatery just as the sun was slipping below the ridgeline—our plan all along—and arrived at the federally protected wetland near the foothills of the Great Smoky Mountains in Blount County while there were still enough daylight to get our bearings. Marcella led the way through a tall grassy floodplain filled with blooming goldenrod, lespedeza, and purplish New England aster. It was early fall at its quintessential best: temperatures in the seventies, little wind, and only a few high pinkish cirrus clouds in the sky overhead.

Arriving at the water's edge, the characteristic domed beaver lodge rose from the center of the sizable wetland. The simplicity of its construction looked perfect in function and form. All around it lay a massive plain of placid water, its smooth surface reflecting the orange, salmon, and fuchsia of the setting sun. "Aren't they marvelous architects?" she whispered. "Let's go see their dam." We then followed the beavers' own pathways through the tall grass along the shore to the east, soon arriving at the bulwark that held back the water, and again discovered a structure wonderfully simple and purely practical. What they are able to accomplish with sticks, mud, and leaves is miraculous. With their assemblage the beavers had changed the small stream that flows into Little River into a vast flooded wetland of well over thirty or forty acres. You had to applaud their engineering skills, and wonder what they could accomplish with concrete and steel.

After our inspection of the dam, we went back and found a place on the shoreline to wait, hoping to get a glimpse of the nocturnal beavers as they began to swim around their watery home before it got too dark for us to see. Mist began to creep along the water's edge, and an Eastern screech-owl called from a faraway ridge, its mournful call really more of a whinny than a screech. Bats also started to fly herky-jerky over the water, one noticeably much larger than the others. "Could be a hoary, they're the largest in the area," Marcella whispered, quickly adding, "You have to pronounce that word clearly when you speak to students or they'll giggle." We then noticed the wake of something moving steadily through the water. Lifting a pair of binoculars to my eyes, I was surprised to see a snake swimming towards us. As a rule, snakes are good swimmers, and this one was doing a splendid job, wiggling back and forth, its head lifted two inches above the surface. It appeared as though it had swum across the entire width of the shallow pond. I have seen such before and always wonder: does it know there's something on the other side? Finally, the reptile seemed to get a sense of us and veered off to the west, coming ashore twenty feet or more to our right in the tall grass.

The seventy-nine-acre broad basin we sat inside is a former lake bed. Today it's owned by the federal government and is protected. This pleases Marcella, who originally acquired the surplus property from the state with the desire to see it remain wild and undeveloped. But it took the work of the beavers to bring in Uncle Sam. The federal government's new mandate is to preserve and re-create wetlands, a habitat that was rapidly disappearing.

"Our Chapter of the Wildlife and Fisheries Society trapped five or six beavers in Blount County and released them in cooperation with Marcella's effort for wetland restoration about 1992," remembers Billy Minser, a research associate and instructor at the University of Tennessee. "Rick Eastridge, now a wildlife biologist for Arkansas Department of Natural Resources, was the student project leader. At the time the beaver population was also expanding naturally up Little River, and so some could also have moved in from there. A similar effort was successfully made by TWRA in 1980 at Royal Blue Wildlife Management Area north of Caryville to help reduce strip mine erosion into the mountain streams, by allowing the beavers to build ponds to retain sediments. The results there were also excellent."

"Other than these two releases," continued Minser, "all the beaver expansion across Tennessee and the whole eastern U.S. has been natural expansion. Beavers sometimes cause people problems, but they also do some good, especially by creating pond and wetland habitats for a wide variety of fish and wildlife. It's good to have them back."

"Middle Tennessee has one hundred wetlands to every one that's left in East Tennessee," said Marcella. These watery places are an essential part of the environment, and that's what beavers create. As we waited, I spoke of Grey Owl and how his early thoughts of conservation had alerted the general public and helped to save the species that now lived before us, a species that one hundred years ago was essentially extinct in our state. My thoughts ran from Archie, the English Indian, to Marcella the Wolf Lady, and how such people can dedicate their lives to noble causes.

Finally, our conversation ebbed, and it grew too dark for us to see. If the beavers were out working, they had chosen to do so on the faraway shore, but such is the way with nocturnal mammals that use the cloak of darkness to hide their movements. We sighed and returned to the car, each knowing that even though we had not seen the wetland's proprietors, we were witnesses to their masterful handiwork.

American Toad
Bufo americanus

I love to hear the voice of the first thunder as of the toad (though it returns irregularly like pigeons), far away in his moist meadow.

Henry David Thoreau
Journal, April 17, 1856

As gray winter begins to melt away to spring, some amphibian crooners—chorus frogs, spring peepers, and wood frogs—begin to sing. These species usually start vocalizing in February or even January if the conditions are warm and damp enough. A little later, American toads add their voices to a smattering of local wetlands and ponds. Never in huge numbers, the toads add a pleasing tremolo to the background dominated by the more numerous high-pitched peepers.

Nature writers walk a fine line. They try to report nature and its processes honestly and accurately, as dispassionate observers. Yet, humans aren't dispassionate beings. We're curious mixes of reason and emotion.

It is said that Thoreau carried two notebooks with him when he walked around his beloved New England. One notebook was to record things he saw in nature, and the other was for the poetry he was inspired to write. There were times when he encountered something that thrilled him so that he wouldn't know which notebook to record it in. In other words, nature itself is sheer poetry. Therein lies the conundrum for the nature writer. Do you write with your head, your heart, or try to balance precariously somewhere in between the two?

I feel this perplexity often but probably never more than when I hear an American toad calling from a nearby wetland. Its sweet song—described by some as a low, melodious trill—is as beautiful and gentle to the ear as anything

I've ever heard. In the Tennessee Valley toads usually begin their trilling in March, as the days lengthen and the temperatures moderate prior to spring.

Totally enamored by their vocalization, I have spent long quiet moments sitting in the bushes just listening to its timeless sweetness. A toad's trill is hypnotic and drifts as delicately as fog over the pond and surrounding countryside. It's a siren's song full of longing, yet these sirens are all males, for it's the male toads that do the singing. Toad trills have floated over Tennessee waters for thousands of sodden springs. No Gregorian chant ever quavered by a Benedictine monk is as serenely pure and life affirming. Its ethereal sound, some would say, is not of this world; it seeps into our consciousness like the wispy fingers of a long-ago dream.

I am not the first to be smitten by toad song. Recalling a pleasant spring day a few months earlier, Thoreau wrote in his journal on October 26, 1853:

> I well remember the time this year when I first heard the dream of the toads. I was laying out house-lots on Little River in Haverhill. We had had some raw, cold and wet weather. But this day was remarkably warm and pleasant, and I had thrown off my outside coat. I was going home for dinner, past a shallow pool, which was green with springing grass, and where a new house was about being erected, when it occurred to me that I heard the dream of the toad. It rang through and filled all the air, though I had not heard it once. And I turned my companion's attention to it, but he did not appear to perceive it as a new sound in the air. Loud and prevailing as it is, most men do not notice it at all. It is to them, perchance, a sort of simmering or seething of all nature. That afternoon the dream of the toads rang through the elms by Little River and affected the thoughts of men, though they were not conscious that they heard it.
>
> How watchful we must be to keep the crystal well that we were made, clear! —that it be not made turbid by contact with the world, so that it will not reflect objects. What other liberty is there worth having, if we have not freedom and peace in our minds, —if our inmost and most private man is but a sour and turbid pool?

To Emerson's attentive eye, we now add Thoreau's perceptive ear, yet keeping our "crystal well" clear, our harmonious connection to the natural world, is not easy. The demands of our cluttered culture scream at us, clouding our perception. Like Thoreau's companion we too become turbid, lost to the beauty that surrounds us. Most people never expect quivering rapture to emanate from such an odd, lumpy creature as a toad, but it does.

Toads are similar to frogs. Both are amphibians, except that a toad is bumpier and spends most of its year on dry land. A frog's life is more aquatic. In the spring, however, the male toads leave their drier environs and move to nearby wet places and trill to attract females into the water. This is where they couple and she lays her eggs. Toads lay long ribbons of eggs, sort of like strings of black pearls. Frogs lay eggs in clumps or masses.

After mating season the toads go back to dry land and live solitary lives. Some may even reside near your home in the mulch around shrubbery or under your back porch. They'll live there, quietly eating insects at night; you hardly know they are there. Gardeners love having the natural insectivores around their homes, but to most people toads and frogs spark little interest. Historically, if they were regarded at all, it was usually in a negative light—especially toads.

As the European settlers began to spread into this country, con men followed, for a fool and his money are soon parted. Mountebanks were scam artists who traveled throughout the countryside selling bottled elixirs they promoted as "wonder cures." The secret recipes—concoctions brewed beforehand in the back of the wagon—probably contained a goodly amount of fermented anything. The quack medicines were said to be, "good for what ails you," and the mountebankery often included a live demonstration.

One scam that was particularly dramatic called for the charlatan to request a volunteer from the gathered audience. In time, a supposed bumpkin reluctantly stepped forward. The mountebank gave the sheepish volunteer a live toad to swallow. After much hesitation and clamorous encouragement from the crowd, the volunteer slowly complied, gulping down the amphibian with a lot of bug-eyed disgust. In fairly short order the poor fool would fall to the ground, twitching and writhing in the throes of death. The flimflam man then came to his rescue and poured a few gulps of his miracle elixir down the dying man's throat. Much to the amazement of the shocked audience, the toad-gulper quickly recovered. (We assume the toad didn't fair nearly as well.)

Of course, the volunteer was in league with the con man all along. Such mountebanks' assistants became known as toad-eaters or toadies. Needless to say, sales of the bottled potion became brisk after the obvious benefits of its curative properties were witnessed by all. This humbuggery worked for two reasons. First, in the days before wonder drugs, people were desperate for a wonder drug. And second, everyone knew that toads were vile creatures; ingesting one had to be foolish or deadly and probably even both.

Perhaps the most widespread myth surrounding frogs and toads warns that handling them will give you warts. This bit of folklore was apparently shared even by the valley's Cherokee. Their name for frog or toad and wart was the same: *wala'si*. Of course, warts are non-cancerous growths of skin caused by viruses; frogs and toads have nothing to do with them.

Since the beginning of recorded time, frogs and toads (collectively known as anurans) have been lumped with snakes, spiders, and all other creepy, crawly things as disgusting beasts and bad omens. They were only loved by small boys, wizards, and poets. In *Paradise Lost,* John Milton describes Satan in the loathsome guise of the amphibian. He writes of the Devil: "Squat like a toad, close at the ear of Eve, Assaying by his devilish art to reach, The organs of her fancy."

Frogs and toads, newts and salamanders are amphibians, which means "life on both sides," in this case land and water. They're unique and specially adapted to living and reproducing in moist, cool environments. The anurans lack ribcages to help their inefficient lungs breathe in air. Consequently, they're very dependent on oxygen being absorbed through their soft, moist skin. This dependence on cutaneous breathing keeps them relatively small, thus maintaining a high ratio of surface area to body size. Also their cool environs help with respiration because oxygen dissolves better in cooler temperatures. Their shell-less eggs must be laid in water or extremely damp locations; otherwise they'd quickly dry out.

Biologists who study amphibians and reptiles are called herpetologists. Like the scientists who study birds, herpetologists have been keeping records of amphibian populations for years. In the late 1980s some of these specialists realized that they weren't seeing or hearing the numbers of amphibia they once had. These declines were believed to be localized because no one had ever attempted a global survey. That's when a group including Jeff Houlahan with the Ottawa-Carleton Institute of Biology in Ontario, Canada, began to pull together data from reports and published accounts from all over the globe. In time the study accumulated information on 936 amphibian populations from two hundred researchers located in thirty-seven countries in eight regions of the planet. What they discovered affirmed their worst fears: the declines weren't just local, but global.

Amphibian populations—frogs and toads, salamanders and newts—have been decreasing since 1960: overall, a steep drop from 1960 to 1966, followed by a smaller but steady slide between 1966 and 1997. The initial sharp downswing in the early 1960s was approximately 15 percent a year. It was followed by a slow fall of 2 percent a year from 1966 to the late 1990s.

The global declines weren't exactly the same in all locations. Both North America and Western Europe showed population loss for the six years after 1960, but only in North America did the slow decline continue after 1966. The initial decline in the early 1960s was more dramatic in Western Europe than in North America, but the continued slump had lasted longer in the latter until, by 1997, both continents had lost about the same in overall numbers. If you do the math, using the annual 15 percent loss for the years 1960 to '66, followed by the 2 percent annual loss from 1966 to 1997, the total decline is over 80 percent in just over forty years. Of the 936 amphibian populations in the study, 61 had disappeared altogether. That's startling, but do we know the cause?

In truth, it has been hard for most people to work up much concern for amphibians. But times have changed. We no longer buy our medicine from traveling salesmen, and we're beginning to view frogs and toads for what they are: hypersensitive creatures keenly attuned to changes in their surroundings, especially their watery habitats. For this reason they are seen as environmental indicators. If amphibians are on the decline, what's next?

Worldwide amphibian decline is probably caused by a variety of factors— habitat loss, ultraviolet radiation, disease, climate change, and chemical pollution—working together. Amphibians need wet places to mate and lay their eggs, and wetlands have long been considered wasted, unprofitable land. Many wetland locations have been drained, dredged, and filled, converted into more suitable sites for an expanding human population. When the first European settlers came to America, they found roughly 230 million acres of wetlands in the lower forty-eight states. A report given by the U.S. Fish and Wildlife Service to Congress in 1991 concluded that, on average, sixty acres of wetlands in the lower forty-eight states were lost every hour between the 1780s and the 1980s.

Congress was partly to blame. The Swamp Land Act of 1850 offered federal wetlands to be given to the states if they would have them drained and converted into useful parcels. Between 1849 and 1860, 64 million acres were given to fifteen states. The problem was exacerbated by our wanton destruction of the beaver population since the industrious mammal is nature's great wetland creator.

The largest wetland area in the United States is in southern Florida. The Everglades and the surrounding estuaries began to be tinkered with—diverted, drained, dredged, and channeled—as early as the late 1800s. Once covering over 4,000,000 acres, the Everglades were reduced by half in just a hundred years. The same percentage holds true for the rest of the lower forty-eight states. In Tennessee, an estimated 1,937,000 acres of wetlands existed in 1780. By the late 1900s only 787,000 remained, representing a loss of 59 percent, with 7 percent of the remaining wetlands considered damaged.

The very term "wetland" is a new one—a creation of ecologists grappling to come to terms with the changing environs. Before their research into the role of such ecosystems, there was no collective label to cover swamps, marshes, bogs, sloughs, riverine bottomlands, floodplains, and all the other wet places that amphibians need to reproduce.

In this country, the loss of wetlands began to be slowed with the passage of the Federal Clean Water Act of 1972. Its primary goal was to restore and maintain chemical, physical, and biological integrity of the nation's surface waters, including wetlands. The Clean Water Act has two primary sections: Section 404 regulates the discharge of dredged and/or fill material into wetlands, and Section 401 mandates that the fill not violate state water quality standards. In effect, 401 lets each state determine these standards and set up mechanisms to regulate them.

In Tennessee the Water Quality Control Act of 1977 requires that a permit be issued before any waters or wetlands in the state are altered. The latest update of the Tennessee Wetland Conservation Strategy, issued in 1998 by the Tennessee Department of Environment and Conservation (TDEC), has established a goal of "no net loss" of wetland functions in the state. Developers must obtain a permit before they can destroy a wetland. They first are asked to avoid impacting the wetland by looking for alternative sites, or they are required to minimize their impacts by reformulating their proposed plans. If the first two fail, they must compensate for the altering of the original wetland by reshaping or re-creating a wetland nearby.

This last step would, in a ideal world, yield "no net loss" of wetlands, but many ecologists bristle at the notion. They maintain that humans don't know enough to create a properly functioning wetland. And by the time you realized it wasn't working, it would be too late; the original wetland would be gone.

Obviously, the loss of half of the amphibian-breeding sites in this country has led to the decline in their overall numbers. But the world's excessive love of chemicals has also played a role. Increased exposure to ultraviolet radiation, or UV-B, has probably contributed to amphibian decline as well. Ultraviolet radiation comes in three wavelengths. The higher wavelengths of UV-A are not absorbed by living tissue, and most of the UV-C is absorbed in the existing ozone layer. It's the midrange UV-B that's the problem. UV-B is particularly harmful to living organisms and the amount of UV-B reaching the surface of the planet has been steadily increasing the past few decades.

Before 1960 sunscreen was something we rarely concerned ourselves with. For someone growing up during the Eisenhower Administration in the 1950s, it wasn't an issue because we had a thick layer of stratospheric ozone blanketing the earth fifteen miles above the ground. The harmful UV-B rays from the sun bounced off the ozone layer and did not penetrate to reach our exposed skin. Little did we know that this protection was being eroded away by ozone-destroying chemicals called chlorofluorocarbons (CFCs). The civilized world used CFCs as propellants in such products as aerosol deodorants and hairsprays and as coolants in refrigerators and air conditioners. Once the CFCs escaped into the atmosphere, they slowly drifted up to the protective layer where they underwent chemical reactions that slowly destroyed the ozone molecules.

In some locations the ozone layer has grown dangerously thin, exposing people and amphibians to increasing amounts of UV-B. CFCs have been banned in America and are being phased out in the rest of the world, but there are still enough existing in the upper atmosphere to continue eroding the ozone layer for many years to come.

In humans, exposure to UV-B leads to an increased potential for skin cancers. Amphibians with hypersensitive skin are even more vulnerable—they can't use sunscreen. Unprotected frog eggs with the developing embryos inside often float at the surface of water where they are warmed by the sun, also receiving UV-B radiation. The effect of this exposure is not clearly understood. It works on different species in different ways. UV-B can kill some amphibians directly or cause slowed growth rates and immune system dysfunction in others. A weakened immune system makes the amphibia more susceptible to disease and parasites.

CFCs are not the only chemicals that are impacting frogs and toads. Air pollution has also had a role in amphibian decline. In Norway "acid rain" has eliminated fish from thirteen thousand square kilometers of fresh water; in neighboring Sweden, it has made twenty-two hundred lakes nearly lifeless. Some researchers believe the polluted precipitation has had a major role in the worldwide amphibian decline. It stands to reason. If a frog wants a drink, all it has to do is sit in water and the liquid flows through its skin into its body as if it were a sponge. Consequently, if that water is polluted, the frog absorbs the toxins.

Acid rain is caused by the release of sulfur dioxide and nitrogen oxide into the atmosphere through the burning of fossil fuels in steam plants and automobiles.

When these chemicals come into contact with water droplets in clouds, they're converted to sulfur- and nitrogen-based acids.

When it comes to acid, the degree of acidity is determined by its pH value. On a pH scale, a reading of 7 is neutral. Numbers falling below 7 are progressively more acidic, with a reading of 1 being the harshest. In other words, a pH of 4 is ten times more acidic than 5, and a pH reading of 3 is one hundred times more acidic. When acid rain falls, it changes the pH of the soil and water, acidifying them. Limited studies conducted in the eastern United States found up to 15 percent of the vernal, temporary pools with lethal levels of acid during the spring, when most amphibians lay their eggs. Another 10 to 14 percent had acid levels that, while not lethal, were still high enough to cause delayed growth in the tadpoles and suppress their immune systems. More than 50 percent of the habitats used by sixteen of the seventeen species that live in eastern Canada have been affected by acid rain.

Closer to my home, research conducted in the Great Smoky Mountains has found that the higher elevations are suffering from "advanced nitrogen saturation." The national park's soils and streams are being acidified to the point at which entire ecosystems are being impacted. The average acidity of rain falling in the Smokies is five to ten times more acidic than normal rainfall. Frogs, crayfish, and mayflies die in water with a pH of 5 or lower.

In addition to acidification, the release of pesticides, heavy metals, and nitrogen-based fertilizers into the environment are probably impacting sensitive amphibian populations. There are approximately nineteen thousand to twenty thousand chemicals classified as pesticides—insecticides, herbicides and fungicides—approved for release in the United States. They're all poisons designed to kill something. In accordance with the Federal Insecticide, Fungicide, and Rodenticide Act of 1942 (FIFRA), all have to be tested to determine a safe level for human and non-target wildlife before they can be approved. A Lethal Concentration (LC) has to be determined on test animals, with the LC defined as the amount it takes to kill 50 percent of the animal group tested. Animals tested are usually bluegill sunfish, fathead minnows, and rainbow trout. Amphibians are not tested because it is believed that they would be more sensitive to the contaminants than the average vertebrate; thus, it's a given that these hypersensitive creatures will fall within the LC limits.

It is estimated that consumers in this country use 300 million pounds of chemical insecticides annually. That works out to be roughly a pound per person. (The U.S. Census Bureau estimated that the population of the United States in May 2006 was 298,752,169.) The insecticides used included compounds that the Environmental Protection Agency says *may* disrupt hormones, impair the nervous system, and cause cancer in humans. Their combined effect on amphibians is unknown.

One widely used weed killer, atrazine, has been tested on frogs. The research of Tyrone Hayes, an endocrinologist at the University of California at Berkeley, has garnered a lot of attention in the past few years. Haynes has determined that northern leopard frogs exposed to small concentrations of atrazine (only one-thirtieth of what is currently approved as the safe level in drinking water) affect the amphibians in an unexpected way. Some of the male frogs developed multiple sex organs, and some had been feminized with shrunken larynxes. Male frogs attract mates by singing, and an impaired voice box would inhibit this. Atrazine didn't kill the frogs outright, but it severely impacted their reproduction.

Whenever I speak to groups about amphibians, if I bring up chlorofluorocarbons or acidification, you can almost see the eyes of those in the attendance glaze over. After all, isn't that chemistry, a subject to be avoided if at all possible? As for me, my last class that dealt with the periodic table was decades ago. When it comes to environmental issues, it's easy to become overwhelmed by the chemistry, which, of course, is exactly what is happening to the environment itself. Even though you and I would not exist without naturally occurring organic chemical components, the artificial compounds that our species has cleverly created are what is causing the problems. The air we breathe and the land and waterways around our cities and beyond are overwhelmed. Because of their hypersensitivity to manmade chemicals, amphibians are often likened to canaries in a coal mine. The caged birds were once carried underground by the miners to detect lethal gases. If the canaries died, the miners quickly evacuated the tunnels.

In 2004 a Global Amphibian Assessment turned up alarming numbers. Of the 5,700 species of amphibians covered by the report, almost one third are threatened and 168 species have become extinct in just the last twenty years. "The last time we saw such a categorical loss was with the dinosaurs. And no one can say that didn't change the planet," says Joe Mendelson of Zoo Atlanta. To the list of other causes for the decline is a newly discovered disease that is rapidly decimating populations. Caused by a fungus that invades the animals' skin and disrupts their water balance, the pathogen is having a big impact and spreading rapidly. In January 2006 *National Geographic* published a map of the world to illustrate the problem. Locations shaded in burnt orange pinpointed places where amphibians are most at risk. The American Southeast was one of the areas highlighted.

In North America the golden toad of Costa Rica and the Vegas Valley leopard frog of the western United States are now extinct. In the United States the relic leopard frog and Wyoming toad are on the brink of extinction, while populations of the western toad and Chiricahua leopard frog have dropped 80 percent in recent decades. The California red-legged, Chiricahua, and mountain yellow-legged frogs, all western species, and the Mississippi gopher frog found in the southern Gulf States appear on the list of Threatened and Endangered Species (TESS).

In the southeastern United States, forty-six species of amphibians are currently listed as being "imperiled," a term now being used to mean endangered, threatened, or in need of monitoring. Of these, thirty-nine are salamanders, and seven are frogs. It appears that the region is not experiencing the dramatic population declines that are happening in the rest of the world, but herpetologists are quick to point out that that may be the result of a lack of historical data, which makes it difficult to establish a baseline for comparison. Most will also say that amphibian habitat in the area is rapidly being destroyed, fragmented, or degraded in some way. Amphibians also have not garnered the attention or research funding that game animals like wild turkey, white-tailed deer, or even many sport fishes have received. Some might even argue that salamanders, frogs, and toads are not that important in the overall scheme of things, and that if we lose a few, so what? It's as though there are two lists: one for animals that have an economic value and one for those that do not. Yet, many of the creatures that would find themselves on the latter list are part of the food chain that supports the glamorous ones on the former.

The Tennessee Valley is home to thirteen species of frogs and toads. Currently none are listed as threatened, endangered, or even imperiled. Yet, knowing exact population sizes is a bit hard to determine because they are so skilled at hiding—that is, unless it's mating season. Then the reclusive amphibians have to make their location and numbers known; at least the males do. At different times during the year, each species goes through breeding season, and the males advertise their exact location by calling. It's also during these vocal times that biologists can get a fix on their overall numbers and range.

All through this narrative, I've referred to frogs and toads as if there were only two distinct groups. The typical frog, or true frog, belongs in the genus *Rana* and has relatively smooth skin and long back legs, while the typical toad, or true toad, is the genus *Bufo* and has lumpy-bumpy skin and short back legs. But nature loves variations. There are groups that fall somewhere in the gray area in between. One of these is the spadefoot. The species that's found around my home is the Eastern spadefoot, perhaps the most curious and secretive anuran in the Tennessee Valley.

To a naturalist, amphibians are intriguing, at least in part because they are so secretive. Thoreau might even say ephemeral. I can think of few things as evanescent as toad song. Therein lies the enchantment: their vaporous existence. By their very nature, frogs and toads tend to live away from humans in wet, sloppy places. Finding them can mean slogging through mud or marsh. It's not often that they come to you, particularly those toads considered rare in many places.

"It was sort of a frog-toad," said Shaney Palmer. "Its front end was rounded like a frog, not pointy like a toad. But its back end was toad-like, with small patches of warts."

Shaney is a middle school science teacher at Webb School of Knoxville, an independent, coeducational day school located in west Knox County. In May 2003 she and her husband, Ed Yost, were chaperones at the eighth-grade dance, so it was a festive occasion. The week had been very rainy—good amphibian weather. Many frogs and toads were out and about enjoying the dampness in dances of their own.

Shaney and Ed were walking across Webb's spacious campus when they noticed something hop on the sidewalk. Ed picked up the small wanderer for both of them to examine. On its back feet they noticed very elongated toes. Ed's degree is in forestry, so he knows the woods. He believed they had found an elusive spadefoot. But on this night, the mysterious creatures weren't that elusive. "We soon realized they were all over the place," said Shaney, an avid naturalist with a strong leaning toward herpetology. "It was a pleasant evening. We had propped the doors open to the lobby and the little guys were hopping around inside the building." Although it's been a long time since I attended an eighth-grade dance, I'm sure having hopping toad-frogs about the premises only added to festivities.

The Eastern spadefoot is about two inches long. It's a species of eastern lowland forests and is usually found in places with loose, sandy soil. Spadefoots have sharp-edged, spade-like projections on their hind feet. These "spades" allow them to dig down quickly into loose soil to hide. During dry times, they remain torpid underground and can lose over 40 percent of their body weight through fluid loss. Other American spadefoot species live out west in more arid areas, where surviving with little water is a must.

Unlike most frogs and toads that reproduce annually, Eastern spadefoots are "explosive breeders." They are opportunists closely tied to weather patterns.

It only takes the right conditions to stimulate mating. A sudden drop in baro-metric pressure, more than two inches of rain and nightfall can trigger a frenzy to find temporary pools, flooded fields, and ditches for egg laying. It's usually a short-lived phenomenon that doesn't necessarily occur yearly. This rush to re-produce may happen anytime during the warm months of April through July.

On these nights, a single spadefoot female can lay twenty-five hundred eggs in long filaments. The eggs are anchored to underwater vegetation and hatch in only one to seven days. The resulting tadpoles metamorphose into adults in just over two weeks before the temporary pools dry up. Rapid development is essen-tial. The obvious danger is that the vernal pools wither before the tadpoles have completed the process. You might wonder: why such a risky strategy? The tem-porary pools used by the spadefoots do not contain any fish, the number-one predator of anuran eggs and tadpoles. By waiting until just the right moment, they completely dodge the number-one obstacle to reproducing in large num-bers: hungry fish. If the right moment only comes every few years, so what?

In fairly short order, the young spadefoots leave their watery birthplace and hop away. They'll soon disappear under leaves and below ground and are rarely seen or heard—that is, until the next "explosion." Since these small secre-tive amphibians are nocturnal and subterranean, they are not easily found or inventoried. Ohio and Connecticut list them as an endangered species. In other states they're considered uncommon, rare or of "special concern." In Tennessee their range is widespread, occurring from the Tennessee Valley westward to the Mississippi River. Determining how changes in the environment are affecting their populations is difficult at best, considering that very little money is avail-able for amphibian research.

In the spring of 2004, Ijams Nature Center educator Kara East and I led a nature walk at Seven Islands Wildlife Refuge that included Kathy Bivens, Remi Joyeuse and his wife, Angela, and their young children, Zane and Savana. The new wild-life area is 360 acres of former farmland located on the French Broad River at Kelly Bend. We were looking and listening for frogs and toads, trying to get a sense of what species lived there. The cool, somewhat unseasonable tempera-tures didn't dampen the group's enthusiasm. By the time the sun dipped low, we had identified three species: chorus frogs, spring peepers, and a lone gray tree frog calling from the wooded parcel that overlooks the nearby islands. As the group was breaking up and returning to their cars, a few of us lingered near a small creek watching an orchard oriole moving back and forth along the water's edge. As we paused to enjoy the setting sun, Kathy and I began to hear American toads trilling from the tall grasses along the stream. First one, then a second, and finally a third. At such moments, as you stand in remote, damp places, your mind begins to drift, caught up in Thoreau's hypnotic dream of toads. The sirens were at work again. I was transported to primeval vernal wetlands when time was new and life fresh upon the land.

Amphibians and their direct ancestors have been on earth for millennia. Their branch of the family tree split away from early land-living four-legged animals roughly 360 million years ago. Following the lead of their ancient ancestor *Ichthyostega*, early amphibians adapted to living on both land and in water. Some might say they were hedging their bets, not firmly committing to either environ. Over the vast reaches of time their forms changed, but they've continued to lay shell-less eggs that need to stay damp to survive. Somewhere along the line, the frogs and toads found their voice and, despite their hypersensitivity, managed to live through the mass extinction that wiped out the seemingly more robust reptiles, the dinosaurs. Yet, today, are modern amphibians on the brink of the same fate?

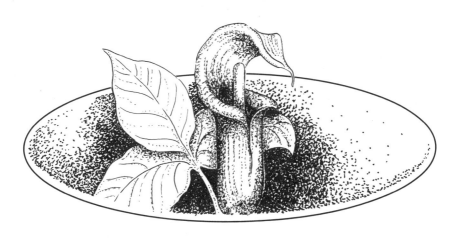

Spring

Freshwater Mussels

Numerous species

The smell of mud, of primeval mud, by Jove! was in my nostrils,
the high stillness of primeval forest was before my eyes; there
were shiny patches on the black creek. The moon had spread over
everything a thin layer of silver—over the rank grass, over the mud,
upon the wall of matted vegetation standing higher than the wall
of a temple, over the great river I could see through a sombre gap
glittering, glittering, as it flowed broadly by without a murmur.

Joseph Conrad
Heart of Darkness, 1899

The first Europeans to venture into the Southeast were the Spanish conquistadors led by Hernando de Soto. The four-year exploration—1539 to 1543—into what they called "La Florida," was the first major expedition into the South's heartland by the self-professed "civilized world," although today many archaeologists, anthropologists, and paleolinguists would argue that, before Columbus, the Americas were far more civilized than the rest of the world. It's just that those cultures did not survive to write the history books. Even though the New World lacked sailing ships and advanced weaponry, it's naïve to think of its peoples as being purely primitive.

In 1539 de Soto was thirty-nine years old and rich from the plunder of Peru. At the time he had been named governor of Cuba and was looking for new conquests. He sought gold and silver or anything of value, but perhaps even more than that he wanted to colonize and control the Island of Florida (today we call it North America). He also sought a northern passage to the South Sea (the Pacific Ocean) and hoped to open a shorter trade route between gold-rich Spain and China, the world's marketplace.

In May of 1539 his army of six hundred conquistadors, half on horseback, plus several hundred servants, camp-followers, and Indian slaves, marched inland and north from Florida's Gulf Coast. His army was loaded, geared for conquest with tons of supplies: gunpowder, cannons, cross bows, lances, armor, helmets, axes, and saws. The troop also sported massive war dogs, mastiffs and great greyhounds wearing armor, and a herd of several hundred pigs.

If de Soto meant to overwhelm, he succeeded. He had seen the weaponry of the natives in South America and knew it was no match. The Native Americans living in the Southeast at the time didn't know it, but de Soto's trip marked the beginning of the end. Their way of life, which had evolved over ten thousand years, would soon crumble.

The indigenous people de Soto's army encountered were the forerunners to the Cherokees, Creeks, Seminoles, Chickasaws, and Choctaws of the eighteenth and nineteenth centuries. These prehistoric peoples were mound builders and had never seen Europeans or armored dogs or weapons of gunpowder or even pigs. Warriors covered in metal on horseback must have stymied them. They also didn't have immunity to European diseases such as smallpox, scarlet fever, whooping cough, and influenza. Archaeological evidence shows that in the 150 years after de Soto's invasion aboriginal populations declined by 50 percent or more. Joyce Hudson writes, "An epidemic of smallpox in an Indian town might kill more than 80 percent of the people living there."

De Soto's expedition also destroyed their social order. Before 1539 the various territories were organized into chiefdoms. The high chiefs were believed to be the divine representatives of the power of the Sun. Their people revered them and, in turn, paid tribute to the chiefs in the form of corn, deerskins, and other valuables. The corn was kept in public storehouses and redistributed to the people in times of need.

De Soto, who had an entourage of nearly one thousand to feed, also coveted the corn. The conquistadors weren't prepared to live off the land; there were too many of them. At times de Soto was able to trade for or finagle provisions. But time and time again, when de Soto entered a province, he'd take the high chief prisoner and loot the village's granaries, enslaving burden-carriers and women. Captives were kept naked "in iron collars and chains." The Spaniards even killed and ate the Indian's small dogs, something the natives themselves did not do.

The high chiefs were held hostage until the conquistadors passed through their provinces and entered another. The humbled chief was then released to return to his vanquished people, but by this time the chiefdom was shattered, the people's respect lost. The sun's divine ones had not been able to protect them. Rarely were the chiefs able to regain authority, and the powerful chiefdoms disintegrated into smaller egalitarian tribes.

The exact route of de Soto's expedition is unclear, a matter for scholarly debate. Four men produced chronicles of the adventure, three in Spanish and one in Portuguese. Three of the writers were actually there at the time; the fourth, Garcilaso de la Vega, wrote his account forty to fifty years later. His source of information was an old soldier who had been part of the expedition. The four accounts don't always agree. Over the years they have all been translated several times, and even the translations vary. The chroniclers also used the Native American names for villages that no longer exist, so knowing exactly where they journeyed is difficult.

It is generally believed, however, that de Soto traveled north from Florida, through Georgia into South Carolina and as far from the gulf as today's North Carolina. The troop then crossed through the mountains into the Tennessee Valley following the river south into Georgia before going west to the Mississippi River. The Spaniards used existing Indian trails, moving from village to village like a plague, trading for what they could and bullying for the rest. Many of the natives gave freely, perhaps partly out of friendliness and partly because they were intimidated.

Although the conquistadors did not find any gold and silver, they did find one item of value. In the province of Cofachiqui, negotiations were cordial. De Soto spoke with a "woman chief" referred to as the Lady of Cofachiqui. She offered the Spaniards lodgings and a storehouse of maize. Garcilaso de la Vega reports that, while talking to Governor de Soto, the female chief began to slowly remove a great rope of freshwater pearls she had wrapped around her neck three times. It is said that the pearls hung down to her thighs. Through an interpreter she offered the string of pearls to the governor, who accepted the gift and gave the lady a gold ring off his finger in return.

In Guaxulle (which some believe is today's Asheville), the natives gave the Spaniards three hundred dogs, which the hungry soldiers promptly ate. Shortly thereafter, de Soto learned of mines of yellow metal, thirty leagues (seventy-nine miles) over the mountains to the north in a province called Chisca. Two Spaniards, Juan de Villalobos and Francisco de Silvera, were sent with Indian guides who knew the land of Chisca and its language. The scouting party went by foot because climbing the rugged terrain of the Appalachians on horseback would have been too difficult. It is generally believed that Chisca was located in the foothills of East Tennessee, perhaps near present-day Knoxville; if so, that scouting party would have been the first Europeans to cross the Smokies into the Tennessee Valley. Ten days later, they rejoined de Soto and reported that Chisca was very poor, with little maize, and that the mines did not contain gold but copper and a "very fine brass."

Still in North Carolina, perhaps on the Little Tennessee River, a chief came to de Soto with a present, another string of freshwater pearls two fathoms long (about twelve feet). The pearls were perfectly matched, about the size of hazelnuts. Governor de Soto was pleased and gave the chief pieces of velvet and other cloth of various colors from Spain. De Soto inquired about the pearls' origin and wondered how they were removed from the shells. Obligingly, the chief offered to show the governor and immediately dispatched forty canoes of hunters to dive all night for freshwater mussels. In the morning, a huge fire was built on a flat part of the riverbank. When the canoes returned, the fire's glowing embers were raked flat, and the night's catch was spread over them. As the shells steamed they popped open, many revealing pearls the size of chickpeas. The pearls were perfect except for the scorch marks of the fire. De Soto was pleased, probably thankful to find something of value to justify his trip.

Later that same day, a soldier came to de Soto in his lodgings. He spoke of eating one of the mussels and finding a pearl inside. Being a good soldier, he offered it to the governor as a gift to his wife, Dona Isabel. The governor thanked him for his kindness but advised the man to keep the pearl and trade it later when they returned to Cuba for a couple of horses and two mares or anything else the fellow might need. He was informed by another that the pearl, back in Spain, would be worth four hundred ducats, a goodly sum for a soldier. This gives us an idea of the perceived value of a single pearl. Today, a gold ducat would be worth just over two dollars.

It is believed that de Soto's large troop crossed into Tennessee in late June 1540 and worked their way southwest down the valley. On Friday, July 2, they arrived at Coste, an Indian village on an island at the confluence of two rivers (maybe the Tennessee and Hiwassee Rivers in Meigs County or the Tellico and Little Tennessee in Monroe County). There the conquistadors found honey from bees "as good or better than can be found in Spain," and in the river they located mussels and more freshwater pearls.

As the summer of 1540 wore on, the expedition moved south into Georgia and west through Alabama to the Mississippi River. De Soto himself did not live to see his plans for La Florida to fruition. The trip did him in. He died of fever on May 21, 1542, and was buried in the waters of the Mississippi River, roughly two years after leaving Tennessee. A biographer writes that de Soto was "neither better nor worse than other conquistadors nor in any way a paradigm of goodness and gentleness." He was ambitious and greedy, passionate and curt. De Soto also delighted in his skill with a horse and lance when used against other humans. Novelist Joseph Conrad might have added that the governor had a heart of darkness, the embodiment of the worst parts of European civilization traveling upriver to exploit the indigenous people of North America.

The Mississippian Period Indians de Soto encountered were mound builders who represented the highest cultural advancement ever achieved in North America before the arrival of the Spaniards. They built large flat-topped mounds that served as the cultural centers of their *talwas* or towns. De Soto witnessed the mounds being built. His chroniclers reported that dirt was carried to the top of the mounds, basketfuls at a time, emptied, and stamped down. The sides of the mounds were so steep they were difficult to climb. Instead, long ramps were constructed in much the same way to afford access to the flat surface on top.

The high chiefs lived in houses atop the mounds. These Mississippian Tradition peoples were craftsmen with high standards, who made a range of items out of stone, metal, pottery, and shell. Garbage piles called *middens* containing discarded mussel shells are often found at sites along the Tennessee River. A historical railroad stop along the river near Jasper in Marion County (west of Chattanooga) was known as Shellmound Station because it was located at the site of immense piles of aged shells. If you've ever eaten at a seafood restaurant on the coast, you've seen much the same sort of garbage pile behind the eatery. Some of the Native American middens contained hundreds of thousands of shells, proving that freshwater mussels were an important food source. Empty shells were also used to a small degree to make tools and utensils such as garden hoes, spoons, scrapers, dippers, and cups. Engraved shell gorgets, worn like pendants, were highly detailed, decorated with symbolic icons. The natives also made pots from clay and added crushed mussel shells to the wet mix to temper the pot so that it wouldn't crack when being fired.

Freshwater mussels are beautiful in their simplicity. Like clams they're bivalves, meaning that they have two valves or shells, perfectly matched mirror images of each other that can close shut. The shells are attached with an elastic ligament that serves as a hinge on the bottom. Inside the valves are animals made of soft tissue that are pinkish to gray in color. Mussels are mollusks like snails: as the animal inside grows, the protective shell outside becomes bigger. Mussels do not have heads, tentacles, eyes, or vertebrates. They do have hearts that usually beat around twenty times per minute with blood that's watery and slightly blue. They breathe and exchange oxygen and carbon dioxide through long flat gills. They also have two dark-colored kidneys that excrete their wastes.

Mussels have one strong hatchet-shaped foot that anchors them to the bottom of the river. They're burrowers: the hinged-half of the bivalve points down, buried in the gravel or sand. With their one foot, they're able to move themselves along slowly, dragging the cumbersome shells through the substrate. Some can move several feet an hour. The open end, where the two shells meet, is generally held slightly ajar. A hollow tube called an *incurrent siphon* extends through the parted shells and pulls water into the bivalve, while a second *excurrent* siphon forces it out. Inside the two shells, minute hairlike cilia on the mantle, gills, and body beat in unison to move the water about. Tiny suspended particles of food, zooplankton, algae, and organic detritus are filtered out of the water and flow into the mouth.

The mussel's shell is made of calcium carbonate, a chalky-white hard substance secreted by the animal. The inner surfaces of these shells are smooth and thickly coated. Called mother-of-pearl, they're layered with calcium carbonate and an organic substance that make the inner surface appear highly polished and prism-like, reflecting a range of subtle colors.

The lifecycle of a typical mussel is more complicated than you might imagine. As a general rule, in most species, the sexes are separate. In their ovaries the females produce unfertilized eggs, which are discharged to lie on portions of their gills; these become brood sacks called *marsupia*. The male's sperm, expelled into the water, is sucked by the female into her body through her incurrent siphon. The eggs are then fertilized in her brood sacks, where the young develop into small larvae called *glochidia* (pronounced glo-kid-ee-ah). The tiny glochidia, with immature heart, mouth, intestines, and foot, are discharged into the surrounding water though the female's excurrent siphon.

Generally, freshwater mussels are either *bradytictic* or *tachytictic*. Bradytictic species are long-term breeders. The females retain their young in their brood sacks over the winter. Tachytictic species are short-term. Typically these females retain their young internally for only a brief period, usually late spring through early summer. Species like rayed bean, purple lilliput, Cumberland monkeyface, rabbitsfoot, and round pigtoe are usually gravid (pregnant) from May through July.

Here's where it gets incredibly interesting. Once discharged, the larvae have to go through a parasitic phase if they are to survive to adulthood. And even though they can't swim or crawl, they must find and attach themselves to a host fish, usually to its gills, fins, or tail. Each species of mussel has a particular host or hosts they must find, otherwise they'll fall to the bottom and die. The purple lilliput mussel, for example, must find a green sunfish or a longear sunfish. This seems astronomically difficult; in part they overcome the odds by sheer numbers. A single gravid female of a large species of mussel can produce as many as three million glochidia. Also to improve the odds, some species of mussel have evolved specially adapted lures. A portion of the soft fleshy mantle (the tissue that lines the inside of the shell) has been modified to look like small minnows or insect larvae, the very things that the needed host fish eat. When it's time to discharge the glochidia, the female mussel wiggles her lure, and the proper fishes move in closer to investigate. At the proper instant the host gets a blast of larvae sprayed in its direction. The fact that the mussel has developed a fleshy faux lure that specifically attracts just the right host fish is an amazing feat of evolution.

The glochidia that successfully find their host remain embedded: the tissue of the fish reacts to the perceived attack and surrounds the tiny invaders with a capsule of tissue forming a cyst. The enclosed glochidia remain there for only one to six weeks while their organs mature. They then free themselves and drop to the river bottom and slowly grow to adult size. As parasites, the glochidia are not particularly demanding. They do feed on the host's cellular fluids, but the host fish is generally not harmed. In a sense, the glochidia are hitchhikers. The young mussels use their hosts to disperse themselves the way a milkweed plant uses the wind to spread its seeds. In this way, the embedded hitchhikers can be moved to new locations before they drop to the river bottom. It then takes several years before the young bivalves grow to adulthood to repeat the process.

The biology of freshwater pearls is equally unique. Pearls are the only gemstone of animal origin, and freshwater pearls are the official state gemstone of Tennessee. But what are these sublime iridescent spheres? Oddly, they are objects of irritation. Attached to the bottom of a river, a mussel may occasionally suck into its inner chamber a grain of sand, parasite, or some other sharp-edged irritant. It's like a husk of popcorn caught between your gums and cheek. Rubbing against the mussel's soft tissue, the irritant must cause some discomfort, and the mussel cannot easily dispel the small object. As a defensive mechanism, it begins to coat the unwanted grain with layer upon layer of a secretion called *nacre,* the same smooth, iridescent substance, called mother-of-pearl, that lines the mussel's inner shell.

The longer the embedded irritant remains, the larger the pearl grows. Different species of mussel secrete at different rates. A species called washboard produces about two-tenths of a millimeter in the first six months, while a black lisp pearl mussel can secrete one to seven layers of nacre a day. It is believed that only one in ten thousand mussels contain a commercially valuable pearl. These are overwhelming odds, but they're much better than those of the typical state lottery. Thus, "pearling" was a popular way to earn money in the Tennessee Valley for several decades in the late 1800s and early 1900s.

The Book of the Pearl, published in 1908 by Kunz and Stevenson, describes the era of the pearl hunter:

> Vivid and picturesque accounts were published in local papers report-
> ing hundreds of persons as camping at various points along the streams,
> some in tents and some in rough shanties, others going from shoal to
> shoal in newly-built houseboats. They were described as easy-going,
> pleasure-loving people, the men, women and children working hard all
> day, subsisting largely on fish caught in the same stream, and dancing at
> night to the music of a banjo around their camp fires.

In addition to the pearls, mussel shells played an important role in the Tennessee economy of the time. If you have an antique trunk in your attic with clothing that's over sixty years old, then chances are these heirlooms have mother-of-pearl buttons. Buttons became a significant part of fashion in the 1200s, when people moved away from loose robes and tunics and started wearing tighter-fitting clothing. Since then buttons have been made from a variety of materials: wood, bone, gold, silver, ceramics, jade, marble, leather, glass, pewter, and, in modern times, plastic. The shells of mussels became a popular medium because several buttons could be made from a single shell. Machines were built that worked like cookie-cutters, punching out round blanks of different sizes.

These discs were polished to a lustrous sheen, and then holes for thread were drilled into them.

In this country the German-born button maker John Frederick Boepple opened a mother-of-pearl button factory in Muscatine, Iowa, in 1891. Boepple choose the small town because it was located on the Mississippi River and had easy access to a seemingly limitless supply of freshwater mussels. His endeavor proved so lucrative that, over the next several years, button factories sprang up along rivers throughout the east. By 1912 nearly two hundred businesses in the United States worked to supply the world with mother-of-pearl buttons. The peak year was 1916. American factories turned out six billion buttons and employed around ninety-five hundred factory workers and another ninety-seven hundred mussel hunters. It is estimated that between 1929 and 1944, Tennessee Rivers supplied 61,476 tons of freshwater mussel shells. In the valley the Clinch, Holston, French Broad, and Tennessee rivers were all heavily harvested.

Clinton, the county seat of Anderson County, was a center for the pearling industry in the valley during the early 1900s. The town is ideally located: the Clinch River serpentines through the location, separating Clinton proper from South Clinton. Pearlers brought their found gems and baskets of shells to market every Saturday from May through September. A historical marker located downtown at 331 Market Street states: "New York dealers came regularly to Clinton during the pearling season. Saturdays were trading days for pearl hunters and buyers. In 1900 Clinch River pearls were featured at the Paris, France Exposition."

Shells for the button industry sold for about eighty dollars a ton, and pearls could sell for considerably more. One buyer, S. M. Hendrickson, bought pearls and thousands of tons of shells to ship to the pearl-button businesses in Muscatine, Iowa. Roscoe Hendrickson recalled the following: "My father, the late S. M. Hendrickson, became a dealer in these pearls and over a fifty-year period bought and sold millions of dollars worth of them. I once saw him buy a large Clinch River pearl for $5,500 and offer $6,500 for one but did not buy it. These prices were when men's wages were $1 a day."

The completion of Norris Dam on the Clinch River upstream from Clinton in 1936 ended the pearling industry in Anderson County. The water released by the dam from the bottom of Norris Lake is much colder than the warm shallow water the mussels thrive in; thus, the mussels soon died out. The Clinch River pearl hunters were forced to move on. By the time of World War II, hard plastic replaced mother-of-pearl as the material of choice for buttons, and the entire pearl-button industry in the United States collapsed. In Knoxville the Lane Street Pearl Button Plant was soon forced to shut down, and in the mid-1960s the last factory in Muscatine, the city once known as the "Button Capitol of the World," closed as well.

A naturalist takes particular delight in knowing that the short-lived Tennessee Gold Rush centered on the secretions of mollusks. Paying fifty-five hundred dollars for an iridescent lump of hardened mussel ooze is hard to imagine. It stands to reason that someone would eventually figure out how to encourage bivalves to make pearls in a controlled environment. Kokichi Mikimoto of Japan dreamed up the process of creating cultured saltwater pearls in the early 1900s. After much trial and error, it was determined that pellets made from mother-of-pearl itself inserted into oysters would work the best. These irritants stimulate them into secreting nacre around the bead, thus forming a pearl. The oysters are raised in special beds, and the pearls are harvested after three years. As you might imagine, a cultured marine pearl looks identical to a natural pearl and can only be distinguished by laboratory tests. A cultured pearl has a larger center and fewer but thicker layers of nacre than a natural one.

John Latendresse is the father of the cultured freshwater pearl. He moved to Tennessee in the 1940s and started the Tennessee Shell Company to sell freshwater mussel shells to the Japanese. They used the shells to make the pellets needed as the nuclei for their cultured saltwater pearls. (The shell business is still active in the state. In 1998 it was estimated that divers harvesting mussels from the Tennessee River made roughly $10 million dollars a year. The mussels are discarded, and the shells are sent to Japan, where they are turned into the seed pellets needed by their cultured pearl industry.) In time, Latendresse decided that he too could create cultured pearls but using freshwater mussels instead. Latendresse tested over three hundred bodies of water to determine the best possible location. In the end, placid Birdsong Creek, a tributary of the Tennessee River in Benton County, was chosen. In 1983, after twenty years of perfecting the technique, Latendresse produced the first marketable crop of cultured freshwater pearls.

In the United States there are about 300 species of freshwater mussels. Tennessee has 130 of these species in its three principal river systems: Mississippi, Cumberland, and Tennessee. Paul W. Parmalee and Arthur E. Bogan, authors of the book *The Freshwater Mussels of Tennessee,* report that the Tennessee River and its tributaries have the most assorted and abundant mussel diversity of any other river system in North America. They list a total of 102 species and subspecies found in the entire Tennessee River system.

The diversity is due to the unique geology, abundant nutrients, and the sheer variety of habitats found in the region. The Tennessee River watershed itself covers more than 40,500 square miles and includes the French Broad, Holston, Clinch, Pigeon, Powell, Little Tennessee, Nolichucky, and Hiwassee rivers as tributaries. The Tennessee River system has fifteen species and subspecies of mussels that are endemic (unique) to the system. Another twenty-one can only be found in two watersheds: the Tennessee and Cumberland. To these you can add another eleven species that were once found in the Tennessee River system but are now extinct because of dam construction and the subsequent changes to their underwater environs.

Parmalee and Bogan list ten mussels that are found in the state only in the Tennessee River system as being endangered species: angled riffleshell, green blossom, shiny pigtoe, finerayed pigtoe, Alabama lampmussel, birdwing pearlymussel, rough rabbitsfoot, Cumberland monkeyface, Appalachian monkeyface, and the purple bean. (The people who gave mussels their names were far more creative than the folks who named most sparrows.) The angled riffleshell and the green blossom are perhaps already extinct, and the others are mostly found in isolated locations, often in the upper headwaters of East Tennessee rivers. The U.S. Fish and Wildlife Service has developed recovery plans for many of the mussels on this list. But is it in time to save their dwindling populations?

The Yuchi Wildlife Refuge at Smith Bend is located on the Tennessee River in Rhea County. The name is derived from an Indian tribe displaced by the Cherokee that once lived there. Located only a few miles downstream from Watts Bar Dam and Nuclear Plant, the new refuge is a twenty-five-hundred-acre tract consisting primarily of river bottom and wetlands with three miles of riverfront. The recent purchase of the property was a joint effort of the Tennessee Wildlife Resources Agency and the Foothills Land Conservancy.

Smith Bend was created where the meandering river takes a hard right, forced to the west by Eaves Bluff, which towers three hundred feet over the surface of the water. The sharp turn slows the current, creating a sandbank where sediments carried downstream are deposited on the inside portion of the hairpin curve. This sandy, sloping bottom at Smith Bend is called Hunter Shoals, and it's the home of several species of freshwater mussels, including three endangered species.

It was a warm January day when I visited the refuge. My winter trip was timed to catch the water levels low so that I could walk the shoreline. It was a sunny afternoon; the steam rising from one of the Watts Bar cooling towers stood out sharply against the azure sky. A belted kingfisher rattled and departed as I approached. In the drying mud I soon encountered the fresh tracks of a raccoon and elected to follow them, thinking I might gain some insight into river life from an expert. Ambling along the slippery shore, I realized that the ringed-tail mammal was more sure-footed than I; after all, it was looking for a meal, and I was just on a gentle walkabout.

Raccoons forage along streams and rivers at night, looking for frogs, crayfish, insects, and whatever other tidbit they can find, including mollusks. Their strong, dexterous front paws are virtual hands that are able to pry open a bivalve and get at the soft creatures inside. Mussel shells, thumbnail- to palm-sized, were strewn about the sandy beach; many glistened pearly white in the early afternoon sun. I had no idea if they had fallen victim to my raccoon or perhaps a local otter or muskrat. At a couple of locations, I discovered sites where beavers had cut and dragged privet branches down to the water to gnaw off the bark. Beavers love privet. Pieces of the highly invasive non-native shrub, stripped clean, littered the water's edge like chicken bones at a church picnic. Often I stopped to gaze into the river, hoping to get a glimpse of a mussel. But no matter how hard I strained, the murky water gave up few of its secrets.

Fortunately, the mysterious bivalves have been divulging their secrets to Dick Neves, professor of fisheries and wildlife sciences at Virginia Tech. He has been working on mussel recovery since 1978, when he first arrived at the university located in Blacksburg, Virginia. Dr. Neves is on the forefront of the propagation and reintroduction of rare mussels. His lab, located at the edge of one of the Agriculture Department's many pastures, is in a long, gray metal building; its plainness belies its ambitious intent. Inside, his group works with a small number of endangered species—Cumberlandian combshell, purple bean, and oyster mussel—found in the Clinch and Powell rivers.

With an enrollment of over twenty-five thousand, Virginia Tech (VT) is the state's largest university. Located in the foothills of Brush Mountain, a part of the Jefferson National Forest, the Blacksburg campus is sprawling and pastoral. It was the first full day of spring when I visited the VT Aquaculture Center. For them, mussel season was just beginning. I spoke with research specialist Rachel Mair, who came to Blacksburg from Connecticut by way of Virginia Beach. She had been working with freshwater mussels for six years. From late winter to early summer, glochidia are collected from the Clinch and other rivers in East Tennessee and Southwest Virginia and brought back to the lab to be raised, giving them a solid start on life.

"When I collect gravid females," began Mair. "I extract the glochidia brooded inside the mussel's gills using a hypodermic needle filled with water. We'll collect fish as well and then put the two together." At the collection site, the captured glochidia, as tiny as grains of sand, are exposed to the proper host fish in a controlled setting. In the confined space, the glochidia are able to locate the host and readily attach to it. The glochidia are basically a pair of tiny shells that quickly close when exposed to salt. "Fish have a saltiness to them," explained the researcher. The young mussel larvae react to the salt by clamping shut. The exposed fish, complete with the hundreds of embedded mussel larvae, are brought back to the VT lab. Mostly the center's aquatic biologists work with endangered species, but more common mussels are also collected and raised so that the group can refine their techniques.

"The glochidia will develop into mussels while they're on the fish," Mair added. "Depending on the temperature, in two to six weeks, they'll drop off. We'll then siphon the bottom of the tank and put the young mussels in sediment, fine sand, things of that nature." For the next couple of months the growing mussels, still tiny but seeable, are cared for inside the lab's row after row of water-filled aquaria. They're fed algae, which is pumped into their tanks. In late summer the young mussels are returned to new locations along some of the same rivers where they were originally collected. At that time of year, the water's flow rate is low. "They have the rest of the summer to grow and settle into a habitat," explained Mair. The program's final outcome is threefold. A higher percentage of young mussels survive since they're introduced to the proper host fish, which in nature might not necessarily be located. Plus, by reintroducing the young mussels into new locations, say, farther up stream, the mussels' range is expanded more quickly than it could manage on its own. The effort is designed to re-establish mussel colonies in places where they were historically. And finally, with each passing year, the researchers learn more about the requirements of each species.

So far, Dr. Neves and his students have produced thousands of young mussels to return to streams where water quality has improved enough to give them a chance. For mussels to recover, it's important to understand the complicated life history of each endangered species, including its preferred underwater habitat, water flow rates, and host fish. When you consider that each species is unique and requires a separate recovery plan, the task seems daunting. Yet, Dr. Neves's group is making encouraging progress. Saving a species pushed to the brink isn't easy, as we'll see later when we visit darters.

At one point in our conversation, I asked Mair: "Are these mussels edible?" Disregarding the fact that many of the mussels that the VT Aquaculture Center work with are protected endangered species, it was a question that I, as an interviewer, felt compelled to ask. There was a noticeable pause as she collected her thoughts. I had insulted her sensibilities. These were creatures she lovingly cared for. Controlling her emotions, she returned, "Why would you want to eat something that's cleaning up our rivers?" Would I ask someone working on bald eagle recovery, "Are your birds edible?" Indeed not; that would be unthinkable. So why should this be any different?

"I can't tell you how many biologists I know that have had some kind of weird bacterial or viral thing they say came from the water," responded Mair. "They have no idea what it is or how to treat it—crazy stuff like you see on TV's *X-Files.*" It's the mussels that rid the water of these sorts of impurities.

Again, you might ask: Why should I care? What's one species of animal that I never see mean to me? (In the case of freshwater mussels, it's actually several species.) When I walked the shoreline at the Yuchi Wildlife Refuge, I could see no mussels in the shallow waters, but I knew they were there. Even unseen, freshwater mussels are ecologically important. They may lack the overt glamour of bald eagles and may not have heads, eyes, or vertebrates, but their unique place in the environment is equally important; some would argue they are even more essential. Often the key components of any ecosystem are the ones that go unheralded. Freshwater mussels play a significant role in maintaining the health of our major rivers and their tributaries. The pure, pristine waters that de Soto encountered were, to a large extent, kept clean by the huge populations of freshwater mussels.

As filter feeders, mussels purify the water by removing large amounts of suspended particles, impurities, and excess algae. In natural settings with large populations and high filtration rates, they clean an enormous amount of water. They're also part of the food chain, serving as a food source for a wide range of other animals: otters, muskrats, fish, shorebirds, turtles, and mud puppies, to name a few.

Because of human interference through water pollution, dam construction, erosion, channelization, fertilizer run-off, coal slurry spills, and commercial harvesting, populations of mussels have dropped sharply in the past 150 years.

Any drop in biodiversity is a concern because it can create a domino effect, and few can predict which domino might be the last to fall. Famed Harvard professor E. O. Wilson is often asked: "If enough species are extinguished, will the ecosystems collapse? And will the extinction of most other species follow soon afterward?" Wilson responds, "The only answer anyone can give is: possibly. By the time we find out, however, it might be too late. One planet, one experiment." Or in my case, one valley.

Whip-poor-will
Caprimulgus vociferus

In the courageous repetition of his name he accents the first and last syllables, the last most; always measuring his song with the same rhythm, while very considerably varying the melody—which latter fact is discovered only by most careful attention. Plain, simple, and stereotyped as his song appears, marked variations are introduced in the course of it. The whippoorwill uses nearly all the intervals in the natural scale, even the octave.

Simeon Pease Cheney
1891

Big South Fork is located on the Cumberland Plateau, half in Tennessee and half in Kentucky. Its one hundred thousand acres are designated as a "national river and recreation area." There are no major urban areas nearby, and because of this isolation, the rugged terrain tends to be sparsely populated. You can go all day and hardly see more folks than it would take to fill up an SUV. While millions flock to the Smoky Mountains, Big South Fork provides a quiet, remote alternative.

If the recreation area has a symbolic heart, it's Charit Creek Lodge. Cradled in a valley less than five miles south of the Bluegrass State, the lodge has few frills: no electricity or thermostats; cell phones go mute. It's just a cluster of rustic, homey buildings, the first of which was built in 1817. Each piece, board, or log is hand-hewed, dovetail- or saddle-notched, lap-jointed. and locust-pegged. It was crafted at a time when building a home tested the true mettle of a man: he was edging his way into *terra incognito* and had a family to protect. The aged home site would have rotted away a long time ago if there hadn't been someone to maintain it and keep nature pushed back to the shadows.

Far removed from the demands and bright lights of the big city, Charit Creek is a trip back in time and temperament, its solitude a tonic. Sitting in a rocking chair on the lodge's front porch, you get a true sense of a bygone era. The voices of Henry David Thoreau and John Burroughs seem to whisper all around, from the creaking planks to the Carolina wren calling from the thicket.

In April 2003 I was naturalist and guide accompanying a group coordinated by Paul James of Ijams Nature Center on an overnight stay at the lodge. Our serpentine hike into Charit Creek Valley took us by dramatic sandstone bluffs, rock houses, and stone arches—all geological formations that seemed somehow out of place, as if someone had carved out chunks of Utah and dropped them into the verdant Tennessee woods.

The weekend was well timed. April is the month of rebirth and homecoming, of celebration and white-hot yearning. Migratory bird song filled the trees, and woodland wildflowers carpeted the hillsides. When a male blackburnian warbler returns from his wintering grounds in the Andes, he sings a hopeful song, a mating call electric. As Burroughs, the great nineteenth-century American naturalist, wrote in 1877: "April, at its best, is the tenderest of tender salads. Its type is the first spear of grass. The senses—sight, hearing, smell—are as hungry for its delicate and almost spiritual tokens, as the cattle are for the first bite of its fields. How it touches one and makes him both glad and sad!"

One of the highlights of our overnight stay at Charit Creek was a gathering around a campfire after the evening meal. As the valley darkened, the footsore travelers chatted and, in time, were joined by a loquacious fourth-grader named Jessica. If you've ever listened to an eleven-year-old tell stories, you know the telling is as much fun as the ending. The tales ramble, like a languid stream that is in no hurry to go any place fast. It was a metaphor for life at Charit Creek: Why hurry? You'll arrive soon enough.

As the fire's embers glowed orange, popped, hissed and popped again, darkness settled in. The newly arrived male whip-poor-wills began their fervent calling, "whip-po-WILLLLLL, whip-po-WILLLLLL." The nocturnal birds are enigmas. They prefer the shadowy edges of clearings in upland secessional forests and are so well camouflaged for life on the forest floor that you'd be hard pressed to find one. Mottled brown like dead leaves, they're rarely seen; their day-to-day lives are cloaked in mystery. During mating season, however, the males must advertise their locations, which is how the females find them. Their energetic calls are sometimes repeated nonstop for hours, staccato. It's like automatic rifle fire that splits the night into uneven pieces. The once-common whip-poor-wills are becoming harder to find throughout the East, their disappearing nocturnal cry another link to our forgotten past.

The strident singing of Charit Creek's evening birds was a curious counterpoint to the flagging energy of the weary hikers. As the fire waned, tired travelers moved one at a time from the circle of light off to bed, leaving the remains of the day to the birds: "whip-po-WILLLLLL, whip-po-WILLLLLL, whip-po-WILLLLLL." It had been a good day, but even good days must come to an end. Human beings are diurnal—daytime creatures. They must relinquish the stage to the shadowy ones, the roamers of the night.

Charit Creek Lodge is reminiscent, both in backdrop and disposition, to the sylvan cabin of John Burroughs, who believed it unwise to build a home on an ambitious spot that overlooked a vast landscape. The exposure and overwhelming vista would become tiresome—even invisible—after a while. Instead, he preferred a "more humble and secluded nook or corner," a place homey and private—in essence, a blind from which to watch cautiously as nature unfolds. When Burroughs was middle-aged, he longed for transformation. When offered a three-acre tract of land, fertile and level, cut off from the vain and noisy world, he seized the opportunity. With the help of a son, Burroughs built a simple cabin to which he gave the rough-hewn name "Slabsides," because the outer walls were covered with long slabs: the throwaway outer, rounded crust of trees destined to become lumber. As he noted at the time, "I might have given it a prettier name, but not one more fit, or more in keeping with the mood that brought me thither," for the great naturalist desired to peel away his own civilized, soot-stained veneer. He desired to blend into the umbra of his new, wild home. As a civilized man, he longed to devolve. "As the traveller who has lost his way, throws his reins on his horse's neck, and trusts to the instinct of the animal to find his road, so must we do with the divine animal who carries us through the world," taught Ralph Waldo Emerson. Trust the innate nature within. The great poet-philosopher concluded: "For if in any manner we can stimulate this instinct, new passages are opened for us into nature; the mind flows into and through things hardest and highest, and the metamorphosis is possible."

For Burroughs the move to Slabsides made his transformation complete. Born in 1837 in New York, he published his first book, a biography of Walt Whitman, in 1867 while employed as a clerk in the U.S. Department of the Treasury in the nation's capital. He built and moved into Slabsides in 1895 to embrace a quiet life, one only punctuated by birdsong and flower. One April morning shortly thereafter, between the hours of 3:00 and 4:00 A.M., he encountered his own whip-poor-will. "What a rude intrusion upon the serenity and harmony of the hour!" he noted. "A cry without music, insistent, reiterated, loud, penetrating, and yet the ear welcomes it also; the night and the solitude are so vast that they can stand it."

A neighbor had told Burroughs that the spirited birds can "whip poor Will" two hundred times in succession without a break. The great naturalist was dubious that such a feat was possible. The small singers seemed to throw all their energy into each phrase; surely they would tire long before that. Lying in bed that long ago April night, Burroughs deemed he'd count the number of repetitions. He tallied as the ardent male repeated its call 1,088 times in one hour; it paused "half a minute" and then whipped Will another 390 times. The ambitious bird then flew a little farther away and commenced whipping yet again. Burroughs drifted off to sleep, as most folks do, long before the passion of the bird subsided.

A few years earlier, Charles Munger noted in *Putnam's Monthly* that the bird known as "Quok-korree" by Dutch immigrants and "Waw-o-naisa" by some Native Americans was "the bird that mourns unseen, and ceaseless sings ever a note of wail and woe. He is not a handsome fowl—rather a plain one to my mind."

The arrival of whip-poor-wills in the spring, with their insistent, penetrating call, is a benchmark of the season—a herald of the warmer, even hot days to come. To the attentive naturalist, it's a moment of such importance that most scramble to their journals to scribe, "first whip-poor-will of year." Naturalists mark the passage of time more by creaking frogs than Gregorian calendars. In 1790, curious about the timing of whip-poor-will song and the crops in the garden, Thomas Jefferson wrote from New York to his daughter Mary in Virginia: "We had not peas nor strawberries here till the eighth day of the month [May]. On the same day I heard the first whip-poor-will whistle. Swallows and martins appeared here on the 21st of April. When did they appear with you? And when had you peas, strawberries and whip-poor-wills in Virginia? Take notice hereafter whether the whip-poor-wills always come with the strawberries and peas."

In the Tennessee Valley, it's early April when the first of these mysterious birds usually migrate through. In 2004 it was April 8 when we first heard one singing on Chapman Ridge behind the house, off in the distance. "Did you hear that?" asked Lindalee as I scrambled for the journal. "Yes, indeed," I returned, knowing the importance of the moment. Hearing the once-common member of the nightjar family at all has developed a new significance because of their declining numbers. It had been at least seven years since one had been heard near our home, even for a single night. Never a breeding bird in our woods, they usually just pause for a few nights before moving on to more isolated locations.

Whip-poor-wills are members of the avian family once erroneously believed to haunt pastures. It was a widely held superstition that members of this group flew around at night sucking the milk from the teats of goats and cows, depleting the beasts to such an extent that the herd animals eventually died. Goat herders in ancient times observed members of the nocturnal family flying with mouth agape about their flocks. The genus name for all members of the family is *Caprimulgus,* Latin for "goatsucker." The Dark Ages were known as such for obvious reasons. In truth, the birds were after the insects that flew around the livestock. Today, a more suitable name is generally used to define the group—nightjar—probably because their piercing calls jar the night.

As a rule, all nightjars are nocturnal, large-mouthed insect eaters. Eight species are found in North America. The common nighthawk is the most widespread; the Antillean nightjar the most limited. Four others are found in the West: common poorwill, buff-collared nightjar, lesser nighthawk, and the common pauraque. That leaves the two species found in the East: the whip-poor-will and the chuck-will's-widow. Their ranges overlap, and the two are closely related, having similar-sounding songs. The "whips" nest in the northern states between the Atlantic seaboard and the Great Plains states, and the "chucks" primarily nest farther south. Both species nest in Tennessee. The call of the chuck resembles that of the whip, but the emphasis is on the first syllable, not the last: "CHUCK-will's-widow," rather than "whip-poor-WILLLLLL."

As *Knoxville News Sentinel* columnist Sam Venable points out, many people hear one and think that it's the other. In fact, when Hank Williams wrote one of his most memorable songs, "I'm So Lonesome I Could Cry," he was perhaps inspired by the chuck and not the whip. Hank was born in Georgiana, Alabama, in 1923 and later moved to Montgomery; and although both species are also found in that state, the two cities are a bit too far south for whip-poor-wills. If this is so, then Hank's song should have begun, "Hear that lonesome chuck-will's-widow, He sounds too blue to fly." Although just as mournful, it's decidedly less melodic. If Hank did make a mistake on his bird songs, let's let it lie, for his version, like the whip-poor-will itself, should not be lost.

The large-eyed whips hunt from a low perch, flying out, open-mouthed, to nab a variety of moths, mosquitoes, and other night-flying insects. They're aided in their efforts by coarse facial bristles, modified feathers that help them scoop up their prey on the wing. The courtship of the mysterious birds is rarely seen; such is their way. Birds that live on the ground utilize subterfuge. In the late 1940s, Juanita Allen lived in a cabin in the mountainous Glades community near Gatlinburg, Tennessee. She watched as a lone male landed on top of an outside table and began to call. He had used the platform on previous nights, but on an evening in mid-June she observed the following,

> He had no more than given four calls, and I had taken my stand near the window, when a female flew in and settled near him. No more calls after this but his chucking was continuous and soon he started a dance. He would strut back and forth before her, keeping his tail feathers spread and stretching out the feathers of first one wing and then the other as though to display the handsome patterns of their brown markings. Meanwhile, his head was kept bobbing up and down with guttural 'chucks' given at each bob, and the outer tail feathers showing pure white in the semi-darkness. The female made no noise, moving along the table twice before flying away with the male close behind her.

Whip-poor-wills lay their eggs on the ground, building no nest. They rely on their dappled, splotchy brown, black, and white plumage to blend them and their clutch into the forest floor. The robin-sized birds synchronize their egg laying to the phases of the moon, insuring that they will be feeding their young by the light of a moon more than half-full.

In Tennessee egg laying peaks in early May. Normal clutches contain two eggs that are incubated primarily by the female for around twenty days. Both parents feed the young while the female broods the cinnamon, down-covered hatchlings during the day. The young make their first flights after only about nineteen days. Life on the forest floor demands rapid development.

Whereas great blue herons have naturally expanded their numbers in the Tennessee Valley and wild turkeys have done the same with considerable help, whip-poor-will populations have been steadily declining. The North American Breeding Bird Survey (BBS) conducted in Tennessee annually indicates a decrease of 5.8 percent a year between 1966 and 1994. Decreases like that add up quickly. Like many other eastern woodland songbirds—the yellow-billed cuckoo, summer tanager, cerulean warbler, and Eastern wood-pewee to name a few—the decline in numbers is difficult to explain. According to BBS data, overall wood thrush totals have dropped 40 percent, olive-sided flycatchers are down 48 percent, and orchard orioles declined by 29 percent over the same period. Perhaps most at peril are cerulean warblers, whose numbers are down 70 percent. In all, there are over 250 species of migratory birds that fly south for the winter; 50

percent of the species are declining in population. To understand the deterioration, you need not only to look at the birds' northern summer homes and their wintering grounds in Mexico and Central and South America but also to be aware of what's happening at all the "stopovers" in between.

The decline in eastern woodland songbirds is perhaps the most complicated issue facing environmentalists and bird lovers today. Each species has its own set of pressures because each has a different lifestyle and occupies a unique niche. "Saving our migratory songbirds may be the most daunting task ever faced by American conservationists," wrote former *Audubon* editor Les Line in 1993.

In some cases, the cutting of tropical rain forests in South America have left the birds that migrate there without a winter home. For example, in 1960, 77 percent of Guatemala was covered by dense forest. By 1990 it had dropped to only 29 percent. In the heavily wooded Amazon, more than 20 percent of the forest cover has been cleared: about 6,500 square miles annually. In Venezuela, it's 540,000 acres per year—roughly the size of the Great Smoky Mountains National Park. To show the affect on just one species, John Rappole of the Smithsonian Institution prepared an analysis of the habitat requirements of the endangered golden-cheeked warbler. The spirited small bird with the bright yellow face spends its summers in central Texas and its winters in Central America. Rappole reports that there is enough habitat to support 220,000 pairs on its breeding grounds but only enough pine-oak forest left to sustain 34,000 pairs in its winter range.

Why such deforestation? Human population growth is the probable cause, and the total population of South American is expected to grow by 100 million between the years 2002 and 2025.

Loss or fragmentation of North American forests and other habitat types due to urban sprawl have left others without a summer home. Suburban sprawl in Fairfax, Virginia, saw 69 percent of its surrounded forests converted to development, homes, and businesses between 1980 and 1995. And then there's the loss of stopover habitat along the coastlines, where flocks stop to rest and refuel during migration.

Fragmentation also gives predators that work the edges of forests, such as raccoons and black rat snakes, more access avenues to nests. Studies conducted in Illinois have shown that low-nesting species (those that build nests no higher than eight feet above the ground) have declined at a greater rate than species that typically nest higher. Raccoon populations have been steadily increasing since 1980, and they relish bird eggs and nestlings. They are also good climbers.

Another problem is the parasitic cowbird, a native bird that lays its eggs in other birds' nests. Historically, cowbirds were nomadic. They followed the huge buffalo herds on the Great Plains, feeding on the insects that did the same. Since their food source was always on the move, cowbirds couldn't afford to linger in one location and raise a family. It was more prudent for them to let other birds do the parenting. As the pioneers permeated the East, cutting forests to build farms, cowbirds adapted to feeding on insects attracted to livestock. They gave up their buffalo-chasing, gypsy lifestyle. But the cowbirds did not give up their use of surrogate parents to incubate and raise their young. One study conducted in the Shawnee National Forest in Illinois found that 80 percent of the nests of canopy birds like scarlet and summer tanagers had been violated by cowbirds.

Neotropical migrants fly south for a reason. They primarily eat insects, and there are not many insects to be found in a North American winter. But where there are insects, there's usually someone spraying insecticides. Could the overuse of these contaminants be creating a second "Silent Spring" like the one Rachel Carson warned us about over forty years ago? In the 1960s bald eagles and osprey were in peril because they ate DDT-laced fish. DDT was banned in the United States in 1972, but it's still being used in Central and South America.

Yet another possible cause of woodland songbird decline has been getting some attention of late: global warming. Many migrating songbirds are timed to arrive in the woods of eastern North America just as the trees are beginning to leaf out and millions of caterpillars hatch. The butterfly and moth larvae appear as the leaves unfurl so that the young leaf-eating insects themselves have plenty to eat. Caterpillars are leaf-munching machines. In turn, many of the migrating songbirds eat the caterpillars.

In early May 2006, I sat on our back deck and watched a red-eyed vireo hop from branch to branch gulping down one caterpillar after another. It seemed as though it was finding them almost faster than it could possibly consume the fuzzy-looking larvae. It's a beautiful, intricate interplay that has been in place for thousands of years. But because we have been experiencing milder winters, the leaves have been appearing earlier in the season, as have the caterpillars that eat them. Bird migration, on the other hand, is determined by day length not temperature. So many of the spring migrants are arriving after a lot of the caterpillars have come and gone. How this will play out in the long run is anyone's guess.

Whip-poor-wills are atypical songbirds. How they're affected by all of these factors is difficult to comprehend. A nocturnal bird adept at hiding in the shadows is not easy to study. Although most people know what the spirited birds sound like, few have actually seen one. You virtually have to step on one to find it.

Wildlife photographer William Burt set out to photograph difficult-to-find birds for his recent book, *Rare and Elusive Birds of North America*. One of his goals was to take pictures of whip-poor-wills in their natural surroundings, but it proved to be easier said than done. Burt had no trouble locating places where whip-poor-wills were singing, but every time he began to sneak in with his camera, the birds would fly away. "So I searched and searched some more," he wrote, "alone and with the help of a few stalwart volunteers, but we found nothing. Plainly, this was one of those things you're not meant to find by *looking*." Luckily for Burt, he learned about two biology professors, Roger Boyd and Calvin Cink at Baker University in Baldwin City, Kansas, who studied the nighttime birds and had devised a methodical way of finding them on their nests. Burt, in turn, got some great photographs.

Whip-poor-wills spend their winters along the Gulf Coast and down into Central America, returning to the valley in April. During nesting season they prefer upland forest clearings like the grounds around Charit Creek Lodge; yet, many of these once-cleared spaces are becoming reforested. Could the drop in the birds' numbers be a natural side effect? Despite the questions, most Tennessee Valley bird lovers agree that whip-poor-wills are getting harder and harder to find, and by "find," I mean hear.

David Trently is a former president of the Knoxville Chapter of the Tennessee Ornithological Society (KTOS), a group affectionately called the "bird club" by its members. David earns his living as research associate in the University of Tennessee's entomology and plant pathology department, but his avocation is the natural world around him. He's rarely seen without a field guide, usually several, and he routinely leads people on searches of winged creatures. If you want to locate a particularly hard-to-find bird, butterfly, or dragonfly in the valley, David is one of the best to call. When I asked him where could I hear a whip-poor-will during nesting season, he responded without hesitation: "Chota, and chucks should be there too."

By Chota, David meant the memorials to the Overhill Cherokee towns of Tanasi and Chota in Monroe County on the shore of Tellico Lake. Hearing either of the nightjars on such sacred ground would be especially poignant. The prospect of hearing both seemed more than I could hope for.

During the 1700s Tanasi (or Tanasee) and adjacent Chota were the principal capitals of the Cherokees. Religious events and national councils were held there. Tanasi (the namesake of Tennessee) was the older of the two. Chota apparently grew as a northern suburb during the 1730s. Tribal business was conducted in Tanasi while Chota developed the mystique of being a holy town because the foremost priest chief, or *uku,* lived there. Cherokee capitals moved from place to place as political influence waxed and waned. After the death of Moytoy in 1741, Chota became the center of influence under the leadership of Old Hop. Tanasi waned in importance, while Chota was central to the Overhill Cherokee throughout the remainder of the 1700s. Chota became the town of sanctuary, a safe haven "where fugitives were protected and no blood could be shed."

Blood, however, was eventually shed. In 1776 the Virginia militia invaded the Overhill country, but they spared Chota, the town of peace. The next military expedition in 1780 wasn't as forgiving, destroying both Tanasi and Chota, along with all other Cherokee settlements in the lower Little Tennessee River Valley. In time, all remnants of the two towns lay buried.

The Chota Memorial is on hallowed ground under the dominion of the Eastern Band of Cherokee Indians and is still being used by the tribe for ceremonies. It's regarded as their most sacred site. Today the memorial sits alone on a narrow point of land surrounded on three sides by water. A tombstone at the south end marks the grave of Oconostota, the great warrior chief.

Oconostota was born in the Little Tennessee River Valley sometime around 1715, perhaps as early as 1710. He grew up in tumultuous times, and his skills soon led him to a position of leadership: a warrior chief. (The Cherokee also had great peace chiefs whose influence was strongest during calmer times.) As a leader, Oconostota performed a balancing act. The British and the French were vying for the control of trade west of the Appalachians because the Cherokee had developed a fondness for European goods. White settlers were also beginning to trickle into the Tennessee Valley, claiming land in violation of established treaties. The traditional Cherokee way of living and their sense of order were slipping away. Tensions flared. Whites killed Cherokees, and their deaths had to be avenged, so Cherokees killed whites; after all, their law dictated "a life for a life." (The problem with this form of justice was that if a white killed a Cherokee, it didn't matter which white was killed or where the murder was avenged.) When the outside world pushed, Oconostota began to push back. If there was to be a battle, skirmish, or fight, he was the one you'd want leading the way. Through the disorder, he was known as a great tactician and strategist. It is believed that he was the only Native American to have successfully captured a British fort. He also prevailed in conflicts with the French and, at times, negotiated with both for he needed European goods that either could supply. The outside world was afraid of him because it knew that if one strong Native American leader emerged, he could possibly unite all tribes to fight as one and drive away both the English and the French. But that did not happen. Despite Oconostota's bravery, ability, and cunning, his people continued to lose ground. The great Cherokee Nation was being carved up and dismantled. By the end of his days, Oconostota, which translates to "Great Warrior," had traveled to New Orleans and earned a commission as captain in the French Army and was inducted into the St. Andrew's Society, a fraternal organization of Scots in Charleston. Both sides courted his favor, and both undoubtedly feared his influence.

Around 1782 the aging pragmatist and warrior-chief stepped down as leader, ending his forty-four years of authority. He spent his remaining days with Indian agent John Martin at his home on the Holston River. His last request was to be buried in Chota, the peace town. Martin honored the old chief's wishes, traveling with him in his waning hours to the former Cherokee capital. Using a canoe to fashion a makeshift coffin, he gave him a Christian burial. Oconostota was also given the Cherokee ceremony reserved for only the greatest in his tribe, and he was reportedly laid to rest near the front entrance of the city's townhouse, the highest form of tribute his people could bestow. It's also written that just before he died, Oconostota said to his friend Martin: "I have never run from an enemy, but I walked fast up a branch once."

By then, Chota itself was a dying town. As the Cherokee were forced out of the valley, the former capital was evacuated, and both it and the warrior chief became a source of legend. In time, many began to believe it was all just a myth, for such is the case of a vanquished people; their lives on this earth are simply erased as though they never existed. Almost 150 years passed, and the location of the mythical town became a matter of speculation, while the location of Oconostota's gravesite was forgotten.

In 1969, as TVA was beginning construction on the Tellico Dam, a team of archaeologists was assembled to learn what they could about the historic Cherokee sites in the area before the Little Tennessee River Valley was flooded. The Tellico Archaeological Project was made up of several agencies, including TVA, the University of Tennessee, and the U.S. Department of the Interior. The archaeologists affiliated with the university included Jeff Chapman, Alfred Guthe, Charles Faulkner, and several other faculty members and graduate students. They would have a few years to excavate before the region was inundated. High on their list was to flesh out the cultural history of Chota. In their first year of fieldwork, the team found the location of the circular structure that was the village's council or town house where tribal leaders had debated important matters. Near its entrance they found a grave; its orientation and contents perfectly matched the description that had been recorded years earlier by John Martin's son. The bones and other items—clay pipes, eyeglasses, iron knife, tin cup, and

white beads—in Oconostota's grave were photographed and then carefully reinterred. They lie there today only a few feet from the circular monument that
marks the site of the council house.

On a visit to the Frank H. McClung Museum, I spoke to its director, Jeff
Chapman. He has been at the museum on the campus of the University of Tennessee for thirty years in addition to having been a member of the archaeological team that excavated Chota three decades earlier. "If you think the site
is beautiful today, you should have seen it before the lake waters covered it,"
he reminisced. "The ground around the memorial has been raised six to eight
feet to keep it above the water line. In theory, the eight concrete columns of the
memorial are in the exact locations of the original eight posts that supported
the townhouse roof." The memorial's cement ring marks the outside perimeter
of the original structure. Inside the ceremonial circle, seven of the concrete pil-
lars represent the various Cherokee clans: Deer, Bird, Wild Potato, Blue, Wolf,
Longhair, and Paint. The eighth column simply reads: "Cherokees in the Little
Tenn. Valley."

David Trently and I arrived at the Chota Memorial two hours before sunset
on our mission to find whip-poor-wills. It was overcast and warm. Narrow-
mouth toads and cricket frogs sang from the marshy area to the east of the
gravel road that leads to the shrine. Red-winged blackbirds, common yellow-
throats, and a yellow-breasted chat sang from the cattails and nearby thickets.
A burnt-orange orchard oriole seemed to follow us as we slowly walked the road
listening. At one point David spotted an osprey, and we watched as it splashed
into the water, missing the fish it had spied before its plunge.

Despite its long anonymity, today the lost Chota survives as a sanctuary. An
overriding sense of peace blankets the isolated location. It's quiet and as purely
serene as any sacred place should be. As the gray sky darkened, we stood inside
the circle near the Deer Clan pillar. To the west, the ashen haze turned pink
while a striped skunk emerged from the tall grass to begin its nightly foray. It
was then that we heard the first chuck-will's-widow: at exactly nine o'clock. "The
chucks start first," said David. "The whip-poor-wills will begin soon." As if there
were an overall master clockwork, and perhaps there is in such divine places,
the whips cranked up six minutes latter. David had positioned us perfectly. For
the next hour we were center stage as several males of both species called and
paused, called and paused, "CHUCK-will-wi-doe, CHUCK-will-wi-doe," followed
by "whip-po-WILLLLLL, whip-po-WILLLLLL." The sacrosanct circle we stood
inside expanded to include the surrounding woody ridges and hills as if the
spirits of the long lost Cherokees themselves seemed to join our jubilation. They
had called the bird *waguli*, a tribal word now lost in time.

Hearing both elusive nightjar species, at times separate and at times together, even overlapping, allowed us to compare the two; their cadence and intonation. Naturalist Burroughs would have been thrilled. As we pivoted around the Deer Clan column, we heard their distant calls, joyous and life affirming, flowing over the water from places both near and far. Cupping our hands behind our ears, we could better pinpoint the whips and chucks, isolating individual singers. As each new bird took its place in the choir, our perceptions broadened. It was a sublime moment, almost as ceremonial as it was naturally pure. The clear voices sang without interruption, time and time again.

On certain occasions, an inherent symmetry falls into place like the inter-meshing gears of an old-time pocket watch—a perfect alignment where all things are connected and work together, moving over the water, the land, per-meating the air. It's an overall sense of balance, of past and present, flowing energy followed by calm—a harmony the Chinese call *Feng Shui*—and for me that evening, the absolute rightness of the place and time rang true. The *Ani'-Yun'wiya* knew the sacredness of the location; they held it dear. And even though the whip-poor-wills are declining and the historic Cherokee are long gone, the peacefulness of *their* Chota endures, now and, let us hope, for evermore.

Periodical Cicadas

Magicicada: six species

I explore, too, with pleasure, the sources of the myriad sounds
which crowd the summer noon, and which seem the very grain
and stuff of which eternity is made. Who does not remember
the shrill roll-call of the harvest-fly?

Henry David Thoreau
Natural History of Massachusetts, 1842

The one sound perhaps the most synonymous with long hot summer days and
sultry nights is the pulsating *zeeeeer, zeeeeer, zeeeeeer* of buzzing cicadas. In
the valley the annual chorus convenes near the end of June, hits full volume by
late July, and slowly fades through August and September. If you are new to the
area, the loudness can be startling. It's often compared to circular saws cutting
through lumber, over and over: *zeeeeer, zeeeeer, zeeeeeeeeeeeeeeeeeer.*

Cicadas, aphids and leafhoppers are members of the insect order Homop-
tera, meaning like-winged, a reference to the fact that both sets of wings are
uniform in texture. The insects in this group are often green and make their
living on vegetation, usually by tapping into and sucking out the plant's sweet
juices and, in some cases, passing excess fluids through their bodies in the form
of honeydew. Cicadas are described as robust with clear wings and big bulging
eyes. In effect, they look like large green flies, up to two inches in length, but
flies have two wings and cicadas have four.

To the native Cherokee the annual appearance of cicadas was a good omen.
They called the summer singer *lalu,* or jarfly, and knew their songs meant that
the beans were ripe and corn would not be far behind. This agrarian timeliness
led to the folk name harvestfly. The common insects are also known as dogday
cicadas because their arrival coincides with the heat of summer. The Dog Days

are the period of time—roughly July 3 through August 11—when the Dog Star, Sirius, rises and sets with the sun. It was once believed that the combined heat from the two bright spheres is what makes the season so hot.

As a boy growing up in the mountains, I used to collect the goggle-eyed summer creatures and carry them around in small jars as temporary pets. They are large, seeable insects that are easy to catch and utterly harmless. If you pick one up and hold it by its sides, its defense mechanism is to buzz and vibrate. It feels like one of those handshake buzzers that were once sold with whoopee cushions and plastic vomit. (It was a simpler time, and practical jokes were a popular sport.)

Thousands of cicada species occur worldwide. To the ancient Chinese they were the harbingers of summer and admired for their punctuality; they became symbols of fidelity and sincerity. It was believed that the large insect ate nothing belonging to the earth and drank only the dew, thus proving their purity and cleanliness. In time they began to be associated with ideas of death and a future life. J. G. Myers writes: "In Taoism the cicada became the natural symbol of the *hsien,* or soul, disengaging itself from the body at death. Disembodied hsien might appear to mortals in the guise of a cicada. According to Taoist rules, it was customary to make use of the image of a cicada in preparing a corpse for burial."

During the Han Dynasty (206 BC to AD 220), the custom of placing a jade cicada into the mouth of the deceased began. Jade had special properties. In essence, it symbolized the good of *yang,* which was locked in an eternal struggle with the destructive, evil *yin* element. The jade was fashioned into the shape of a cicada, the emblem of resurrection. It was believed that the amulet would aid the immortal soul in leaving the departed. The jade tongue amulet was the last high honor that could be given to the deceased.

The Native American Oraibi also believed that the cicada lifecycle symbolized resurrection. They noted the physical changes each cicada goes through and felt that because it had the power to renew its own life, medicine made from a cicada's body could renew life in others. Wounds received in battle were treated with this powerful healer. Cicadas were likened to the Phoenix, the bird of Egyptian mythology that after five hundred years burns itself to death and arises anew, reborn from its own ashes. When you look at cicada biology, you easily see where such images of death and rebirth were derived.

After harvestfly cicada eggs hatch, the nymphs crawl to the ground and burrow down, literally leaving the light of day for up to five years. Initially, they tap into the roots of grass or other herbal plants and suck out nourishment. As they grow, they burrow farther until they find the roots of trees. This is were they live, molting and growing, until it's time to return to the surface. As underground larvae, cicadas have front legs that are large and claw-like for digging. They're also wingless, but that will soon change. As they emerge from the ground, the cumbersome larvae climb a nearby object, attach themselves and wait until their skin dries and cracks down the middle. The adult cicada works itself free from the old skin, and after its new wings dry, it flies away like a phoenix reborn. Each species of cicada has a slightly different buzzing song, or they sing at a different time of the day to distinguish themselves. Even though each individual harvestfly spends several years below ground, each summer there are enough of its kind to mature and fill the trees.

The Dutch have a word for it: *uitwaaien.* It means, "to walk in windy weather for fun." Isn't that a beautiful concept? Wind makes the trees, indeed the entire woodland, come alive. There's yet another phenomenon that passes through the valley every decade or so that produces the same sort of wonderful animation in the forest canopy. But this one is not caused by the mixing of warm and cold air but by hordes of six-legged creatures.

The real champions of the death and rebirth motif are the periodical cicadas that disappear underground much longer than their harvestfly cousins. There are six different species: three have lifecycles of thirteen years, and three live a whopping seventeen. That's a long time out of sight, tunneling in the dirt, and a long time for an insect to live; only some queen ants and termites live longer. When these cicadas emerge from the ground en masse, they create a swirling, whirling wind of oscillating sound. The trees are alive, and walking through them is as invigorating as any breezy day.

Periodical cicadas look like harvestflies, except they're smaller and bluish and have bright red eyes. Their wings are golden. The six species have separate populations called broods around the country; a Roman Numeral is used to designate each group. The emergence of each brood is synchronized so that almost all of the cicadas climb out of their holes within a few weeks of each other. The thirteen-year cicadas have three broods: XIX, XXII, and XXIII, the seventeen-year cicadas have twelve broods: I through X, XIII, and XIV.

Periodical cicadas are only found in eastern North America. Principally, the seventeen-year broods occur in the northern part of the country and the thirteen-year broods are found in the south. But Tennessee is centrally located, and both groups occur in the state. In fact, in the Tennessee Valley the two ranges overlap. There are seven counties—Blount, Loudon, McMinn, Monroe, Meigs, Rhea, and a part of Hamilton—that periodically have either Brood XIX (thirteen-year cicadas) or Brood X (seventeen-year cicadas) crawl from their underground homes in unison, and because the lifecycles are staggered, once every 221 years, in those seven counties, both broods emerge at the same time. The last time the two groups lined up was in 1868, and the next time their cycles terminate the same year will be in 2089.

When it's time for just one of the broods to emerge from the ground, they appear in Biblical proportions; one report estimates 1.3 million periodical cicadas per acre. A single tree can have forty thousand buzzing males. Because of the Biblical scale of their arrival, colonial accounts refer to them as locusts, and to some their coming foretold of impending calamity. Some Native Americans also felt their arrival had an evil connotation. Thomas Matthews, son of the governor of Virginia, wrote about an emergence in the late 1600s believed to be Brood VIII.

To Matthews 1675 was a scary year. He chronicled three natural phenomena that in his mind were ominous presages. The first was the appearance of a comet, the second the passing of a huge flock of migrating passenger pigeons "in breadth nigh a quarter of the mid-hemisphere, and of their length was no visible end." Matthews reported that the weight of the roosting birds broke branches of large trees. He noted that the previous passage of a large flock in 1640 was the last time the Indians had committed a large massacre of white settlers and that surely a second coming did not bode well.

The final ominous occurrence of 1675 was the emergence of periodical cicadas: "The third strange appearance was swarms of flies about an inch long and big as the top of a man's little finger, rising out of spigot holes in the earth, which eat the new-sprouted leaves from the tops of the trees without other harm, and in a month left us."

Early American Colonists knew of the Biblical descriptions of locust plagues in Egypt during the time of Moses. It was well described in the Book of Exodus. They knew that the insects had covered the earth and eaten every plant in the land of the Pharaoh. The early settlers had never seen a plague of locust or periodical cicadas until their farms were covered with thousands of them. They must have felt a deep sense of alarm; being on the edge of the unknown in a strange new world was unsettling enough. Was this a warning? Of course, the locusts of Exodus weren't cicadas; they were grasshoppers. But that information would have been of little comfort to the colonists.

European settlers would have first encountered periodical cicadas in the Tennessee Valley in the late 1700s. The move into the valley really began in earnest when long hunter, explorer, and settler Daniel Boone entered the watershed of the Watauga River in northeast Tennessee in 1760. "Within fifteen years," writes historian Wilma Dykeman, "settlement would be trickling and then flooding across the mountains into Tennessee." In the southern end of the valley, Brood XIX of the thirteen-year cicadas would have crawled from the ground in 1777 and again in 1790. Brood X of the seventeen-year variety would have emerged in the upper half of the valley in 1783 and again in 1800. We imagine that even adventurer Daniel Boone himself must have been mystified.

Growing up in Motte, Ohio, Luke Smith witnessed every emergence of Brood X of the seventeen-year cicadas in the 1800s. The first in 1817 happened when he was a schoolboy. In 1891, Smith fondly reported: "I remember how it delighted me as I passed along the woody school path to give the drooping limbs of the forest, bending with these winged insects, a sudden jerk and see them hunt other resting places." Smith also recalled that the gray squirrels in 1834 became quite fat eating the plump cicadas, and he looked forward to being around for the next occurrence in 1902.

Professor E. A. Andrews of Johns Hopkins University reported on the emergences of Brood X in 1902 and 1919 in the rural and suburban areas north of Baltimore. Andrews was more than a passive observer. He was curious and set out to learn all he could about the mysterious visitors. In the years preceding the 1919 emergence, he dug into the sod to find the cicada nymphs. He found many tunnels smaller than a finger several inches long. The tubular holes might be two or more feet below the surface, and inside each was a "clumsy light-colored gnome-like creature with grotesquely large and powerful front legs and claws." Each nymph had a closed-in face with a concealed tube for sucking the juices out of tree roots. This nourishment allowed the odd-looking creatures to grow to the "size and plumpness of a peanut."

In the spring of 1918, a full year before their time to emerge, Andrews observed that the plump nymphs began to burrow toward the surface, and by early 1919 all the pupae had inched upward. By May the ground was full of straight and smooth vertical tunnels pushed close to the surface. Each had a hollowed-out dome of earth at the top and one expectant nymph sitting braced against the smooth sides of its own tunnel. They were poised and waiting for their time in the sun they had not seen in seventeen years.

If an obstacle like a board lay on the surface, the tunnel made a hard right angle and lay horizontal to the ground until it reached the board's edge. In some locations, if the spot was dark and well shaded, the tunnel actually broke the surface and formed an extended chimney made from pellets of mud carried to the surface. Some rose up to five inches in height above the ground. In a small dark shed with a dirt floor, Andrews found a great number of cicada chimneys poking out of the soil. Inside each a larva was waiting. There they sat, millions of plump, goggle-eyed creatures, biding their time, waiting for their D-Day. The thought of the Brood X horde spread across several states and waiting to break through the surface is sensational and somewhat creepy. That year, in the Baltimore area, the first emergence was recorded on May 16. In Professor Andrew's own yard, D-Day happened on May 22.

From then on, every evening between 8:00 and 10:00 P.M., more and more cicadas crawled from the ground and moved towards the closest tree or tall object. The nymphs left their tunnels just after sunset while there was still enough daylight left for them to get their bearings. It appeared that the warmer the soil, the sooner the emergence. The ground on the north sides of buildings was cooler than the south, and locations separated by only a few hundred feet might have emergences seven days apart. (A temperature of sixty-seven degrees, four inches deep, seemed to be ideal.) In 1919 it took the millions that climbed from the ground in the Baltimore area about three weeks to complete the task.

What Andrews reported next was somewhat ghoulish. Once each nymph broke the surface, it paused to look around in different directions, and as soon as its mind was set, the nymph began to move deliberately and directly in a straight line to the nearest tall object. "Standing under an isolated tree," Andrews wrote, "it is a remarkable sight that presents itself when from the north, south, east and west and all intermediate radii the emerging pupae, as if all of one mind march steadily toward the tree trunk at the center. . . . The cicadas which emerged from the ground under this big pear tree, went toward the trunk as if drawn by a powerful magnet."

This description sounds like a zombie scene from *Night of the Living Dead*, with legions of creatures climbing from the ground to march in unison toward a common goal. Once the tree was reached, each nymph began to climb slowly until it found a horizontal branch. Then it crawled toward the end of the limb to the tip of twigs and leaves, where its journey came to an end. There each nymph waited as its skin began to dry, splitting down the back. Here the small phoenix completed its rise from the ashes. The soft white adult slowly began to pull itself free of its last underground skin. The tearing of tissue and stretching of sinew was a slow process, like any birth, as the newborn fought to pull free. Once the old skin was shed, the chalky white cicada soon began to attain its adult coloration; damp wings, at first folded, began to unfurl. Through the night, the hatchlings hardened.

The next morning, the new glistening adults vibrated their wings and flew away "with great speed and strength of flight." What Andrews witnessed and recorded in his own yard must have been exhilarating, perhaps the first to record such a detailed account. Around one pear tree he collected 4,983 nymphs over a thirteen-day period.

Farther south, the territory covered by Brood X dipped down into East Tennessee. May 1919 was atypical: it was cooler and damper than normal in the valley that year. The month had seen sixteen rainy days and the coldest single May day in thirty-six years. On Monday, May 12, the newspaper in Knoxville, the *Journal and Tribune*, reported that the first of the "Seventeen-year Locust" had been seen in several sections. On the following Sunday, the paper declared that "Scientists, near-scientists and 'bug-ologists' are having the time of their lives chasing and obtaining specimens." The cicada swarms were occurring in small numbers in many sections of East Tennessee, and it was believed that the unusually cool weather had delayed their emergence. Numbers were expected to increase as soon as the clouds parted and the sun was able to shine through. The largest swarms were reported in the area of Huffaker's Ferry on the French Broad River just downstream from the Sevier County line. It was recorded that the trees were literally alive with the emerging insects. Word had quickly spread, and the riverside location attracted many curious people making day trips to view the natural phenomenon.

In May 1919 the buzzing cicadas would have been a pleasant distraction, marking a return to a sense of normalcy. The five-year-long World War I had just ended, and the local newspapers were filled with stories about the Huns, Bolsheviks, and Anarchists. An armistice had been signed at the eleventh hour of the eleventh day of the eleventh month in 1918, but the formal terms of the peace treaty had yet to be agreed upon. Emotions were still running high on both sides of the Atlantic. The German National Assembly was not happy about the terms they were being forced to accept at Versailles, France.

Locally, the Knoxville paper published accounts of war hero and favorite son Sergeant Alvin C. York, who returned from Europe after winning the Congressional Medal of Honor and the French Croix de Guerre. York, a mountaineer from Pall Mall in Fentress County, entered the war as a conscientious objector for religious reasons (he thought it was wrong to take a human life) but became the war's most celebrated hero when on October 8, 1918, he killed over 20 German soldiers and captured 132 others. His actions effectively silenced an entrenched machine gun nest near Chatel-Chebery in the Argonne Forest. A superb marksman, York had reportedly honed his sharpshooting skills hunting squirrels in the woods around his boyhood home. Back on American soil—after the same "war to end all wars" that saw Archie Grey Owl being wounded—the tall, redheaded doughboy was honored by the Tennessee Society of New York at a testimonial dinner in the Big Apple's Waldorf-Astoria. Hundreds attended the gala. Two weeks later, York returned to Fentress County to marry Grace Williams and move to a fifty-thousand-dollar farm stocked with "the best animals money can buy"—a gift from the people of Tennessee.

The *Journal and Tribune* also reported that some people worried about the ominous appearance of cicadas. The populace was war weary. A headline read, "Seventeen Year Locusts Appear in Battle Array." It was believed that the natural black W-shaped marking on the outer end of the cicada's front wings foretold of "war" and that global hostilities would return before the next cicada emergence in 1936.

History saw these fears realized. Adolph Hitler became German Chancellor in 1933, and his newly reconstituted army marched into the Rhineland in March 1936. This aggressive move, two months before Brood X was to emerge again, violated the peace treaty signed at Versailles and marked the inevitable chain of events that led to the Second World War.

Believing that an inch-long insect, even a few million of them, can predict what we humans do to ourselves is an unfair burden to place on the cicadas, a throwback to a darker, more superstitious age. But the sudden appearance of periodical cicadas is unnerving, particularly if it's unexpected. Why would a creature develop such a curious life history in the first place? Why disappear underground for thirteen or seventeen years? For one thing, it keeps the predators off balance. There's really no way that predator populations can fluctuate to be in tune with the cicadas. The normal predators that do exist, like gray squirrels and blue jays, eat their fill of emerging cicadas in a few days and the rest go unmolested. Cicadas are described as "predator-foolhardy." They're bite-size morsels with little defense. By hiding underground for so many years and then emerging by the million, periodical cicadas can overwhelm the opposition with sheer numbers.

Yet, without a balancing predator population, wouldn't cicada broods grow to astronomical numbers? As it turns out, there is a small check and balance in place. A fungal disease, *Massospora cicadina*, preys on the cicadas, and it also has an unusual life history. The resting spores of this cicada pathogen remain viable in the ground for thirteen or seventeen years, perfectly timed to keep the cicada populations from inundating the environment.

Even with this fungal disease in the natural forests in the east, periodical cicadas are "spectacularly abundant." But, there's evidence to suggest that in artificial locations like orchards and suburban lawns with trees, periodical cicadas exist in even larger numbers. This may be because the fungal disease spores have been somehow destroyed when the former forest was tilled and converted to human use.

After spending so much time underground in the dark, the millions of periodical cicada adults that emerge to fill a neighborhood do not live very long—only a few weeks. Their sole purpose is to find a mate and reproduce. To this end, the males begin to collect in a large tree or shrub and sing their buzzing, pulsating song. The female cicadas are mute. As the singing intensifies, it attracts more males, which add their buzz to the choir. The gathering place is called the "chorus tree," and as the days pass, the choir grows.

The buzzing song is not produced vocally. Instead, the sound-making organs are a pair of stiff concave membranes located on the sides of the cicada's abdomen. They're called *tymbals,* and each has a strong muscle attached to the inside. These muscles can pop the membranes in and out, causing a click in each direction. Air sacs below the tymbals amplify the sound. Cicadas can generate 390 clicks a second, which creates their loud squawking buzz. In time, females are lured into the noisy maelstrom, where the males grab them.

Once mated, each female uses her knife-like ovipositor to make slits into branches. They prefer twigs that are roughly the size of a pencil. Into each slit she lays twenty-four to twenty-eight eggs; her total egg output is between four hundred and six hundred eggs. After six or seven weeks the eggs hatch, and the tiny white ant-like newborns crawl out of the slit and drop to the ground, where they disappear for thirteen or seventeen years depending on the brood. Once back in the ground, the tiny phoenixes have returned to their own ashes. For Brood X, their resurrection is short-lived, but the centuries have taught them that it's safer underground.

Needless to say, I approached May 2004 in a heightened state of alert. Brood X was due to reappear in the Tennessee Valley, but where? As it turned out I didn't have to wait long or go far to find the creeping horde. The first report came from a coworker at Ijams Nature Center. On May 6 Ben Nanny was moving nursery plants around on the west side of the park and discovered the little tunnels and larvae under some pots. This was something I had to see for myself. As I lifted away the same black nursery containers, I found the holes Ben described. Many still had the odd nymphs waiting at the top of their tunnels just as Professor Andrews had described. As the morning sun filled the depression, the plump creatures scurried back down into the darkness of their holes. Like a David Lynch movie, it was unsettling, even eerie, a word I'd hear often over the next three weeks.

The same day the cicadas turned up under the potted plants, On-site programs coordinator Misty Gladdish and Kara East were leading school groups on walks around the nature center's homesite and saw oodles of the red-eyed insects near the ground. They were emerging from their shells, leaving their last nymphal skins like death masks attached to trees scattered around the property.

On Sunday afternoon, May 9, I drove out to the former site of Huffaker's Ferry. In 1919 it had been a focal point of the cicada emergence. Located on the French Broad River, a few miles upstream from the beginning of the Tennessee River, the onetime ferry business was founded by George Michael Huffaker, who moved with his family to Seven Islands in east Knox County in 1781 or early '82. Years ago, before the construction of the many bridges in the valley, a series of independent ferry operations existed up and down the Tennessee River and its tributaries to carry wagons and then cars from one shoreline to the other.

Exploring the southern riverbank, the fields, trees, and shrubs where the ferry operation had been, I found nothing unusual, no cicadas. Was I too early? Driving away disappointed I soon encountered a slow moving truck coming towards me. "Have you seen any cicadas?" I asked the woman behind the steering wheel. Karla Hunt looked at me with a hint of suspension; her husband, Scott, and son Trey were in the back, sitting on the open tailgate, leading a reluctant, small horse home. Karla's suspicion gave way to recognition. "Yes," she replied. "I've seen a few in my yard. Do you want to see?"

In their backyard on Huffaker Ferry Road, we quickly discovered numerous small round holes all over, particularly under a stately hackberry tree. The more we looked, the more we found. Hunt's oldest son, Seth, lay in a hammock casually reading a Harry Potter novel. He seemed only mildly interested in my tale of cicadas until our collective excitement infected him as well. Finally, the magic of the moment (periodical cicadas genus name is *Magicicada*) overcame the charm of Hogwarts; he too became caught up in our search, which ended in the discovery of hundreds of discarded shells all around the house. Overhead it was quiet, only a faint murmur coming from a distant ridge but nothing remarkable. Yet, I left knowing that the invasion of Brood X had begun.

The next report came from Steve Davis, who had taken a day off to be with his son. "Cicadas were dripping from the trees," he said. The box elders in his front yard were crawling full. The trunks, branches, and leaves were festooned with the colorful insects like small Japanese lanterns. Three-year-old Ben was having cicada races around his swing set while piles of empty nymphal shells crunched under his feet. The Davis family have three acres on Stock Creek off John Sevier Highway near the Blount County line—as the crow flies, not that far from Huffaker's Ferry. When Lindalee and I visited the following week, the gyrating drone from the caterwauling males almost hurt our ears. It was like living inside a grade-B movie, with spaceships overhead, crunching dead shells underfoot. As we walked along a trail mowed through the trees and meadow, the golden-winged insects flew all round, bouncing into us blindly. Steve enjoyed the bizarre surrealness of it all; they reminded him of the sound the Martian flying saucers made in George Pal's 1953 movie *War of the Worlds*, just before they fired their lasers. It was otherworldly, like the electronic theremin etched into the soundtracks of those 1950s sci-fi movies we all remembered from childhood.

Helen Picou lives in Lovell Heights in west Knox County. She'd noticed the creeping cicadas "boiling up from the ground. It's eerie," she said as she held her phone outside for me to hear.

By May 19 the cicada chorus was at full throttle. What had started as a distant hum had become a permeating, oscillating drone, a pervasive spookiness. It undulated as the clusters of males moved from tree to tree. It's difficult to imagine something as earthy as a cicada sounding so unearthly, but en masse they did.

Brood X actually consists of three separate species—*Magicicada septendecim, M. cassini,* and *M. septendecula*—each with a variety of buzzing calls. Although considered the most widespread population, Brood X has a spotty emergence. It is primarily a northern phenomena, with Tennessee and Georgia at the southern edge of the emergence. In the Volunteer State, the emerging cicadas appear primarily in the Tennessee Valley, excluding Sullivan and Claiborne counties. Middle and West Tennessee see only a few in isolated pockets. As we drove around the valley with the windows down, we'd hear them in some locations, while others were strangely normal—although, in this case, normalcy seemed oddly out of place, as if the location had somehow been left out.

In addition to front page news stories, the *Knoxville News-Sentinel* ran a full page feature under the headline "Cicada Mania," quoting local resident Cathy McCaughan: "Although the alien-sounding hum of the cicadas doesn't bother me, the crunching as I walk across the lawn is worse than fingernails on a chalkboard. The worst thing about this invasion is the Ziplock baggies full of shells that my 8-year-old son keeps bringing into the house."

Perhaps pushed to the edge by the hypnotic whirl, accounts began to surface that cicadas were actually edible. Newspapers, the Internet, and television published recipes that quoted the *Eat a Bug Cookbook*, written by David George Gordon. Well, why not? Many cultures all over the world regularly eat insects. Squirrels, raccoons, birds, and domestic pets were chowing down, so what's the harm? If you're ever going to knowingly eat a bug in your lifetime, wouldn't this be the time to do it? The supply was ample and certainly readily available.

Caught up in the media frenzy of May sweeps month, Knoxville's local NBC affiliate, WBIR, planned to do a live one-hour broadcast from Ijams. Walking the grounds of the nature center a few days beforehand, I discussed possible segment topics with executive producer Steve Dean. With the golden-winged cicadas buzzing in the trees over our heads, I commented, "There's so many of them, we're talking about cooking a few. We've actually got a recipe."

"You're kidding," returned Dean, the creator of the "Heartland Series" and an expert at ferreting out odd and unusual stories. "If you're going to eat a bug, let's do it live on air. That's great television!"

On Friday, May 21, Channel 10 broadcast *Live at Five*—unscripted and unrehearsed—live from Ijams. The news-and-local-interest program ended with cohosts Russell Biven and Sara Allen, plus reporters Herryn Riendeau and Beth Haynes and several members of the nature center's staff, sitting around a formal dinner table outside, eating cooked cicadas. Following an 1887 recipe from the bug cookbook, the harvested insects had been battered—in either flour or corn meal—and fried by Peg Beute, the nature center's resident cook supreme. As she discovered, coating them in batter makes the culinary oddity somewhat more palatable. "It's important you cover those little red eyes," Peg reported as she dropped them into the batter. It was another surreal scene punctuating a bizarre, *Twin Peaks* kind of week.

Peg also provided ranch and honey Dijon dressings, salsa, and chocolate dipping sauces, and with true television panache, everyone waited to take their first bite until the cameras were on. Therefore, reactions were real. If any retching occurred, it would also be real, but surprisingly that did not happen. The responses were positive. "Tastes like fried squash," most seemed to agree, albeit a bit crunchy. The oddest sensation was the feel of scratchy wings and legs sliding down your throat. A chorus of comments arose from the diners: "Don't think about what you're eating." "It's like popcorn shrimp. Just pop 'em in your mouth and chew." "There's plenty for everybody." "I think I've got a leg caught between my teeth." Overhead in the trees around us, the unearthly drone continued as we snacked on sautéed members of Brood X. Native Americans had roasted cicadas on rocks around campfires and eaten them like baked wontons. Over two hundred years later, we had simply added a bit more pomp and circumstance to the indulgence.

By month's end, the treetop wailing was subsiding. Lives returned to normal as the media moved on to something new. Dead or dying golden-winged cicadas began to fall from the trees like autumnal leaves. Standing on sidewalks littered with twitching insects, you were filled with a sense of loss. A sudden rainstorm hit the nature center a few weeks after the cicadas were gone, and the roof gutters along the rear of the visitor center overflowed. Surprised that the gutters weren't doing their job, Ben Nanny climbed a ladder to discover that the metal downspouts were clogged with dead cicadas. Their presence was making itself known one last time.

Studies conducted in part by Bard College professor Felicia Keesing determined that the sudden appearance of thousands of dead cicadas on the forest floor caused a dramatic spike in nitrogen in the soil. Graduate student Louie Yang published findings in the journal *Science* that seem to indicate that the rush of soil nutrients could explain marked tree-ring growth in oak trees in infested areas at regular thirteen- and seventeen-year intervals. Keesing compared it to someone pouring a pound of fertilizer per square yard throughout the forest where the cicadas were found, underscoring yet again that nature has profound cycles, although some are easier to observe than others.

Although I did not ever see cicadas in biblical locust proportions, I did see hundreds, heard thousands, and even ate a few. "I'm really going to miss them," someone said with a sigh. Seventeen years is a long time to wait for a second chorus, or from a bug-eater's point of view, a second course.

As a follow-up to the story, you might wonder how thousands of these cicadas remain in sync. The fact is, they don't. In 2005 I spoke to Rikki Hall, managing editor of the *Hellbender Press,* an East Tennessee environmental journal. Rikki is also an insect aficionado who keeps up with the comings and goings of the six-legged creatures around the valley. He lives in Rockford in Blount County and told me that he actually heard a few Brood Xers in late spring 2003 (one year early) and at least one lone male buzzing away in 2005 (one year late), which illustrates that this natural cycle isn't perfectly in tune. After my conversation with Rikki, I wondered if the nature center had any cicadas buzzing one year out of sync with the rest of their brood. In 2004 the trees around the parking lot had been full of them, so on May 26, 2005, I stood in the same location as I had the year before and listened. Sure enough, one lone male periodical cicada was buzzing away. As Rikki later reminded me, perhaps there was an out-of-sync female that was able to keep him company. You never know. As the great naturalist Constantine Rafinesque wholeheartedly believed, in nature anything is possible.

Gray Bat

Myotis grisescens

There is nothing to do but wait. It is always like this for naturalists, and for poets—the long hours of travel and preparation, and then the longer hours of waiting. All for that one electric, pulse-revving vision when the universe suddenly declares itself. A ravishing tug on the sleeve of our mortality. A view of life so astonishing as to make all of life newly astonishing: a spotted bat.

Diane Ackerman
The Moon by Whale Light, 1991

It's a dark scene we all remember from high school, a time when we were too young to appreciate the pathos. The story began with thunder and lightning, in a cavern with a boiling cauldron surrounded by three witches. As the trio threw ingredients into their pot they chanted, "Double, double toil and trouble; Fire burn, and cauldron bubble."

"Fillet of a fenny snake, In the cauldron boil and bake; Eye of newt and toe of frog, Wool of bat and tongue of dog . . ." The fortunetellers were conjuring prophecies for the ambitious Macbeth, the Thane of Glamis, who longed to be more. And he briefly accomplished it by slaying Duncan, the king of Scotland, while he slept—truly a deed most foul.

But, why *those* ingredients for the prophecy potion? Why wool of bat? Shakespeare's play was about fear and dark deeds; the witch's mixture was meant to repulse; and bats have long been associated with evil doings. Early representations of the devil often picture him with bat-like wings. Yet, as the treacherous Macbeth found out, things are not always as they are presented; our mental images of bats are but insensible, chimeric notions. If you've ever spent an evening looking closely into the flattened little faces of these nocturnal mammals, you see them for what they are: small, vulnerable creatures as remarkable as they are mysterious.

Bats are mammals, and like all others in that class, they have fur and nurse their young with mammary glands. But, unlike any other mammal, they have wings. The Germans called the animal *die fledermaus,* or the "flitter-mouse"; in France it's *chauve-souris,* or "bald mouse." But bats are not flying or hairless mice or any other rodent; in fact, bats are in an order all to themselves. Worldwide there are 925 known species, making them second only to rodents as the most numerous mammalian group. In the tropics, one out of every two species of mammal is a bat, and many tropical trees are bat-dependent, needing the flying creatures for pollination or seed dispersal or both.

Bats belong to the order Chiroptera, from the Latin for "hand-wing," a reference to their most miraculous features: wings that are made up of two layers of skin held outstretched on elongated bony fingers. These fleshy membranes are without fur and contain an elaborate network of elastic fibers, blood vessels, and nerves; when stretched and taut, they're powerful and lightweight. Although thin and translucent, the wing skin is durable, even rubbery, and quite resistant to puncture or wear.

Perhaps the best known and oddest behavior of a bat is its habit of sleeping upside down, hanging from a branch, cave ceiling, or some other horizontal surface. Why is this? In order to fly, an animal has to be incredibly lightweight. Birds accomplish this by having hollow bones, which reduce their overall weight, but a bat's bones are solid. To reduce its weight, the bones and muscles in a bat's legs are underdeveloped and light compared to non-flying mammals of similar size. When it stands on the ground, the bat's legs are so weak that they cannot support its upper body for long periods of sleep or hibernation. However, these same limbs are strong enough to allow it to hang upside down. The knee joints bend in the opposite direction of our own, which helps the bat navigate in flight and hang by its feet, but due to this unusual physiology, the bat moves awkwardly on terra firma and cannot lift up enough to become airborne efficiently. Yet, if the animal drops from a suspended position, it achieves flight easily. (Chimney swifts clinging to the vertical wall of a chimney take to the air in a similar manner.)

Bats are masterpieces of bioengineering. All the species found in the Tennessee Valley are insect eaters with small eyes. Although folklore has it that they are blind, they're not. Their vision is poor, but it's not a hindrance; their most developed sense is their hearing. The flying mammals use echolocation: high-frequency sound waves they produce in bursts that bounce off objects and back like sonar used by submarines. Their flattened faces and large ears catch the returning echo. This enables them to locate and catch winged insects and even fly through caves in total darkness.

It had been a warm day in late May. The sun was just beginning to slip below the tree line when I arrived in Fentress County at a rural location in north Tennessee. I was there to visit a research team led by Mary Kay Clark, curator of mammals at North Carolina's Museum of Natural Sciences in Raleigh. Joining her from Kentucky and Ohio were environmental scientists Jo Hargis and Katie Dunlap, representing R. D. Zande and Associates Inc., an environmental consulting firm.

"Bats became my specialty," said biologist Jo Hargis. Fresh out of college, she worked with her mentor, Dr. Virgil Black, conducting surveys of the endangered Indiana bat. The company she now works for is based in the Midwest and studies endangered species. That night in the Fentress County woods, they were seeking Rafinesque's big-eared bats; medium-sized fur balls that bear the name of the early American naturalist, Constantine Rafinesque.

"Fifteen years ago, very little was known about the Rafinesque when I started to work with them," recalled Mary Kay Clark. This is part of what lured her into their nocturnal world.

The night I joined them we met on a lightly graveled, washed-out road with more furrows than a new-plowed field. The location was somewhere in the wooded countryside near Jamestown. I arrived just before dusk, which for bat enthusiasts is when the action starts. It's at twilight that many bats emerge to begin their night of foraging for night-flying insects.

Bats must be caught in order to get a closer look at them. Biologists use mist nets, fine-meshed netting that is placed like invisible curtains at promising locations. That was what Clark, Hargis, and Dunlap did during their Fentress County field study. As darkness seeped into the Tennessee woodland and American toads began to trill from muddy puddles in the roadbed, three nets were raised. It wasn't long before the first bat was caught as it flew from the horizontal, slanted mouth of a small cave.

Once entangled in such a net, the bat hangs safe, although perhaps somewhat bewildered, until someone can very carefully remove it. I watched as Hargis's experienced, nimble fingers freed the bat's delicate wings and tiny feet. It's a tedious process done in low light. The small, furry creature squirmed and fussed, fighting to get free. Once unfettered, the bat's species, sex, maturity, reproductive status, weight, and forearm measurement were determined and recorded on the night's data sheet. It was fascinating to watch as the biologist opened her hand and the bat, realizing it was no longer tethered, flew away. As the evening progressed and P.M. gave way to A.M., more bats were caught, examined, and set free.

Rafinesque's big-eared bats are not listed as endangered. Its designation is "of special concern," which affords it no federal protection and really means that more information is needed to understand its status. Like the local species known simply as the gray bat, it could be endangered; it's just that no one knows. It's one of the least known bats in the Southeast, and as the name suggests, it has enormous ears, four times bigger than its tiny face. When it's asleep, its ears curl up against its head. When active or agitated, however, they unfurl like a ship's sails to quickly get a sense of its surroundings.

"They're intriguing to me because they look so different from most of our bats and they behave so differently," said Clark. They fly slower and are able to hover like a helicopter. Clark said that they "likely glean insects instead of hawking them" like other bats. It is believed that the "Rafs" actually use their lower frequency echolocation to scan the texture of leaves and other surfaces. This enables them to detect the bumps that might in fact be insects crawling or resting on the surface.

In May the females form maternity colonies, often in abandoned buildings. Babies are born in late May and early June. While I was with the team, only male bats were caught, probably indicating that all the females were busy in their nurseries. Males do not help raise the young; in summer they roost alone.

"When I started," said Clark, "very little was known about the Rafs." She explained that "discovering their secrets, being out after dark, seeing and experiencing parts of the night and wildlife that most people will never see and experience" was part of her motivation. As you can imagine, closely observing such an incredible little creature is enormously compelling. As I watched in the dark, Clark's interest and affection for the tiny mysteries she was holding was inescapable.

The story brings up a curious point. How do you know if an animal is endangered when little is known about it in the first place? Perhaps Rafinesque's big-eared bats have always existed in small, secretive populations, uncommon throughout their known range; perhaps their population is holding steady, neither increasing nor declining.

But there once was another species that had flown over southeastern skies in huge dark clouds, thousands and thousands strong. Decades ago the gray bat was quite common, much like the passenger pigeon. Today, it's the only mammal from my home county on the endangered species list. What happened?

The research conducted inside caves and other dark, nighttime locations by modern biologists has increased our understanding of the status and natural history of the only true flying mammals. Bat appreciation has come a long way since the days of Macbeth.

Historically, indigenous peoples living in both North and South America had different myths surrounding bats; in many cases they were associated with death and darkness. The Maya believed that the underworld, through which a dying man had to pass, was inhabited by *Camazotz,* or the Death Bat. In Mexico pregnant women went to a cave in Veracruz to give offerings to the bat gods to ensure that they would have successful deliveries. The South American Arawak told a story of an immense monster bat that lived on Bat Mountain. During the night it would swoop down on villages and carry away anyone foolish enough to be outside.

The Cherokee saw the bat in heroic terms. They had a story of how the bat got its wings. It happened, according to this legend, on the field of competition before a game—the precursor to modern lacrosse—that the Cherokee played with netted rackets and a ball. As the legend was told, there was once a great game in which the animals of the land challenged the birds of the air. The land animals were led by the powerful bear and the birds by their captain, the eagle. The land animals rejected one of their small four-footed members as being too insignificant. Downhearted, it climbed a tree to join the side of the birds. The feathered ones consulted and decided to make the dejected furry animal a pair of wings out of the head of a drum. The newly winged creature dodged and circled in the air, never dropping the ball. It proved to be one of the most agile flyers on the team and won the game for the birds. The game's hero went on to become *Tla'meha,* the bat.

Worldwide, bats have long been mystical ingredients in potions. The three witches in Shakespeare's *Macbeth* weren't the only ones brewing concoctions. Medicinal mixtures were widespread in Europe; everyone was searching for a miracle panacea; and since humans have been around for thousands of years, the search has an equally long history. The dried head of a bat mixed with three fingers of syrup and vinegar was once said to cure tumors. Gout could be treated by boiling three bats in rainwater and adding an ounce of flaxseed, three raw eggs, a cup of oil, dung of an ox, and an ounce of wax. Luckily, this concoction didn't have to be drunk; rather, it was spread over the swollen joint.

The Arab physician Ibu al-Beithar prescribed rubbing bat's blood on the thighs of children to remove the growth of hair. And in India, bat wings were crushed and mixed with coconut oil and other ingredients, then buried in a closed vessel for three months. After this lengthy process, the contents could be rubbed though the scalp to prevent hair from falling out or turning gray.

In his *A New Voyage to Carolina,* published in England in 1709, John Lawson reported: "The Bat or Rearmouse, the same as in England. The Indian Children are much addicted to eat Dirt, and so are some of the Christians. But roast a Bat on a Skewer, then pull the Skin off, and make the Child that eats Dirt eat the roasted Rearmouse; and he will never eat Dirt again. This is held as an infallible Remedy." (Personally, I would rather eat dirt.)

In the late 1700s European settlers began to trickle into the country's interior and set up housekeeping. The pioneers didn't own much beside their livestock, but one thing they brought with them was their culture—the customs and beliefs they carried with them from the Old World. In many cases, these were mere superstitions that helped them translate their strange new world. Traditionally, many animals—wolves, snakes, wild cats, bats—were demonized in the old folk tales. The most infamous were stories of vampires, but not until Bram Stoker's *Dracula,* published in 1897, were bats so closely associated with the blood-sucking undead. Prior to that, the vampires of Slavic gypsy legends could appear in the form of many animals: horses, dogs, frogs, spiders, even fleas. In old Yugoslavia there were tales of vampire snakes and even vegetables or household items that could harbor the dark spirits. Today, it's difficult to work up much of a fear for fleas or pumpkins, but back then it was believed that evil could be hiding in just about anything.

As Professor Schele de Vere wrote in *Appleton's Journal* in 1871:

> Among the prejudices cherished by the masses against harmless animals, few are stronger than that felt almost universally against bats, arising probably from the simple fact that they are children of the night and forced to carry on their search after food in the darkness. . . . A poor, lost bat need but fly into a room filled with company, and every body is frightened. Superstitious people tremble at their mere presence as an evil omen.

On the edge of the unknown in aboriginal America, many demons were conjured up; after all, the woods were dark and deep. "This was the age of superstition" wrote George Sheldon in 1886. He was reflecting on "Forty Years of Frontier Life" and added:

But over all a grave earnestness prevails; there is little laughter or mirth, and no song to cheer the tired workers. If stories are told they are of Indian horrors, of ghosts, or of the fearful pranks of witchcraft. . . . Tales of events like these, so fascinating and so fearful, sent the adults, as well as the children to bed with blood chilled, every sense alert with fear, ready to see a ghost in every slip of moonshine, and trace to malign origin every sound breaking the stillness—the rattle of a shutter, the creak of a door, the moan of the winds or cries of the birds and beasts of the night.

And the new world was brimming with strange birds and beasts, especially bats. Early accounts have long dark columns with hundreds of thousands of individual bats flying over the Southeast on summer evenings.

A report in the *Atlantic Monthly* in 1867 described a colony inside a cave in Kentucky:

I found these creatures clinging by thousands, literally blackening the wall, and hanging in festoons a foot or two in length. The manner of forming these festoons was curious enough: three or four bats having first taken hold of some sharp projecting ledge with their hindmost claws, and hanging thereby with their heads downward, others had seized their leathery wings at the second joint, and they too, hanging with downward heads, had offered their wings as holding places for still others; and so the unsightly pendent mass had grown, until in some instances it contained as many as twenty or thirty bats.

And then in 1868 came another account, this one from Wyandotte Cave in Indiana:

Descending a steep declivity, some forty or fifty feet, they entered a spacious apartment, on whose lofty ceiling could be discerned large, irregular, dark-colored clusters, resembling swarms of bees. The doctor quietly requested Sylvester to discharge his pistol. He did so. The cluster suddenly dissolved, and the air was filled with myriads of bats. The ladies screamed and pulled their hoods closely over their faces. Several of the candles were extinguished by their wings, and for several minutes the cave resounded with their rustling flight and sharp twittering cries.

After hearing such ominous stories, many believed that something clearly needed to be done about these loathsome vermin. In some cases, fires were deliberately set inside caves. The thick dark smoke that rose to fill the ceiling vaults suffocated whole colonies of sleeping bats. (Wolves, snakes, and bats have all suffered through years of such human persecution.)

Surprisingly, many bat colonies experienced declines as a direct result of the Civil War. As the conflict was winding down, a successful blockade by the North cut off supplies to the South. The Confederacy began to run low on the ingredients for making gunpowder—particularly potassium nitrate, also known as saltpeter. This valuable chemical compound can be extracted from bat droppings, and in the South there were huge buildups several feet deep in roosting caves of gray bats, including Hubbards Cave in central Tennessee. The fires built to light the interior of the caves while the guano was harvested destroyed many colonies.

This is not the only time that bats have involuntarily aided an American war effort. During the Second World War, an American dentist named Lytle S. Adams concocted a plan to use bats carrying small incendiary bombs to help fight the Japanese. Adams petitioned the White House about his bat-bombs, getting the attention and interest of President Franklin Roosevelt who signed off on the plan; after all, desperate times called for desperate measures. The top-secret U.S. Navy operation, known as "Project X-Ray," spent two million dollars over a two-year period testing the procedures. As contrived, bats that roost in buildings were captured and fitted with tiny one-ounce napalm charges. Planes were to fly over key Japanese cities and drop canisters slowed by parachutes. Each tubular cage was to hold around seven thousand bats that would escape when automatic devices opened doors before the metal container reached the ground.

If all were to go as planned, the bats would fly away and seek shelter in random buildings: homes, factories, and ammunition dumps. Chemical timers then triggered the devices. Each incendiary bomb was designed to burn for eight minutes, long enough to set thousands of structures on fire, causing widespread chaos. Tests were conducted, and it was determined that the Brazilian free-tailed bat that inhabits caves in the Southwest was the most suitable because it could carry a bomb the equivalent of its own weight for ten to fifteen miles. Caves inhabited by this species were leased by the U.S. Navy, and marines were posted to guard the entrances (as if someone might want to steal the bats). Tests were carried out, but the bats were decidedly uncooperative. Even so, the oddball plan might have worked because one day during the operation, six armed bats escaped and sought refuge in buildings at Carlsbad Auxiliary Army Airfield in New Mexico. The control tower and barracks was accidentally destroyed when the errant bat-bombs ignited. This incident prompted project officials to build an imitation Japanese village—authentic in architecture and building materials—in the deserts of Utah to practice their sorties. Eventually, however, Project X-Ray was scrapped, probably because of another top-secret project underway at the time: the development of the atomic bomb that ultimately was dropped on two Japanese cities instead.

As illustrated by these stories, the real threat to bat populations is ill-advised humans, but wartime only created a small disruption. Other factors have had a far greater impact. As with freshwater mussels, each endangered species must be evaluated separately because each has a unique life history.

In the United States, there are forty-five known species of bats. Six are currently federally protected under the Endangered Species Act of 1973: lesser long-nosed, greater long-nosed, gray, Indiana, Ozark big-eared, and Virginia big-eared. The first two are nectar eaters found in the desert Southwest, and the last two are subspecies of the Townsend's big-eared bat found in isolated locations. The two others, the gray and Indiana bat, are both found in the East and once existed in large numbers, but their populations have suffered dramatic declines in recent history. Human interference—habitat destruction, direct wanton killing, pesticide use, cave vandalism, and hibernating and maternity colony disturbances—have perhaps all played a role in their decline.

Gray bats are only found in a handful of states in the South, mainly Arkansas, Missouri, Kentucky, Tennessee, and Alabama. After their late summer shed, their fur is a uniform dark gray, but it slowly fades to a chestnut brown over the course of the year. Historically, the gray bat was once one of the most abundant mammals in the Southeast. Hundreds of thousands would pass overhead in great columns every summer evening on their way to eating tons of night-flying insects. The highly gregarious grays like to forage over water.

In 1958 Merlin Tuttle moved to Knoxville with his family. As a teenager, he attended Little Creek Academy and soon began to explore Baloney Cave with his newfound high school friends. Located slightly more than nine miles from my Chapman Ridge home, the cave's odd name comes from a drapery formation it contains that looks like a string of round sausages. It's an eight-foot drop into the cave's entrance, which makes getting in somewhat difficult. "Our biology class inadvertently discovered a moonshine still in the entrance," says Tuttle. "The local sheriff was notified, and there was a major raid on the still that night."

The early cave explorations changed the course of Tuttle's life; he became fascinated with bats. In the late 1950s it was believed that gray bats lived in the same caves year-round. Tuttle noticed, however, that thousands of grays flew into the cave near the Tennessee River in the fall and again in the spring; it appeared to him to be migratory behavior.

Tuttle persuaded his parents to take him to the Smithsonian Institution, where he sought out bat experts to discuss his observations. The specialists were so impressed by the boy's interest that they issued him bands through the U.S. Fish and Wildlife Service and encouraged him to learn more about the gray's movements. By October 1960 the eager student used the bands to tag several hundred gray bats. Fate often steps in at points such as these, and one's destiny is often determined by being in the right place at the right time. Two months later Tuttle and his father recaptured a few of these banded bats in a cave one hundred miles north of Knoxville. He had proven not only that the gregarious grays had traveled to winter hibernation caves but also that they had migrated north rather than south.

Twenty years later, the boy had become a man. Along the way he had banded 40,182 gray bats at numerous locations in six states. Perhaps more important, Tuttle had recaptured over 20,000 of his bats, which gave him a firm understanding of their migration movements. Tuttle did his undergraduate work at the University of Tennessee in Knoxville and completed his PhD dissertation in population ecology at the University of Kansas. The story could have ended there, but the data collected over those two decades led to another profound conclusion. Gray bats were in huge trouble. In fact, they were declining at a remarkable rate, but no one knew why.

Although most bat species hibernate in caves, they often do their summer roosting in trees, buildings, or under bridges. Gray bats use caves year-round, albeit distinct caves at different times of the year. Winter hibernation is spent deep in vertical caves with large rooms that maintain a temperature of 58–77°F. Because of their specific requirements, today about 95 percent of all gray bats hibernate in only eight caves: two in Tennessee, three in Missouri, and one each in Kentucky, Alabama, and Arkansas. One of the locations houses 50 percent of the entire hibernating population. Herein lies the problem. Being so dependent on so few locations makes the entire population vulnerable.

In the summer, after migration to suitable foraging sites that may be as far away as two hundred miles, females form large maternity colonies in caves with restricted rooms or domed ceilings capable of trapping the colony's combined body heat. Frequently the caves also have streams. Males and non-reproductive females form separate summer "bachelor" colonies in yet other caves. Because of these very specific requirements, it's believed that fewer than 5 percent of available caves are suitable.

Gray bats mate in September and October, and soon thereafter the females move to hibernation colonies, followed in time by the males. However, fertilization is delayed, and the mated females store the sperm internally. They don't become pregnant until after emerging from hibernation in the spring. Having sufficient stored fats to meet the energy requirements of a long hibernation is risky enough, but a female bat with a developing fetus requires even more energy reserves. By delaying fertilization until the colony becomes active in the spring, all the females that mated over a two-month period the year before are in sync and will each have one baby in late May or early June. All of the new mothers will be attending their newborns at essentially the same time and place. Young gray bats are able to fly independently in twenty to twenty-five days.

Gray bats are gregarious for a reason; their survival depends on it. Maintaining the proper temperatures in their maternity colonies requires a large number of individuals that share the cost of heating a roost through their collective body heat. Once overall numbers fall below a threshold point, the growth of the baby bats slows. The colony is destined to fail. Biologists call the phenomenon "the passenger pigeon effect," which recalls the extinction of the native bird that also required huge numbers to survive.

Dr. Tuttle became aware of failing nursery colonies in the 1970s. A colony in Alabama at Hambrick Cave disappeared in one year, which prompted him to take a second look at some of the 120 caves where he had found gray bats in the course of his studies. In 1976 he revisited twenty-two isolated colonies in caves he felt were the least likely to have been disturbed. To his chagrin, he discovered a 54 percent population decline in just six years. The largest maternity colony had completely disappeared. Combined numbers revealed that the total population of 1.2 million had dropped to 635,700, followed by a decline to 293,600 in 1976. That's a fall of almost 76 percent in one man's lifetime.

A similar study in Missouri revealed that twenty-seven maternity colonies with a total of 238,000 gray bats had fallen to only eleven colonies with a population of 46,500 bats—a drop of 80 percent in just fifteen years. Clearly, something had to be done, or, as Barbour and Davis wrote in *Bats of America* in 1969, gray bats faced probable extinction. At Dr. Tuttle's request, the U.S. Fish and Wildlife Service officially placed gray bats on the endangered species list on April 28, 1976, giving them full federal protection. The next step was to figure out what was causing the decline and formulate a plan for their recovery.

Gray bats are insectivores. Could the use of pesticides be causing the problem? Dr. Tuttle sent guano samples to the Putuxent Wildlife Research Center in Laurel, Maryland. Residue analysis turned up elevated levels of toxins, organochlorine pesticides, PCBs, and even lead. Mayflies, a principle component of a gray bat's diet, are sensitive to aquatic pollution, so poisoning was a possibility, but was it enough of one to kill thousands?

Early in the research another problem became even more obvious. Because of their habit of living in very large numbers in only a few isolated caves, loss of any of these locations was devastating. Direct human interference through cave exploration, vandalism, and commercialization were having a profound effect. Hibernating colonies awakened in winter by spelunkers or even well-meaning biologists caused the bats to use up precious fat reserves. It's estimated that a single disturbance can cost a bat the energy it would normally need to survive two or three weeks of hibernation. Low on fat reserves, bats may leave the cave too early in the season and starve to death. In maternity colonies, mother bats spooked by cave explorers may flee, dropping their flightless pups in the process.

It became painfully clear, therefore, that because gray bats only use a small number of suitable caves, those caves had to be protected, and "protected" meant that they needed to be gated with bat-friendly barriers that allowed bats access but kept people out at critical times on a seasonal basis. Over the years conservationists have perfected effective barrier designs. Four important nursery caves—Hambrick, Cave Springs, and Blowing Wind Caves in Alabama and Nickajack in Tennessee—had all lost their maternity colonies; with protection and locked gates all four were soon occupied by new nurseries.

Important hibernation sites had to be protected as well. The largest known winter site, Fern Cave in Alabama, was acquired by the U.S. Fish and Wildlife Service, and in 1985 Hubbards Cave was gated through a joint effort of several conservation groups. The barrier, thirty feet tall and thirty-five feet wide, consisting of concrete and 130 tons of steel is the largest ever constructed to protect cave-dwelling bats. Historically, the cave, located in central Tennessee, was the winter home to thousands of gray bats that migrated from as far away as 350 miles to the south. The new gate only closes off the bat section during the important hibernation season: mid-August through mid-May.

In 1982 Dr. Tuttle founded Bat Conservation International (BCI), which is dedicated to saving bats worldwide through raising public awareness, conducting research, and forging partnerships with other like-minded environmental groups. Saving the gray bat became one of its first priorities, and at present, protection of cave habitat seems to be working. Ironically, the gray bats' chief vulnerability was turned into a plus. Once it was recognized that their existence depended on a very few caves, protection of those safe havens turned the tide. Today, the overall population of gray bats is said to be stable and growing.

One of the principal maternity sites had been Nickajack Cave located in Marion County, twenty miles west of Chattanooga. The location is one of the most historic in the Southeast. Native Americans used the spacious cavern for shelter, and river pirates once hid out there. During the Civil War, the Confederate army mined saltpeter at Nickajack, and Federal troops shelled it for that reason. Using tourist caves as social sites for dances began in the early 1800s and lasted well into the 1900s. In 1878 property owner James W. McReynolds opened the cavern to commercial tours, and a dance platform was built just inside the cave's entrance to service steamboats that came and went on the nearby Tennessee River. Appropriate caverns were essentially cool and spacious covered ballrooms. Nickajack's rectangular entrance is 140 feet wide by 50 feet tall. A short distance inside the cave opens up to be nearly 200 feet wide, plenty of room for summer cotillions.

In October 1967 singer Johnny Cash reportedly crawled into the dark recesses of the cave to attempt suicide but gave up the idea when he "sensed God's presence." When the Tennessee Valley Authority completed Nickajack Dam a short time later, the resulting reservoir flooded the cave entrance, reducing its height to around twenty-five feet and making it accessible only to boat traffic. Social cruises into the underground darkness replaced the dances. When it was determined that the storied cave was key to the survival of the endangered gray bat, it was closed to the public. A fly-over barrier (essentially a heavy chain-link fence) was built across the entrance in 1981 to keep boats out. It became Tennessee's first nongame wildlife refuge. Gray bats soon returned to Nickajack. They are there from April to October, and once again the cave is a thriving nursery.

It was late afternoon on a hot summer's day when I drove to the Chattanooga Nature Center (CNC). I met with about twenty-five other curious visitors for a program about bats in general and gray bats specifically, presented by the center's senior naturalist, Kyle Waggener. After the short program at the center and with our heads full of bat facts, we formed a caravan heading to Marion County on I-24. Twenty miles to the west the sky was darkening, wispy and rose colored as we arrived at Maple View Public Use Area on Nickajack Lake. The public park is near New Hope, a fitting name for a site so key to the recovery of an endangered species. In 1985 the location was designated a wildlife observation area, and a few years later TVA built a wooden platform roughly eight feet above the water to aid bat watchers.

The observation deck faces the cave's entrance but keeps viewers from getting too close. Waggener had predicted that the bats would begin to emerge around 9:05 P.M., and in one of those perfect moments in which naturalist and nature are in sync, the bats did just that. Located on the western shoreline, the deck is surrounded by cedar trees. Looking up into the dwindling light, we began to see bats dart about in unpredictable paths, in and around the aromatic evergreens. The first one I got a really clear view of pirouetted in the fading light just over my head. As the sky darkened, the number of bats increased until the emergence developed into the frenzy of an urban rush hour, except the traffic flow was not in straight lines but erratic, like a swarm of bees. Occasionally a bat dipped low, just above us. The crowd gasped, becoming giddy with excitement, turning this way and that like slow-moving dancers; yet our gaze remained skyward. With binoculars you could peer across the cove to the opposite tree line and see just as many, if not more, bobbing and weaving over the landscape.

It's now believed that the maternity colony's population has returned to number between 60,000 and 100,000 bats. (Estimates are made by how much space the roosting bats occupy, knowing that roughly 1,828 gray bats fit into a square meter.) It took a while for that many bats to fly out and begin their night of foraging. "The bats will disperse and fly up to 4 miles from the cave," related Waggener. "Each will eat about 3,000 insects tonight; and most will return to the cave intermittently to rest or nurse their babies. But by morning, just before sunrise, the entire group will return to the cave to roost all day."

"This is one of the great natural spectacles of our region," added the CNC naturalist in charge. And it was wondrous indeed to see, but more than that, the realization that, just a few short years prior to our visit, gray bats had disappeared from the site made the experience somehow sweeter. Witnessing their emergence from the cave's gaping mouth with the understanding that it had been precipitated by a conservation effort made it decidedly more satisfying.

Today there has been a spectacular turnaround in the gray bat population, so much so that the animals could soon be taken off the endangered species list. This would not have been possible without the efforts of Merlin Tuttle and Bat Conservation International, the organization he founded. If "vigilance continues to protect sites like Nickajack," Dr. Tuttle told me in an e-mail, "yes, I am confident they will soon be de-listed."

In the end, all life is tenuous. We do not need a witch's prophecy to comprehend such infallible truths, or that evil doings lie in the hearts of men, not in small, furry mammals. As it turns out, the fate of these beneficial bats now seems rosier than that of Shakespeare's truly dark Macbeth, who thought he was somehow indestructible; yet, as Macduff proved with a vengeance, he decidedly was not.

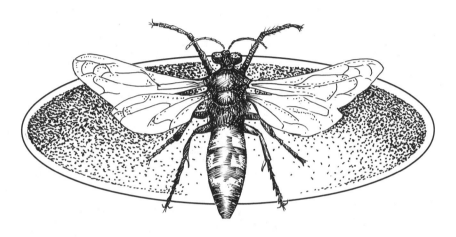

Summer

Passionflower
Passiflora incarnata

In the valleys we saw the laurel and the dwarf rosebay, the passion flower and the Turk's-cap lily, and on the mountain sides the poplar or tulip tree, the hickory, the Chincapin, the alder, and the chestnut in profusion. . . . For miles around the country is grand and imposing.

Edward King
"The Great South," 1874

Unlike most rivers in this country, the Toccoa flows northwest. It begins in the mountains of north Georgia in Lumpkin County, works its way through the Chattahoochee National Forest past Margret and McCaysville, and crosses the Tennessee state line just south of Copperhill. When it leaves the Peach State, its name changes to the Ocoee. It then continues northward through the Cherokee National Forest knifing between Licklog Ridge and Little Frog Mountain.

Over the past several millennia, the river has carved the Ocoee River Gorge, a dramatic winding channel hewn from solid rock. Today, as any kayaker knows, it's the home of turbulent whitewater. The tousled water passes through three dams before it enters the Tennessee Valley. There the current is calmed, and it eventually enters the Hiwassee River in Polk County. From there on the water's journey is more leisurely, like that of most rivers as they encounter rich, fertile bottomland.

Although inhabited by Native Americans for thousands of years, the remote and rugged region of the Ocoee was largely ignored by white settlers until 1843. That's when copper was discovered near Ducktown in extreme southeast Tennessee. The discovery brought a boom to the area, even attracting miners from as far away as Cornwall, England. The original inhabitants knew of the deposits and had even smelted copper from the site, but by 1843 all of the Cherokee had been forcibly removed. In 1847 casks of ore were transported by mule to Dalton, Georgia, and in 1853, a wagon road that followed the Ocoee River curve for curve was completed to transport the high-grade metal from the thriving sixty-thousand-acre Copper Basin, out of the mountains and down into the valley to Cleveland. This Old Copper Road was later used as the roadbed for today's U.S. Highway 64 that snakes through the rugged gorge.

The name Ocoee comes from the Cherokee. Accounts vary, but it means either "place of the river people," a reference to the Catawka who once lived there, or "place of the apricot vine." Most sources cite the latter, but if this is true, just what is apricot vine?

In the botanical lexicon, a vine is described as "a climbing plant with woody or herbaceous stems that climbs, twines, adheres or scrambles over other taller objects—shrubs, trees, walls, fences, arbors, porches, gazebos, etc.—in order to reach sunlight." In short, it's a tenacious thing much like the Ocoee itself.

The Cherokee's apricot vine is a northern member of a large, primarily tropical family of plants. They climb with the aid of tendrils (modified leaves or stems that grow rapidly as slender strands of plant tissue). A tendril is sensitive to touch, creating a process botanists call *thigmotropism*. The tendril's tip grows in a spiral pattern. When it touches a solid surface, it rapidly encircles it, grabbing hold. Within only five to ten minutes, its grasp is complete, and with the added support, the tendril is able to pull the plant along, advancing its growth.

Apricot vine is a perennial. Each spring, new three- to five-lobed leaves begin to appear as the vine spreads. The flowers that follow are often described as "strikingly spectacular." It is certainly the most ornate wheel-like blossom in the Tennessee Valley. Its structure is complex, boasting five outer sepals and five inner petals that are white to lavender in color. Inside the whorl are five drooping stamens with five anthers (male, pollen-producing) suspended around a three-styled pistil (female, ovule-bearing). As if this weren't enough, the entire floral structure is surrounded by a purple and pink-banded, fringelike corona two inches or more in diameter. It's easy to get lost in this floral description; suffice it to say, the apricot vine is sensationally ornate like a Victorian lampshade.

You might think such a memorable flower would produce a noteworthy fruit. In this case it does, as Captain John Smith of Jamestown discovered. But before that, a bit of background: Settled in 1607, the Jamestown Colony in Virginia was the first permanent English settlement in North America. It took three ships—the *Susan Constant, Godspeed,* and *Discovery*—to ferry the one-hundred-plus colonists across the Atlantic Ocean. Upon arriving in the New World, Captain Smith learned that he had been appointed in "secret orders"—sealed before the trip by King James I—to serve on the new colony's governing council. This surprised all of the English farmers and Polish woodcutters who made up the settlement because Smith had been arrested for mutiny during the long voyage over. The reversal of fortune saved Smith's life since his ship's captain was going to have him hanged. Released from his chains, Smith served as "councelor" until being elected president of the council in 1608. At one point in his Virginia adventures, Smith was captured by Chief Wahunsunacock of the Powhatan, who controlled all of the coastal tidewater area. About to be put to death, his life was spared a second time when Pocahontas, the chief's young daughter, threw herself between Smith and his executioner.

This is one of the most embellished stories in American history, and it's generally believed that it has been romanticized a little too much. The intervention by Pocahontas was probably part of an established initiation ritual, and Smith was never in jeopardy. At this point, the colonists were perhaps still something of a novelty and had not yet worn out their welcome. Pocahontas was actually the ten- to twelve-year-old girl's nickname; it purportedly meant "playful one." A goodwill ambassador, her true name was Matoaka, and she was described by colonist William Strachey as being a "well featured but wanton young girle," beloved by both sides and known for turning cartwheels in the nude, an act so purely innocent and primal it surely lightened the mood of any village.

Despite the playful one's good-natured efforts, hostilities finally broke out between the two groups in 1610. Four years later, her frolicsome days over, Matoaka married tobacco grower John Rolfe, adopted Christianity, and changed her name to Rebecca. It was perhaps more of a diplomatic union that brought the Anglo and Indian camps back together and ended their war. Captain Smith eventually returned to England and wrote three books about his adventures in the new land, the people he met, and the food they ate. In 1624 he reported that the Native Americans in Virginia planted "maracocks": "In the watery valleys groweth a berry which they call ocoughtanamnis very much like unto capers. These they dry in summer. When they eat them they boil them near half a day; for otherwise they differ not much from poison. . . . During summer there are either strawberries, which riped in April, or mulberries which ripen in May and June. Raspises [raspberries], hurts [huckleberries]; or a fruit that the inhabitants call maracocks, which is a pleasant, wholesome fruit much like a lemon."

The maracock was also described by Strachey as "of the bigness of a green apple," and "like as a pomegranate, a good summer cooling fruit." The Powhattan called the fruit "mahcawq." Over the course of the centuries, maracock or mahacawq became apricot or maypop; the latter name has been the one that's still most often used because it seems most appropriate. If you squeeze the fruit when ripe, it "may pop," or burst like a small balloon.

For the Cherokee the apricot vine must have been vastly important. The fruit was eaten raw or was strained into a juice. The sweet liquid could then be thickened with flour or cornmeal for a summertime beverage. In an interview in the 1970s, Cherokee descendant Betty Lossiah remarked that the fruit could be peeled "like eggs" or used as a potherb; the plant's leaves could also be parboiled, washed, and then cooked in hot grease.

Apricot vine was also an essential part of Native Americans' medicine kits. For earaches, a warm infusion of the beaten root was dropped into sore ears. The pounded root was also applied as a poultice to "draw out inflammation" of boils or briar and locust wounds. The plant has an analgesic, or pain-killing, property; plus, its flavonoid compounds have a relaxing, anti-anxiety, and sedative effect. The Aztecs used the plant to promote sleep.

It was also said that the vine could bring people together. If a couple had lived together for many years, petty things they did could start to wear on their nerves. An herbalist would recommend that drinking a tea brewed from the vine's leaves would calm the situation: "Pretty soon you start to relax and the little things don't bother you so much and you get along fine." A pharmaceutical with this talent would be valuable in any generation.

Native Americans did not have a drugstore down the street. They used what they found growing in the fields. Apricot vine was common throughout the Southeast. Its properties were well known to them. Obviously, a plant so useful must have been revered. Early Jesuits saw the natives covet the fruit, saw their fervor for the plant, and took it as a sign that they were "hungry for Christianity," and with "great zeal" they began to convert them.

The European holy men looked farther and found divine symbols in the apricot vine. The plant's leaves stood for the Roman spears. The flower's five sepals and five petals represented the ten apostles who remained loyal to Jesus. The five anthers stood for the five wounds; the plants tendrils symbolized the scourges; the central column of the ovary stood for the cross; the stamens the hammers used to attach Christ to that cross; and the three stigmata, the three nails used in the crucifixion. The fringe-like filaments that surround the centerpiece were the crown of thorns the Savior was forced to wear.

To them the plant became known as *flor de las cinco llagas*, or flower of the five wounds, or simply *flos passionis*, the passion flower. It was believed by the Jesuits that it had appeared in a dream of St. Francis of Assisi as the flower that grew on the cross. Such vaulted esteem is a lot to place on a single wildflower but seeing such an embellished wonder for the first time must have stirred their imaginations. It is just that remarkable. As time went on, the name passionflower slowly caught on.

Before we all rush out and look for some Powhatan maracock to calm our nerves, we should consider what we're doing. Folk remedies like passionflower (*Passiflora incarnata*) have been widely used, with lots of trial and error, for thousands of years by intelligent people. The herb is still available in many health food stores. A study published in the *Alternative Medicine Review* in December 2001 states that passionflower extract worked as well as oxazepam in treating generalized anxiety disorder (GAD). Oxazepam is a modern drug given to treat GAD sufferers. The double-blind study also found that passionflower actually had a lower incidence of "impairment of job performance."

The real problem with herbal medicine is knowing the proper dosage, any possible side effects, and reactions it might have with prescription drugs that are already being taken. There is a romantic notion that since a herbal remedy is natural, it has no adverse effects. This is not true. A doctor should always be consulted.

In January 2000 the *Journal of Toxicology: Clinical Toxicology* cited the case of a thirty-four-year-old woman who took passionflower at therapeutic dosages and ended up very ill. The article on the toxicity of *Passiflora incarnata* reports that she had developed "severe nausea, vomiting, drowsiness, prolonged gastrointestinal toxicity and episodes of nonsustained ventricular tachycardia [abnormally fast and ineffective heart rate]." The case report goes on to say that the patient "required hospital admission for cardiac monitoring and intravenous fluid therapy." The true cause of her illness went undiagnosed for a while because doctors were unaware she was taking *Passiflora incarnata*.

John Muir, the founder of the Sierra Club, was also one of this country's pioneering conservationists, but he didn't start that way. Early in his life he was torn between two worlds: earning a living or following his heart. I'm sure many of us can relate to his quandary. Muir's free time was spent outside studying plants, but inside he worked in a factory making carriage parts. One evening, as he was repairing a broken machine belt at his workplace, the file he was using flipped up and struck him in the eye, blinding him. While recuperating, he had an epiphany: should his vision return, he'd spend the rest of his life doing what he wanted to do—outside. He lived in a country rich in natural history and hoped he'd get a chance to see it.

Luckily for the Sierra Club, Muir's eyesight returned, and as he had promised himself, he quit his job. On September 1, 1867, he left Indianapolis "joyful and free, on a thousand mile walk to the Gulf of Mexico," taking note of the unusual plants encountered along the way. Muir's long trek is one of the most famous solo walks in American history. On September 12, after passing southeast through Kentucky and crossing the Cumberland Plateau, he walked down Walden Ridge—the eastern edge of the plateau—and entered the Tennessee Valley, reaching Philadelphia and Madisonville two days later. Muir was dependent on the kindness of total strangers he met along the way. On September 15 he "Reached a house before night, and asked leave to stop. 'Well, you're welcome to stop,' said the mountaineer, 'if you think you can live till morning on what I have to live on all the time.' Found the old gentleman very communicative. Was favored with long 'bar' stories, deer hunts, etc., and in the morning was pressed to stay a day or two."

Muir accepted the old man's offer and spent a few days botanizing the valley before climbing the mountains along the Hiwassee River into North Carolina. He wrote in his journal that "almost everything that grows is interesting to me." In Georgia, along the Savannah River, passionflower caught his eye. He noted that it had been common all the way back "into Tennessee," and scribed, "it is here called 'apricot vine,' has a superb flower, and the most delicious fruit I have ever eaten."

Muir's thousand-mile walk to the sea changed his life. Gretel Ehrlich writes that "his passions had begun to order themselves into what could be called a life's work. He was on a leafy path to salvation; his damaged sight absorbed all that came before it—mountain, fern, vine, brier, pine, sedge, aster, goldenrod, human being, river." We should also add the passionflower's maypop, for it's the little things that weave themselves into the fabric of our lives and set our resolve. John Muir went on to dream of a system of national parks and influenced President Theodore Roosevelt to make it so.

Almost three decades after Muir's walk, a World's Fair was held in Chicago. For the 1893 celebration, states were asked to choose State Flowers. It was a novel idea, and the Territory of Oklahoma, perhaps eager to prove itself, was the first to choose; it picked mistletoe as its floral symbol, an odd choice since the plant most associated with Christmastime and stolen kisses is actually a parasite that preys on trees. It also couldn't be called a state flower because the Sooners didn't become a state until 1907, but you have to start somewhere. On February 1, 1895, Vermont, which was a state, named red clover as its official blossom. Afterwards, there was a rush to proclaim allegiances to flowers. That same year Montana picked bitterroot, Delaware choose the peach blossom, Nebraska grabbed goldenrod, and Maine championed the white pine-cone and tassel. Technically, this last one isn't a true flower. Pines are conifers, which means cone-bearing. They have male pollen-producing cones and female seed-bearing cones. But since Maine's nickname is the "Pine Tree State," what else could they do?

It wasn't until 1919 that Tennessee joined the fray. By then thirty-one other states had chosen their flowers. On Monday, January 6, 1919, the Sixty-first General Assembly of the State of Tennessee convened in Nashville. Soon thereafter, Knox County Representative W. K. Anderson sponsored House Joint Resolution No. 12, which provided that a committee be selected to choose an official state flower. It was signed by the Speaker of the House on January 15. Meanwhile, two state senators, John C. Houk and E. E. Patton, who represented Knox, Polk, Loudon, and Monroe Counties, sponsored Senate Joint Resolution No. 13, which did the same. The Speaker of the Senate signed this measure on January 23, so both the House and the Senate had a resolution to find an official, symbolic flower.

On Sunday, January 26, 1919, the *Nashville Banner* ran a story titled "School Children to Vote on State Flower." It seems the Sixty-first General Assembly regretted that the Volunteer State "has not been represented in the list of those commonwealths which have adopted official floral emblems." It had been determined that in the fall, when the new school term began, the school children of Tennessee would decide the matter. Before the year was out, the kids voted, and passionflower became the state's official flower.

Fourteen years later, in 1933, sentiments or memories shifted. The cultivated iris had become all the rage in Nashville, and the state capital became known as Iris City. Garden Clubs around the state had become quite popular, and many were dissatisfied with the lowly passionflower. After all, it was little more than a roadside weed and lacked the noble stature worthy of a proper garden. They encouraged the passage of Senate Joint Resolution 53, which named the iris as the official state flower. The 1919 resolutions were not rescinded, and it remained that way for forty years, with Tennessee having two state flowers. All that time, supporters of both flowers argued over which was the one true representative floral emblem of the Volunteer State. The debate was at times passionate and over-heated. It was not until 1973 that the Eighty-eighth General Assembly found compromise and named the iris the official State Cultivated Flower and the passionflower the State Wildflower. Tennessee is the only state with such a distinction.

In 1982 the U.S. Post Office released a set of fifty commemorative stamps representing all the states. Each stamp is unique and shows a different state's official "State Bird and Flower." Tennessee's stamp has a mockingbird and an iris. The passionflower was snubbed once again, even though it had seniority.

Letting the story end at this point on such a sour note seems unsatisfying. On a hazy day in July, I drove to Polk County, planning to walk and drive the roads near the Hiwassee and Ocoee Rivers, looking for passionflower in bloom; after all, that's where this narrative started. The John Muir National Recreation Trail begins near Reliance on the Hiwassee. The river's name comes from the Cherokee word, *Ayuwasiu,* meaning "meadow at the foot of the hill," and indeed, the Hiwassee River valley is just that. The official nineteen-mile Muir trail begins farther up into the mountains. It was restored in 1972 by the Youth Conservation Corps and the Senior Community Service Employment Program to commemorate the path that Muir took through the rugged terrain on his "Thousand-Mile Walk to the Gulf." The trail follows the river through the Cherokee National Forest. It was hot the day I walked along the footpath; the heavy southern humidity hung like a smothering blanket over me. I could hear the refreshing roar of the river, but through the thick growth of the floodplain, it seemed unreachable—a tantalizing audible mirage. The trail appeared little used; Muir would have liked that. Tall plants—river cane, blackberry, lespedeza, pawpaw, and a host of other vegetation—sealed in the simple dirt path, at times obscuring it like a tropical jungle. I imagined the botanist Muir perusing the thick undergrowth. The only flower I found in bloom was the chest-height wild sweet William, or meadow phlox, which grew close to four feet tall. There was no passionflower.

Southwest of Benton on Highway 411, there's a roadside historic marker located at the gravesite of Nancy (Nanye'hi) Ward, Native American. Nanye'hi got her English surname when she married British trader Bryan(t) Ward. Her memorial overlooks the ambling Ocoee, and it seemed an appropriate place to find the plant her people held in such esteem. In her day Ward had earned the title of "War Woman of Chota," having fought with Oconostota against the Creeks in North Georgia. (She entered the battle when her first husband, the Cherokee named Kingfisher, was killed.) Afterwards, Nanye'hi attended council meeting with the men who knew her as *Ghighau,* or "Beloved Woman." She is buried on a hill under an aged cedar with a small rock cairn and a metal plaque that reads, "In Memory of Nancy Ward, Princess and Prophetess of the Cherokee Nation, The Pocahontas of Tennessee, The Constant Friend of the American Pioneer, Born 1738–Died 1822."

The Pocahontas of Tennessee? I wondered if she had shown the pioneers the marvels of the Powhatan's maracock. This only stands to reason; she became a friend to the white settlers and a liaison between them and the Cherokee, several times preventing bloodshed and soothing ruffled feathers. What better way to ease tensions than an infusion of passionflower tea? Nanye'hi was highly respected by both sides and is credited with introducing milk cows and other European improvements in homemaking to her people. Yet, like the Pocahontas of Jamestown, her diplomatic efforts were not enough to keep the two sides at peace. The Cherokee were forced to give up their cows and other Anglo adaptations a few years later when they were marched west on the Trail of Tears, but luckily for Nancy Ward, she did not live long enough to see that happen.

A curved walkway leads clockwise from the parking lot up the slope to the iron fence surrounding Nancy Ward's grave. Along the walk, native flowers have been planted: purple and gray-headed coneflower, butterfly weed, coreopsis, beautyberry—but no passionflower. Finding the plant here would have been a fitting conclusion, but in the real world, stories do not always have tidy endings.

Frustrated, I pressed deeper into the mountains, up the historic Old Copper Road that follows the river into its gorge. Several people along the way knew of the flower but weren't quite sure where I could find it. At overlooks I searched the steep riverbanks. Queen Anne's lace and chicory were widespread, while winged sumac and mullein were just beginning to bloom. At one spot a giant swallowtail delicately visited the yellow flowers of bearsfoot, while below the Ocoee churned its famous whitewater. It was murky and olive green and seemed angry, filled with the water from the heavy rains that fell the day before. On a trail that parallels Goforth Creek, I snacked on tart blackberries while an ardent indigo bunting sang overhead. Still no passionflower.

Farther up the two-lane road, there's a section of river channel that widens, revealing a sizable portion of the underlying bedrock: near-vertical layers of alternating argillite and metagraywacke, two metamorphic rocks created by heat and pressure deep underground. Water has worn these exposed layers until they are smooth and rounded, suggesting an organic life within, like sleeping whales or reclining nudes. It's difficult to not be anthropomorphic in describing these forms, for they resemble the eroded human shapes created by English sculptor Henry Moore. The rock also has the most marvelous rusty-orange patina, a stain that's created by the constant bath of iron and pyrite that flows down the mountain.

It's at this spot, in a river bend, that the Ocoee Whitewater Center is located. It's also where, after several hours of searching, on the back stone terrace below a sandstone bench that I found Tennessee's forgotten State Wildflower blooming alone and inconspicuous a mere fifteen feet from the water, its roaring namesake. My journey had come, as perhaps it should, to a quiet and inauspicious end.

Darters

Numerous species

I look for his name in the water, his face in the airy foam. He must
be here. Wherever there are deer and hawks, wherever there is
liberty and danger, wherever there is wilderness, wherever there
is a living river, Henry Thoreau will find his eternal home.

Edward Abbey,
Down the River, 1980

On the surface of it, Sunday, August 12, 1973, was a day like any other of the dog-day summer variety—hot, humid, hazy. It was a lazy, gone fishin' kind of day. The forecast for the Tennessee Valley called for temperatures in the mid-eighties with a slight chance of an afternoon thunderstorm; some locations would see a bit of rain, but most would not. That, at least, was the surface of it, but that was just the thing: Dr. David Etnier wasn't on the surface; he was below it, snorkeling in the cooling depths of the Little Tennessee River at Coytee Springs. It was one of those mornings that was destined to change a person's life. Dr. Etnier happened upon a two-inch fish that he was able to cup in his hands, and since he was an aquatic biologist and a professor of zoology at the University of Tennessee, he knew he had found something special, something he had never seen before. Dr. Bob Stiles from Samford University, who was with him that day, had not seen anything quite like it either. That is what separated their morning from the rest of the mornings being enjoyed up and down the river.

Outside the valley, the national concerns were focused elsewhere. The front page of the *Chattanooga Times* featured no less than four articles on a growing scandal known simply as "Watergate." Thirty-seven days of live televised hearings conducted by a Senate select committee had just concluded. The hearings that were designed to get to the bottom of a bungled criminal break-in had ultimately laid bare the White House of President Richard Nixon and had left those on the committee, including Senator Howard Baker of Tennessee, asking, "What did the president know? And when did he know it?"

Meanwhile, Dr. Etnier knew what he knew, and he kept quiet about his little find. He was a man of science and did not want to tip his hand too soon. He only showed his mystery fish to other aquatic biologists, and none of them could identify it either. Little did anyone realize that if his foundling was as rare as he thought it might be—and he had never seen it anywhere else—it too would find its finned self embroiled in a national controversy all its own. But that would come later. In time, Etnier determined that his happenstance catch of the day was unique—one of the twenty-one species of animals he would write the first scientific description of in his career. Dr. Etnier gave his Coytee Springs fish the name *Percina tanasi*, in effect, "little perch of Tennessee." Yet, most people know it by its more common moniker: snail darter, perhaps the most famous little fish in North America. Certainly, the most famous little fish to ever swim in the Tennessee Valley.

Darters are little perches belonging to the biological family *Percidae*. There are at least 153 native species of North American freshwater fish in this diverse family, and all but three—the yellow perch, walleye, and sauger—are darters. As a group, darters are small, highly colorful (especially during breeding season), benthic (bottom-living), and current-loving fish that have a minimal or even absent swim bladder. This lack of an internal floatation device gives them slightly negative buoyancy, so rather than swim, they generally spend their time perched on the bottom, balanced by their two front fins and tail, hiding under boulders or wedged into the gravel. Startled, they do as their name suggests; they dart away.

Initially, most people who encountered them believed they were just young-sters, small fry that would grow up to be larger, better-known fish. It was early naturalist Constantine Rafinesque who first realized that they were a distinct group in their own right and gave them the scientific name *Etheostomoid*, from *Etheostoma* (ee-thee-os'-toe-mah), which means "to filter-mouth," probably a reference to the fish's small mouth. Most little boys splashing through summer creeks simply called them Johnny darters or just Johnnies.

Today, all darters are broken into two groups: *Etheostoma* and *Percina*. The latter contains the more primitive species, including the snail darter. Some are widespread, found in lots of places, but with at least 150 known species, many are listed as endemic, which means they are found only in a very limited area; sometimes they only occur in a particular river or even a single portion of a river or its tributaries. The heart of darter biodiversity is the southern Appala-chian highlands and the myriad of watersheds that surround them. Darters quietly live in the creeks, streams, and rivers that drain the cool mountain waters. This isolation makes them infinitely interesting but highly vulnerable, and over the course of several thousand years, they have evolved unique lifestyles.

Fully grown, snail darters can reach a length of up to three-and-a-half inches. Their coloration generally matches the sand and gravel of their habitat. A strongly developed set of blotches, dark saddles that straddle their backs, is interspersed with pale brown. These markings break up their outline against the variably colored gravel in the depths of their hiding places. On a more uniform background of sand, they are able to blanch out their dark saddles to better blend in, or they can simply burrow beneath the loose sand and gravel on the bottom. Thus, a snail darter is able to remain sedentary for long periods of time without being detected. In their element they're practically invisible. As the name implies, 60 percent of their diet is made up of river snails, while various insect larvae—caddisfly, midge, blackfly, and mayfly—make up the rest.

Spawning comes early in the year. The males venture to shoal areas in early February. Like many other darters, the males develop nuptial iridescent colors; with snail darters it's blue-green. As the season progresses, more and more females join the males. The males court them with head butts and by stroking the females' backs with their pectoral fins. A mature female can contain as many as six hundred eggs and probably mates with several males. After the eggs are laid, they hatch in eighteen to twenty days, after which the young drift a considerable distance downstream with the current. Their nursery period lasts five to seven months. By late summer, older and stronger, the juveniles begin to migrate back upstream to their spawning grounds, where they remain the rest of their lives. It's generally believed that a few individuals can live as long as four years.

There is a widely held misconception that swirls around the snail darter. It is generally believed that the three-inch fish almost stopped the completion of the Tellico Dam. It did. And that it and it alone was the only obstacle to the project. It wasn't.

Opposition to the project ran deep and had been around since the dam first appeared on the drawing board. Many grew to despise little *Percina tanasi* because they felt it stood in the way of progress, but essentially it was just a pawn in a larger battle. Since the 1970s environmentalists have been labeled "tree-huggers" or "snail-darter types," as though anyone who cares for plants and animals—that is, the environment—are extremists. This unfortunate name-calling is a ploy to polarize liberals and conservatives in this country. In truth, environmentalists come from both sides of the political aisle and include a wide range of outdoor enthusiasts who enjoy canoeing, hiking, camping, fishing, hunting, bird watching, and nature study, as well as those who simply want to conserve nature in parks, wilderness areas, green spaces, refuges, and sanctuaries. Someone who enjoys trout fishing and wants to see the fish's watery homes protected is not an extremist. It's also the duty of every generation to save and protect the environment for future generations.

The irony is that the building of the Tellico Dam polarized people within the Tennessee Valley Authority (TVA) before the snail darter was ever found. But the sides ran counter to what you might think. The notion to build the dam was opposed by TVA's conservatives, who thought that it was the result of a too-broad interpretation of the original TVA charter. From the perspective of this faction, the leadership within TVA that pushed for the dam was too liberal in its views, too suggestive of President Franklin Roosevelt's New Deal. The TVA conservatives felt that the government-run utility was not in the business of creating jobs through public works. That smacked of socialism and job creation and was better left to the private sector.

By 1959 the very popular Aubrey "Red" Wagner was general manager of TVA. Wagner championed the Tellico Dam project because he sought to unite the agency under a common cause and regain lost momentum with a "new mission." But he knew the unfavorable cost-benefit analysis that had haunted the project since its early planning days would never make it past any congressional appropriation committee. Wagner's dream got a boost in 1960 with the election of President John F. Kennedy, a neo–New Dealer and a public works supporter. Kennedy was also pro-TVA.

The opposition to the Tellico project outside of TVA had been growing quietly. At a public meeting at Greenback High School on September 22, 1964, Wagner had hoped to calm local critics but was surprised by the turnout. Over four hundred highly vocal people attended, and it was estimated that 90 percent of them strongly opposed the dam. The congenial Wagner was overwhelmed. One person in attendance, Judge Sue Hicks, proposed a local referendum on the project, but Wagner refused, stating that it was designed to benefit more than just the local residents. A public vote held in the affected counties, Monroe and Loudon, could have killed the project then and there. Behind the scenes, TVA would remain steadfast, maintaining that the dam was for the "public good," even if the public didn't know what was good for it.

. Supporters of the project insisted that it would bring new industry and development to the Little Tennessee Valley, thus raising the standard of living. Those opposed to the project felt that the costs far outweighed the projected benefits. During the summer of 1971, Keith Phillips, a UT economics professor assigned a class project: an analysis of the cost-benefit ratio of the Tellico Project. Known as the "Phillips Report," the 106-page document produced by his students challenged TVA's reported Tellico benefits, arguing that the agency's claims were badly bloated.

Although construction had been underway since 1967, by 1972 formidable and varied opposition still stood in the way of the completion of the Tellico Dam. This opposition was principally composed of landowners, some local businesses, historical preservationists like the Fort Loudoun Association, and members of the modern-day Cherokee Nation, who opposed it because the resulting reservoir would flood the historic sites of Chota and Tanasi. Many area sportsmen, particularly trout fisherman, saw the loss of the Little Tennessee River as a threat to their avocation. Other influential people and groups opposing the project included officials of the Tennessee Game and Fish Commission (forerunner of the Tennessee Wildlife Resources Agency), the Tennessee Outdoor Writers Association, some Knoxville and Maryville industrialists, a member of the Knoxville Chamber of Commerce, the editor of the original *Knoxville Journal,* the Environmental Defense Fund, and Winfield Dunn, the Republican governor of Tennessee. And no less than a highly respected Supreme Court justice weighed in on the affair. Avid outdoorsman William O. Douglas visited the Little Tennessee River and penned an article for *True Magazine* (originally it had been planned for *National Geographic*) titled "This Valley Waits To Die." The passionate account helped rally national support against the damming of the river. An issue that had been primarily regional began to be bandied about across the country.

Local public opinion polls produced by both sides gave conflicting results. One conducted in 1972 indicated that 37 percent of the respondents opposed the project, 36 supported it, and 26 percent had no opinion. Another poll released by project supporters showed 70 percent in favor of the dam, 14 percent opposed, and 16 percent with no opinion. Clearly the two groups were not polling the same people.

In late 1973, three events that would ultimately and unfairly frame the controversy entered the picture, and these would eventually intersect. First, in August, Dr. Etnier found the previously unknown snail darter in the Little Tennessee River; second, the U.S. Congress passed, and President Nixon signed, the Endangered Species Act; and third, Zygmunt "Zyg" Plater arrived in Knoxville to take his post as assistant professor in the U.T. College of Law. In *TVA and the Tellico Dam, 1936–1979,* William Bruce Wheeler and Michael J. McDonald write, "In some ways Zyg Plater embodied the upheaval within the American legal profession in the late 1960s and early 1970s. In those years a new breed of young attorney had emerged, advocating the causes of the dispossessed—the poor, the blacks, the 'victims' of society—against powerful entrenched interests"—in other words, the "Establishment." Plater was not considered a wild-eyed radical. But he was a force: charming, intelligent, and energetic. His legal specialty was environmental law, a field of expertise that was relatively new at the time. He almost instantly joined the opposition to the Tellico Project, energizing the cause and rallying its varied components. Joining Plater were other talented people from within UT's College of Law, notably Peter Alliman and Sharon Lee. There were several avenues of argument that Plater could pursue in the courts—protection of Native American historic sites, fiscal irresponsibility (the cost-to-benefit issue), or the unconstitutionality of the land acquisition and the right of eminent domain—that is, the lawful power of the state to expropriate private property without the owner's consent, either for its own use or on behalf of a third party (over 350 families were being uprooted from their homes supposedly for the "public good"). However, Plater gradually realized that Etnier's newly found snail darter was probably his best course of action. Completing the Tellico Dam was in clear violation of the new federal Endangered Species Act. But from a legal standpoint, this approach was a venture into uncharted waters and a lot to place on the back of a tiny fish. Undoubtedly there were people within TVA who found themselves in an awkward position; they were seemingly on the wrong side of an environmental issue. Many, including Aubrey Wagner, considered themselves environmentalists. Rank-and-file TVA scientists who had spent their careers seeking ways to restore habitat and biodiversity in the valley now found themselves working for an entity that seemed hell-bent on destroying a portion of it. Damn! A messy situation had gotten even messier.

The late 1960s and the 1970s saw several measures passed that focused on correcting environmental mismanagement. They were popular acts of legislation, and legislators want to be popular. In addition to the Endangered Species Act, there were the Air Quality Act of 1967, the Clean Air Act of 1970, the Clean Water Act of 1972, and the Resource Conservation and Recovery Act of 1976. Of these, the new law protecting endangered species has probably caused the most controversy, and very early in its existence the center of that debate was located in the Tennessee Valley. Should the existence of a small, endemic fish stop the completion of a dam that had already been started and was almost finished? Millions had already been spent; wasn't it a little too late? Also, how big and glamorous does an endangered species have to be before it merits protection? Few people would have objected to stopping the Tellico Dam if it meant saving bald eagles from extinction. But a tiny fish that few people ever see—how important can that be?

The arguments raged for years, friend against friend and neighbor against neighbor. Suffice it to say, it was the most divisive environmental debate ever to rock the valley. People on both sides of the issue have written thousands of words and even entire books on the pros and cons of the project, among them Wheeler and McDonald's aforementioned work and *Tellico Dam and the Snail Darter* by Jim Thompson and Cynthia Brooks.

One of the best ways to relive an era is to sit down at a microfilm scanner and scroll through the daily newspapers of the time. I did just that, beginning with the Sunday papers for August 12, 1973, the day the snail darter was first encountered by Dr. Etnier. Of course, I knew it wouldn't have been considered newsworthy at the time, but I was curious to see just how long it would take to break into the spotlight. As I spooled through the papers, I soon recalled that it had been a turbulent year in governmental affairs. On October 10 Vice President Spiro Agnew resigned and soon pleaded *nolo contendere* to charges of money laundering and tax evasion. His resignation, though unrelated to the burgeoning Watergate scandal, fed the general mood of disillusionment and cynicism associated with that dark chapter in American politics. On October 23 Attorney General Elliot Richardson resigned after refusing the president's request to dismiss special Watergate prosecutor Archibald Cox; then Nixon fired Deputy Attorney General William Ruckelshaus for refusing to do the same; and finally the president fired Cox himself. Known as the Saturday Night Massacre, it was one of the most explosive events of the year; talk of Nixon's impeachment began soon thereafter. On November 26 the president's secretary, Rose Mary Woods, testified that she had accidentally erased eighteen minutes of a secret tape recording that had been subpoenaed. The erased tape contained a conversation between Nixon and top aide H. R. Haldeman three days after the botched break-in at the Democratic national headquarters at Watergate, the event that started the whole affair. The gaffe became the most famous eighteen minutes of blank tape in the history of recording devices.

On November 19, meanwhile, the U.S. Supreme Court denied the request by the Environmental Defense Fund for an injunction to halt the work on the Tellico Dam project until a lawsuit could be heard by a lower court. The suit maintained that TVA had not complied with the National Environmental Policy Act. Eight of the nine justices joined in the decision; the lone dissenter was Associate Justice Douglas. Clearly, the country was on edge as 1973 came to a close.

TVA had long been a hero in the valley, but now many people were beginning to question its practices. To kick off 1974, *Knoxville News Sentinel* staff
writer Carson Brewer began a twelve-part series of articles titled "TVA: Saint or
Sinner?" The series explored all aspects of the "growing attacks" on the agency
and its practices. Part ten of the series looked at the fight over the construction
of the Tellico Dam, a battle that "has raged for nearly a decade—in the Congress,
the courts and in thousands of public and private arguments. Regardless of what
else happens, the argument will go on for years." The snail darter was never mentioned, for at this point only Dr. Etnier and a handful of scientists even knew it
existed. At the end of the series, Brewer concluded that TVA had an impressive
environmental record and cited numerous examples, including education, water
quality improvements, and heightened efforts to increase the valley's forest and
recreational land acreage.

As I spooled through the microfilm searching for news of the tiny fish,
Watergate continued to dominate. On February 26 President Nixon vowed to
fight impeachment. On March 1 seven of his top aids, including John Mitchell,
H. R. Haldeman, and John Ehrlichman, were indicted by a federal grand jury for
being aware of the Watergate break-in and the cover up that followed. On July 28
the House Judiciary Committee voted 27–11 to impeach President Nixon. And,
finally, on August 8 the president resigned, and newly appointed Vice President
Gerald Ford replaced him.

Watergate was emblematic of the era. During the ten years that had preceded 1974, there had been a growing empowerment among the citizenry: the
general public learned that they could and should question the establishment.
According to Wheeler and McDonald, protests over the Vietnam War, the civil
rights movement, and now Watergate had emboldened the people. During
the months prior to the president's resignation, Tennessee state officials also
worked out the provisions of a sunshine law that would eventually open all state
governmental meetings to the public and news media; it was designed to elimi-
nate decisions made behind closed doors. The people had a right to know what
their elected officials were discussing. An age-old paradigm was changing.

I continued to spool through the microfilm, but still no word on the snail
darter. The first anniversary of Dr. Etnier's find passed before me two weeks
after the death of pilot Charles Lindbergh, the first man to fly solo across the
Atlantic Ocean. As unlikely as it seems, I pondered a parallel. I realize it's a sizable stretch to compare a famous aviator with a little fish, but both Lindbergh
and the snail darter were thrust into the national spotlight virtually overnight.
Lindbergh was never comfortable there, and although it's impossible to get into
the mind of a little fish, I can only suspect it didn't enjoy the scrutiny either.

After all, darters live such short, unassuming lives. But for me, sitting in the library, watching days swirl before my eyes, its saga was yet to come.

Finally, on October 13, in his weekly column, *Knoxville News Sentinel* outdoor editor Sam Venable reported on a research trip to the Little Tennessee River made up of biologists from the University of Tennessee, U.S. Fish and Wildlife Service, TWRA, and TVA. It was a "final look at Little T fauna before Tellico Lake waters bury everything." Several types of darters, shiners, chubs, and a banded sculpin were brought up from the depths. Then finally, "Someone let out a war-whoop and danced a chest-wader jig. In came a snail darter, a species recently discovered in the Little Tennessee. The fish is so new and rare, it does not yet have a scientific name. Everyone seemed happy."

The snail darter had finally found its way into the popular press. Two weeks later, the significance of the find was also reported by Venable in a headlined story at the top of the outdoor page: "Snail Darter is Endangered; 'New' Fish Could Stop Tellico Dam." He went on to write: "The Interior Department's Office of Endangered Species and International Affairs is drafting documents which would classify the snail darter—a species unique to the Little T—as endangered. In doing, it may bring about the strongest test yet of the Rare and Endangered Species Act. The Federal statute makes it unlawful to destroy an endangered species or habitat critical to its survival."

The cat was out of the proverbial bag—and what a cat. "I knew the story was dynamite," related Venable recently. "I took the photo that ran with the story, placing the darter on top of a car and a quarter beside it for scale." The darter was only about three times bigger than the coin. His caption read: "Little 'T' Snail Darter. Tiny fish . . . with a clout." That impromptu photo ultimately ran in a lot of other publications.

"In those days, I even laid out the outdoor page, so I put the story at the top. I knew it was big," Venable added. He was a young reporter at the time and had only worked at the *News Sentinel* for four years, but even though he knew the story was that important, it took the rest of the world about six months to pick up on it, including his own paper. In the meantime, he received a lot of ribbing from other newsmen and even locals who claimed to have seen snail darters everywhere—even bucketfuls of them. When finally the snail darter's significance made it to the front page of the *News Sentinel*'s front section, Venable was able to walk in with a smile and say, "Where have you boys been? I scooped you. I wrote about the snail darter six months ago." They were flummoxed when the youthful reporter produced a copy of what had already run in their own paper. It would seem that the newspaper's veterans were caught red-faced.

Six months later, on October 9, the species was officially classified in the Federal Register as endangered. The varied opposition to the Tellico Dam project believed they had been dealt a card that vastly improved their hand, for now completion of the dam was in direct violation of the recently passed federal Endangered Species Act. The little darter became a pawn, and everything about its existence was placed under the microscope of public opinion. Now everyone who had been arguing about the Tellico Dam had something new to raise their hackles over. Watergate was over, and the discussion at local diners and barbershops turned to the darter. The *New York Times* quoted Jack Lett, a hardware store owner from Greenback, just upriver from the dam site: "Some's for it and some's against it, which is the way it usually is with TVA. It's a mess. I've been on both sides, but finally I concluded that things have gone too far to turn back for a little fish and we ought to finish building it."

The little fish was also debated in the courts and in congress; lawyers prepared briefs and congressional subcommittees listened to hours of testimony. Today, Marcey Wheeler lives in West Knoxville. She is the daughter of the late Richard Bruce "Dick" Fritz, an aquatic biologist with TVA in the 1970s. Although she was a little girl at the time, Marcey clearly recalls going with her father to his lab at Norris. He "showed me an embalmed snail darter in a jar," she said. "Daddy told me that he was going to prove that the fish lived all over the place." Fritz was one of the TVA employees who testified at the congressional hearings. "Our lives (mom's and mine) were a living hell with the local media unable to take 'no, and leave us alone' for an answer." With her mother recovering from an operation, Marcey was left alone to answer the telephone and field the questions. It was a tense and memorable time in her young life.

By 1978 the little fish had worked its way to the U.S. Supreme Court, a long way from the gravel shoals of the Little Tennessee. In court, the darter won the day. By a six-to-three vote, the highest court in the land ruled that the law was the law and completing the Tellico Dam would violate the Endangered Species Act. The opposition had chosen the correct legal strategy. Not to be outdone, dam supporter and Tennessee senator Howard Baker pushed the passage of an amendment to the act that set up an Endangered Species Committee with the power to grant exemptions to some federal projects if, "on balance," the project was deemed more valuable than the species in danger. Nicknamed the "God Committee," it met in Knoxville and Washington early in 1979 and, much to the chagrin of Senator Baker, ruled not to exempt the Tellico Dam from the Endangered Species Act. The little fish appeared to be saved from a death sentence once again, but it couldn't take the credit for its own reprieve. Committee member Charles L. Schultz was dubious about the economics of the dam, stating: "I can't see how it would be possible to say that there are no reasonable and prudent alternatives to the project." The committee chairman, Secretary of the Interior Cecil Andrus agreed, commenting at the time: "Frankly, I hate to see the snail darter get the credit for stopping a project that was ill conceived and uneconomical in the first place."

Senator Baker wasn't thrilled by the committee's decision. A few months later, on June 18, U.S. Congressman John Duncan Sr., representing Tennessee's Second Congressional District, quietly attached a rider to the Energy and Water Development Act that was working its way through the House of Representatives. Reading the amendment aloud was waived, and as the *Knoxville News Sentinel* reported at the time, "it was passed immediately by a mumbled voice vote—apparently with few in the House aware of what was happening." The parliamentary move happened late in the afternoon with a small number of representatives present, and many who were on hand didn't realize that Duncan's amendment exempted the Tellico Dam from the Endangered Species Act. The Tennessee congressman had skillfully moved the political hot potato across the floor and out the door on its way to the Senate, and no one even noticed his oven mitts.

"I have strong reason to believe this will stick this time because it is in a bill that contains a number of other water and resource development projects all across the country," Duncan stated. The opposition cried foul, pointing out that the addition to the funding bill had not received a proper hearing, but nothing could be done to change it. The die was cast. "This was an amendment that had its origin in the dead of night," commented Senator John Culver of Iowa, "and I doubt if it's anything to brag about. . . . There were 15 members [of the House] present, it took 42 seconds." The last-minute add-on provided $1,846,000 in federal funds and authorized TVA to finish the dam.

Meanwhile, in early September in the waters of the Little Tennessee River, juvenile snail darters that had hatched a few months earlier slowly moved upstream to their home shoals. It was a seasonal migration that had been going on for perhaps thousands of years. Back in Washington, the gears were turning. After an earlier attempt in July had failed by a vote of forty-five to fifty-three, Senator Baker, a Republican, maneuvered the $10.9 billion appropriations bill with Duncan's addition through the U.S. Senate on September 11. On that side of Capital Hill, Senator Jim Sasser of Tennessee, a Democrat, sponsored the Tellico Dam amendment. This time the measure passed by a final vote of forty-eight to forty-four. The vote was bipartisan, with twenty Democrats and twenty-eight Republicans voting for the bill and thirty-four Democrats and ten Republicans tallying against it. Several senators were not back from their weekend breaks. Sasser proclaimed that it was "a great victory for East Tennessee and supporters of the Tellico Dam project."

By 1979 the controversy had actually outgrown the issue of the snail darter's survival. Efforts to transplant the three-inch fish into other suitable waters in the Tennessee Valley seemed to be going well. TVA biologist Dick Fritz reported that a quantitative check had found twenty-five hundred in the Hiwassee River and only three hundred in the original parent population in the Little Tennessee. Public opinion polls in Tennessee indicated that a majority now favored completion of the dam; after all, it was 95 percent finished. Senator Sasser estimated that $111 million had already been spent, and an unfinished dam would have become a large concrete monument to governmental waste. Environmental groups opposing the dam feared that if the Endangered Species Act could be circumvented once, it would open the floodgates to other such attacks. They lobbied President Jimmy Carter to veto the bill, but with mixed emotions he signed it into law. The president was on record against the Tellico project, but like many others involved, he wanted other provisions in the bill, including his Water Resources Council, an independent body that would judge future projects. Signing the act on September 25, 1979, the president from Georgia remarked, "I accept, with regret, this action as expressing the will of the Congress."

At the time, a new report prepared by TVA and the U.S. Department of the Interior concluded that the twenty-three megawatts of electricity produced by the soon-to-be-completed Tellico Dam would be offset by operational costs yielding an annual deficit to the agency of $750,000. Yet, despite the documented impracticality of the venture and almost fifteen years of bickering that bordered on outright rancor, the bitter end had come. Two months later, TVA workers closed the sluice gates of Tellico Dam, and the lake began to fill. The historic Cherokee sites of Chota and Tanasi, the state's namesake, were inundated. Many also believed that the only known natural population of snail darters would soon be lost.

There was an epilogue to the snail darter story. The little fish proved to be more resilient than its supporters had realized. One year later, while seining the South Chickamauga Creek in Chattanooga, Dr. Etnier and several others discovered a second natural population of snail darters. This prompted the recovery team to conduct additional searches, and much to their surprise, other populations were found in Big Sewee Creek in Meigs County, Sequatchie River in Marion County, Little River in Blount County, and the lower French Broad River in Sevier County. On July 5, 1984, the little fish that had been the topic of so much heated debate was down-listed and reclassified as no longer endangered, but threatened. There is a study underway at this time to see just how widespread the famous little fish truly is in the hope that it can be down-listed once again and removed from even the threatened list. Preliminary findings seem to indicate that although it is widespread, as TVA biologist Dick Fritz had predicated, it doesn't seem to occur in large numbers anywhere.

It is somewhat ironic that a debate that began publicly in the early 1960s and progressed through Watergate and its associated shady dealings to an era of sunshine laws and openness in government should find its end initiated in a bit of legislative sleight of hand. Perhaps by 1979, everyone just wanted the issue to go away. The little three-inch fish survived to spawn another day, but in the end that really wasn't what it was all about.

In many ways, the controversy that swirled around the snail darter proved to be both a blessing and a curse. Its status alerted the general public to the plight of small nongame freshwater fish, and public awareness of an issue is beneficial. The curse for many researchers is that the famous fish is the only darter most people know. You can almost see a cringe on the face of an aquatic biologist when they say they're working with darters because they inevitably get the question, "Oh, you mean snail darters?"

Today, researchers are looking at the bigger picture. Although snail darters have proven to be in better shape than originally believed, the story doesn't end there. Of the 149 species of perch living in the Southeast, 49 are believed to be imperiled. That's almost a third of the entire perch family, and all of them are darters. If you add to this number the other small imperiled fish—chubs, madtoms, daces, and shiners—it's easy to see why many environmentalists are concerned. "If our waterways are too degraded to support them," writes biologist Pat Rakes, "it spells trouble for all of us." To address the problem, Rakes and his partner J. R. Shute cofounded Conservation Fisheries, Inc. (CFI), in 1992. Both have master's degrees in zoology from the University of Tennessee, and both are former students of Dr. Etnier. Located in Knoxville, CFI is a nonprofit organization and the only private hatchery in the country that is successfully raising rare and endangered nongame fish.

It was an overcast Monday when I visited CFI, located only a few miles from the university campus. Hurricane Katrina had just made landfall east of New Orleans, and the projected rain it would bring to Tennessee had altered Rakes's plans for the week. At CFI's nondescript concert-block building, I met Rakes, his partner Shute, and Hatchery Manager Crystal Ruble, who joined the group in 2004. The austerity of the building is somewhat deceiving for it hides the groundbreaking work being carried out within its plain white walls. Inside Rakes gave me a tour of the facility, essentially a cluster of offices that fronts one large room containing almost five hundred aquaria: containers of various sizes filled with a combined total of approximately seventeen thousand gallons of water. The assemblage houses thousands of rare and endangered fish of various ages, from tiny, hard-to-see young fry to adults several inches long.

The water temperature is controlled by the ambient conditions of the room itself, and since all the fish that CFI work with are native to local cool rivers and streams, the thermostat is set low. In the winter, the temperature inside the huge room can drop to 40°F, and in summer it doesn't get warmer than 75°. The photoperiod is also controlled to reproduce an artificial-day length that approximates outside conditions because the fish's breeding cycles are controlled by seasonal changes.

The aquaria are of different sizes, ranging from trays holding a few quarts of water to three-hundred-gallon tubs sitting on the concrete floor. Each contains different species of fish, segregated for easier observation. Various populations of the same species from parent stocks collected in different locales are also kept in separate containers that are neatly labeled and arranged on shelves or pallet racks. All were connected to an array of tubing, filters, and bubbling air stones. In each the researchers were attempting to create a freshwater flow and substrate that closely mimics the natural conditions the fish were especially adapted to live in. As simple as that may sound, it's not, because each species is unique, evolved to live, feed, and reproduce in a totally individual way. Each container has to be fed every day, and some need it twice a day. Needless to say, it's a major job to keep track of it all.

As for breaking down the life-history secrets of each species, it takes a lot of trial and error, educated guesswork, and acute observation. The goal is to re-create the proper conditions that are conducive to stimulate reproduction and to raise young fish to maturity. Rakes has a sort of "wet thumb," an intuition about how to keep fish alive and healthy. When CFI gets it right, their fish successfully breed, and the outcome is batches of captive fish that can be reintroduced into southeastern waterways where the water quality has improved enough to support them. In some cases, the fish are released into sections of streams where historically they once had been; in other cases, the locations closely match the habitat requirements each species needs and where it likely occurred but was never documented. Like Dr. Tuttle's work on the gray bat, understanding each species' uniqueness is the key to saving it.

One of CFI's biggest success stories is the duskytail darter. A key to successfully raising duskytails was the discovery of where the female lays her eggs. As surprising as it may sound, she swims upside down and attaches her eggs to the bottom of flat, slightly concave rocks. By the time she finishes, she may create a mass of eggs in a single layer as flat and round as a small pancake. To find the eggs, researchers turn over submerged flat rocks and look on the bottom. In the case of the duskytail, it's more productive to find natural egg nests in the wild and bring rock and all back to the lab. Some nests may contain two hundred to three hundred eggs, far more than CFI can produce artificially. In the hospitable conditions created in the lab, CFI is able to hatch the eggs and raise the young free from predators; consequently, a much higher percentage of the brood survives. Duskytail darters' spawning season runs from mid-May to mid-June or even earlier, depending on the water temperature, so the key is to be in the right place at the right time with favorable water conditions to find the nests because the eggs hatch in about a week after being laid.

CFI has been stocking young duskytails into Abrams Creek in the Great Smoky Mountain National Park since 1993. The reintroduced population is now apparently thriving. "They have taken off in Abrams," said Rakes with a mix of enthusiasm and pride. Duskytail darters are most active at dusk. To do a proper census you have to look for them in the dark, using underwater dive lights. On a recent night snorkel, Rakes discovered a higher percentage of duskytails present than are usually found in Citico Creek, where their source population lives. "Half of what we saw were young of the year," added Rakes, "so they are established and reproducing."

With the Abrams Creek reintroduction going well, CFI has started to stock the same population into the Tellico River, but as Rakes points out, they don't stock the entire river because they are limited in the number of eggs they are allowed to remove from the wild—usually only several hundred a year. If they spread them all up and down the river, the little bottom-dwellers would never find each other. Instead, they stock the same location—carefully chosen as being the right habitat—for five years or more until the population is dense enough to be not only self-sustaining but also capable of spreading to new locations on its own.

CFI has also started to raise a second population of the sand-colored duskytail darters from Little River. Nests collected near Rockford in Blount County have been hatched and raised in the lab. The young darters are then returned to Little River but farther upstream, past Heritage High School, where the water quality is cleaner and the fish stand a better chance than their parents, which live closer to the city where the water is more impacted. They also hope to reestablish a population as far upstream as Townsend, much higher upstream than the small darters could ever venture on their own because of a mill dam that now blocks their way. A lot of biodiversity was lost from the upper reaches of

Little River because of the logging operations along that waterway over one hundred years ago.

With each new species CFI studies, there come a few surprises. In the case of tangerine darters, CFI discovered that the *Percina* with the colorful name were very nervous, easily stressed fish; they didn't like the regular glass aquaria, even large one-hundred-gallon tanks. In 2005 the tangerines were moved to an even larger, opaque fiberglass tank and placed in a situation Rakes calls a "living stream." In the darker, more private container, the fish settled down and spawned for the first time, making CFI the first group to be able to propagate these large, beautiful darters in captivity.

"Even though we haven't produced many tangerine darters," reports Rakes, "we're fine because we've figured out how to do it."

In the process, they have discovered a lot of unexpected life-history uniqueness they weren't expecting. "We're finding out that for a lot of darters," continued Rakes, "after the larvae hatch and have absorbed their yoke sacs, they don't feed on the bottom but swim up into the water column near the surface or just below the surface, and they stay there for a week to a month." Essentially, unlike their bottom-feeding parents, the tiny fry hide in plain sight. They are too small for the predators that swim at these shallow depths to fool with. The young darters feed there, so CFI has to make sure they have plenty of proper food available at that level in the aquarium.

"A lot of fish are more opportunistic than we give them credit for. We may think we know their life history and ecology, but it is not always as simple as we think. Each species is different," added Rakes.

In some cases, CFI works with surrogates, sister species that are closely related to endangered ones. The surrogates should have similar life-history attributes: their spawning techniques are the same, they lay eggs in a similar way, and their young grow and feed in a comparable manner. By developing methods of raising and propagating the surrogates, the same techniques can be used on the rarer ones should funding become available. In the past, CFI has worked with warrior darters as surrogates for endangered vermilion darters.

In addition to the thousands of fish they raise, CFI researchers also cultivate a variety of live fish food such as brine shrimp and *Ceriodaphnia dubia,* small water fleas. As with any environmental endeavor, money always defines its limitations. CFI works with several small grants. The species they propagate are the ones for which they've received research funding. As codirector J. R. Shute points out, the work is expensive. The electric bill alone to keep five hundred tanks running and at the proper temperature can be over eight hundred dollars a month. In addition to funding issues, there's the mountain of paperwork:

permits, applications, and reporting that has to be done, principally in the off-season. Because CFI collects and works with threatened and endangered species, permits are required from U.S. Fish and Wildlife, plus scientific collection permits from every state in which they gather specimens. For work done in the Great Smoky Mountains, Big South Fork, Obed River, and Blue Ridge Parkway, permits must be obtained from the National Park Service. All of the required paperwork alone fills one large notebook.

When asked why they do what they do, Rakes had a quick response: "Why? Because we can. If you can do something that no one else has the ability or will to do, that is as rewarding as this is, and as much fun—at least in the field and hatchery when not behind a desk or in front of a computer—you'd be crazy not to! Or just plain lazy or apathetic." As a footnote, he added, "But it is a lot of work."

Like so many dedicated people, Rakes found his calling early in life. Growing up in northwest Arkansas, he had a passion for water and everything that lives in it. He loved to fish, float, and snorkel and even kept aquaria. "I initially planned to study marine biology and then discovered what was in our own backyards and came to UTK to study under Dr. Etnier. The rest is history."

Then he became philosophical. He saw the metaphor, the undeniable parallel between our own lives and what they study at CFI. "You know, all of our lives are the result of as fascinating and unlikely a sequence of contingencies as any of the natural processes, adaptations, et cetera, that science strives to observe, explain, and understand."

It was a sequence of contingencies that created the rich aquatic biodiversity of the Tennessee Valley, and millennia later it was another sequence that lured white traders and settlers, copper miners and loggers into the fecund, fertile land—a move that set off a chain of events that altered the grandeur of the valley itself. Some were looking for a home, some for profit.

But the contingencies did not stop there; they played on, placing the unassuming snail darter in the path of a dam-building juggernaut in the 1970s. Like the popular toy of that decade, the Rubik's Cube, one sequence affects another; the interrelationships constantly change and seem frustratingly endless. But like the colorful cube, should there not be a solution? An amiable balance? Today, Pat Rakes and J. R. Shute of CFI and a host of other concerned people like them have maneuvered themselves into the continuum, and because of their conscious decisions to work on the puzzle, perhaps all of the many darters have a fighting chance.

Pawpaw
Asimina triloba

And sich pop-paws!—Lumps o' raw
Gold and green,—jes' oozy th'ough
With ripe yaller—like you've saw
Custard-pie with no crust to . . .

James Whitcomb Riley
"Up and Down Brandywine," 1916

The Hoosier poet Riley was describing a distinctly native American delectable, arguably the most exotic fruit found in the valley: the papaw or pawpaw.

The ripe "lumps o' raw gold" he was praising look like yellowish-green potatoes. Some appear to be wearing ill-fitted corsets, making them oddly shaped, yet voluptuous. Pawpaw is the northernmost New World member of the primarily tropical *Annona* (custard apple) plant family. The trees like to grow in a colony near water or fertile bottomland and can often be found on stream banks throughout the valley. Oddly though, unlike their tropical cousins, a pawpaw tree requires a minimum of 400 hours of winter chill and at least 160 frost-free days, making them the only Annona found in the temperate zone. It is not found too far north or south and is seldom found on the Gulf or Atlantic coasts, so it's a tree well adapted to the major inland river valleys in the east, making it a true species of the heartland.

Ruth and Carl "his friends call him Duke" Lawhorn are from Elkhorn, West Virginia. Growing up in the Mountain State, the Lawhorns had seen plenty of pawpaws, perhaps too many. Ruth used to pick them for her mother, but after moving to the Tennessee Valley in 1962, they had not seen any for quite a while. The Lawhorns once owned and operated the Dixie Lee Motel and Restaurant at

Dixie Lee Junction located at the eastern edge of Loudon County. In the early 1990s they retired and bought a condominium on a quiet street. A short time after moving in, they discovered pawpaws again, growing in a wooded area across a fence. You might say that after all those years the exotic fruit had reentered their lives. Ruth calls me every so often in September to let me know that the exotic, long-ago fruits are ready to be picked because she knows I like them. This gives me a good reason to go visit and talk about the "good old days."

Pawpaws have been called "poor man's bananas" for good reason. For some people growing up when "times were hard," they were a special treat. The fruit can weigh as much as a pound and is normally from three to six inches long. They are the largest edible fruit native to our country. (Watermelons are originally from the African tropics, while cantaloupes and honeydew are from France.) Riley's "jes' oozy through" flavor of a ripe pawpaw is otherworldly. Your first bite leaves you grappling for words to describe it. It's like nothing you've ever placed in your mouth. You swish your tongue around relishing the taste, puzzled. It's pleasant but not subtle, just difficult to categorize. Is it mango- or papaya-like? Writer Janet Lembke describes it as having "the creamy smoothness of banana, enlivened by the light but definite hint of pineapple, a dollop of clover honey and a dash of vanilla." Personally, I think there's a smidgen of kiwi in there as well, but taste is such a subjective thing.

The fruit's texture is also exotic, like yellow egg custard loaded with large brown seeds the size of lima beans. You really can spoon the pulp out of the thin skin like pudding. My favorite part, however, is the jungle-island aroma. A ripe pawpaw lying on your kitchen counter fills the house with a tropical, sultry perfume that to some is actually too pungent. A fruit—any fruit—is a temptress, its color and scent meant to be alluring. My guess is that every opossum in the neighborhood is aware of it when I have a pawpaw in the house.

It has long been believed that pawpaws were first discovered by the outside world during the de Soto expedition. As Napoleon later remarked, "An army marches on its stomach," and de Soto's conquistadors, despite their thieving, were often hungry. One of the chroniclers of the trip was a man from Portugal. He wrote his report anonymously under the pen name "A Gentleman from Elvas." His account is filled with the everyday detail of the journey, and he often wrote about foods like the maize, cooked beans, cornbread, walnut oil, and *mazamorras* (hominy mush) provided by the villagers. He also recorded the edible native plants used by the Native Americans—treats like wild apples, grapes, mulberries, pecans, and plums.

The last chapter from the report by the Gentleman from Elvas was written at the end of the expedition after de Soto's death. It was a look back, a recollection of things he perhaps had not thought of recording at the time. He muses that the fruits of the New World were of great perfection and more healthy than those of Spain and writes of chestnuts being common in the mountains and strawberries in the open fields and a fruit that "like unto peares riall . . . hath a verie good smell and an excellent taste." He also reported that the natives "through all the countrie" cultivated the exotic plant.

The Europeans mistook the good-smelling delectable for another tropical New World fruit, papaya, and called it such. Over the course of time, the word papaya has been transformed by generations of lackadaisical tongues into pawpaw.

De Soto's expedition gives us a glimpse into the Southeast and Tennessee Valley in the mid-1500s. The native peoples living there cultivated what they called the "Three Sisters"—corn, beans, squash—and a variety of other plants. It is generally believed by paleoethnobotanists that Native Americans planted, tended, and protected plants like pawpaws, persimmons, plums, and maypops. The seeds of all four are often found in archaeological digs.

Compared to the conquistador's four-year spree of dog-eating, kidnapping, and rape, the cultivation of maize and pawpaws is rather civilized. It was once believed that the early aboriginal farmers had brought the pawpaw from the tropics of South America; after all, corn had arrived in North America the same way. But fossil evidence now proves that pawpaws are native to the continent. However, the range of the plant was probably broadened by its widespread use by the indigenous people from eastern Nebraska to the Carolinas.

John Lawson was a young English adventurer. In 1700 he was assigned to conduct a reconnaissance survey into the unexplored backcountry of the Carolinas. In 1709 his *A New Voyage to Carolina* was published, detailing his findings. In the book's preface Lawson reveals his motivation:

> 'TIS a great Misfortune that most of our Travellers, who go to this vast Continent in America, are Persons of the meaner Sort, and generally of a very slender Education; who being hir'd by the Merchants, to trade amongst the Indians, in which Voyages they often spend several Years, are yet, at their Return, uncapable of giving any reasonable Account of what they met withal in those remote Parts; tho' the Country abounds with Curiosities worthy a nice Observation.

We're lucky Gentleman Lawson took the time to set down the "nice obser-vations" he made on his fifty-nine-day journey through the Carolinas. He didn't make it as far west as the Appalachians or cross them into the Tennessee Valley, but he did run into pawpaws. Under the subhead "Of the Vegetables of Caro-lina," Lawson relates that "the Papau is not a large Tree. I think, I never saw one a Foot through; but has the broadest Leaf of any Tree in the Woods, and bears an Apple about the Bigness of a Hen's Egg, yellow, soft, and as sweet as any thing can well be. They make rare Puddings of this fruit."

In addition to rare puddings, Native Americans enjoyed pawpaws in a vari-ety of ways. The Iroquois mashed the ripe fruit into little cakes that were dried and stored. Later, these cakes were soaked in water and cooked into a sweet sauce that was served with cornbread. Other tribes dried them in the sun or over a fire and carried the dehydrated fruit chunks wherever they traveled. The Cherokee and others used the plant's inner bark for cordage, string, ropes, and fishnets. Pawpaw fiber has been found in many archaeological digs throughout its range.

The fact that the Indians were able to cultivate pawpaws speaks a lot for their ingenuity because the plant is notoriously finicky. Finding a ripe pawpaw can be a challenge; the small trees don't produce that many. They grow in colonies called "pawpaw patches," with young trees springing up from root suckers. The saplings prefer shade or filtered sunlight near a creek or wetland. Older, mature trees prefer more sun. The trees don't readily invite pollination. The small flow-ers hang upside down and have wrinkled red-violet to red-brown petals that look like spoiled meat, with a scent to match. You might think that a flower that looks and smells like rotting flesh wouldn't be very alluring, but the plant's chief pollinators are blow flies. From a biological point of view, it's a good strategy. Why be sweet-smelling and compete with all the other flowers of spring when putrescence-seeking flies can do the same job? However, one source reports that these carrion-loving insects are somewhat unenthusiastic about their task. It's an example of a plant that has adopted a strategy that works, albeit not that well.

Should they be pollinated, the flowers have several ovaries and can produce multiple fruits hanging from the same spot. There is a complication, though: the female part of the flower (pistil) matures much sooner than the male (stamen), so timing is critical. This makes the flowers *protogynaus,* meaning "ladies first," and ensures that the female part of the flower is open and receptive to pollen long before the pollen of the same flower is mature, thus preventing the flower from pollinating itself. Pawpaws are also self-incompatible, which ensures that they must be cross-pollinated by an unrelated tree, and since most trees growing close together are related, pollen must be brought in from someplace else. Because of these complications, it is estimated that only around 0.5 percent of all flowers—that's one in every two hundred—ever manage to produce a fruit, and many of these are eaten by wildlife or knocked from the tree by summer storms long before they ripen.

Pawpaws face another difficulty. The voluptuous fruits are not ripe for very long—only about three days. After that the savory tutti-frutti perfections are too overripe to eat. They'll keep longer in a refrigerator—that is, if you can find a ripe pawpaw in the first place.

Agricultural researchers have been working for years to create a domestic pawpaw that's easier to grow and keep. One of the country's foremost proponents of the fruit, Neal Peterson, an agricultural economist with the U.S. Department of Agriculture, founded the Pawpaw Foundation in 1988. The nonprofit foundation works to raise public awareness of the benefits of all things pawpaw. To this end, the foundation oversees orchards of more than a thousand trees at the University of Maryland. Since 1990, Kentucky State University has had a comprehensive program working to improve the viability of a commercial pawpaw. They're seeking to improve fruit taste and size, pulp-to-seed ratio, resistance to disease, and overall productivity. The fruit is being cited as a highly profitable replacement crop for tobacco because it grows in roughly the same part of the country.

Pawpaws are chemically very active. Many people cannot eat them because they have strong allergic reactions. A researcher at Purdue University, Jerry McLaughlin, recently reported that he has isolated a chemical compound derived from the pawpaw that is one million times more potent than the cancer drug Adriamycin. McLaughlin adds that this compound acts on cancer cells in a new way: it pulls the plug on cell energy, causing the tumor to shrink. McLaughlin became interested in the pawpaw when he remembered that one he had eaten as a child had made him throw up. Recalling this moment from his youth, he realized then that the golden lump must contain something very potent.

Whether or not the odd plant becomes a miracle cure remains to be seen. As an edible fruit, however, the pawpaw's approval rating has gone up and down over the years. It was once very popular in the South, but its appeal was of the love/hate variety. Pawpaws were sold in large quantities in cities and towns near to where the tree grew naturally. They were highly sought after by some during the Great Depression as folks scratched and clawed just to get by, but their popularity began to wane after World War II, as other fruits with longer shelf lives became more readily available in supermarkets. The odd native fruit was all but forgotten for decades.

My uncle Alvin Latham grew up with my mother, Helen, and a house literally full of brothers and sisters during the Depression. Their Panther Creek home was located among the cedar glades and rolling hills in the Sevier County lowlands. During that era, the food you ate was either grown, found, or traded for. Actually buying groceries was difficult because that required money, which was in short supply in the 1930s. On a recent visit, I asked Uncle Alvin about wild fruits: did he eat pawpaws back on the farm? He looked puzzled and said he couldn't remember.

My visit was well timed, as it happened to be early fall, pawpaw season, so I left to search a patch I knew of on an island near downtown Sevierville. It was raining, at times hard and soaking, as I waded through a shallow section of the Little Pigeon River. Wandering around the tall grass on the soggy island, I wondered: was I the first to search this place barefooted looking for food? I doubted it. During those long-ago Depression days, shoes were as hard to come by as groceries. And what about the Native Americans? The McMahan Indian Mound is located less than a mile from the secluded dollop of land. The rounded earthen structure, built during the Dallas Phase (AD 1200–1500), is 16 feet tall and has a circumference of 240 feet. Today, civilization and its jabbering entourage—fast-food restaurants and motels with enough beds to sleep all of de Soto's dog-eating army—surround the burial mound. Traffic noise lies as heavy on the scene as the rain that rolled off my shoulders. Yet, somehow the pawpaw island just upriver has survived, still lush, still wild—too small to develop, yet too big to be swept away.

Returning to my uncle with several pawpaws in a small, wet bag, I handed him one not quite ripe. He sniffed and a long-ago memory was sparked. He laughed and flashed his signature smile. "Oh yeah, I remember these. I didn't like 'em then and I won't like 'em now." He recalled their flavor as being much too strong. It seems that even when food was in short supply, taste mattered.

Despite their unusual flavor, the demand for the poor man's banana is slowly returning, at least in part because of its exotic nature. In 1998 pawpaws were sold at the Lexington Farmers Market in the Bluegrass State for a dollar apiece. Bray Orchards, located in Bedford, Kentucky, has developed a pawpaw ice cream and pays five dollars per pound for the hard-to-find fruit's pulp. In Louisville the prestigious Oakroom Restaurant at the Seelbach Hilton features an Appalachian cuisine menu that includes pawpaw sorbet, pawpaw brandy, and a compote made with pawpaw and green tomato served on a French rib pork chop. For dessert, you can order Pawpaws Foster, a dish of flambéed pawpaw and banana with a ginger liqueur. (To cooks working in their own kitchens, pawpaw can be substituted in any recipe that calls for bananas.)

Nutritionally, pawpaw has a high calorie and protein content and is rich in vitamins A and C. The fruit is also loaded with essential fatty acids and minerals, which are a blessing since the golden fruit helped sustain the men on the Lewis and Clark expedition during the closing days of their famous journey.

President Thomas Jefferson had a keen interest in the largely unknown American West. On January 18, 1803, he sent a confidential letter to the U.S. Congress seeking $2,500 to fund an expedition to the Pacific Ocean. Jefferson had several goals in mind:

> Gentlemen of the Senate, and of the House of Representatives . . . The Indian tribes residing within the limits of the United States, have, for a considerable time, been growing more and more uneasy at the constant diminution of the territory they occupy, although effected by their own voluntary sales: and the policy has long been gaining strength with them, of refusing absolutely all further sale, on any conditions; insomuch that, at this time, it hazards their friendship, and excites dangerous jealousies and perturbations in their minds to make any overture for the purchase of the smallest portions of their land. A very few tribes only are not yet obstinately in these dispositions. In order peaceably to counteract this policy of theirs, and to provide an extension of territory which the rapid increase of our numbers will call for, two measures are deemed expedient. First: to encourage them to abandon hunting, to apply to the raising stock, to agriculture and domestic manufacture, and thereby prove to themselves that less land and labor will maintain them in this, better than in their former mode of living. The extensive forests necessary in the hunting life, will then become useless, and they will see advantage in exchanging them for the means of improving their farms, and of increasing their domestic comforts. Secondly: to multiply trading houses among them, and place within their reach those things which will contribute more to their domestic comfort, than the possession of extensive, but uncultivated wilds.

Much of the western lands in question, the 827,500-square-mile Louisiana Purchase, were obtained the same year from the French with no real consultation with the Native Americans who had been living there for hundreds of generations. Although French ruler Napoleon Bonaparte had aspirations in the

New World, he knew that defending territory so far from home would be costly; he would be constantly sending troops he could ill afford to lose. In the end, his finance minister, François de Barbé-Marbois, convinced him that Louisiana had little worth to the French. The transaction was negotiated in Paris by U.S. Minister to France Robert Livingston and James Monroe, a special envoy to the president, and was announced in Washington on July 4, 1803.

In addition to the city of New Orleans, President Jefferson was curious about what he had just bought for $15 million (that's $184,319,183.96 in today's dollars). His famed "Corps of Discovery" began its historic trip on May 14, 1804, five months after France transferred the territory to the United States. In addition to establishing trade relationships with the native tribes, Lewis and Clark's mission was to explore the region and find the elusive—if it existed—all-water route to the Pacific Ocean: the fabled Northwest Passage. De Soto was looking for the same thing but got mired down stealing corn in the Southeast; he had too many mouths to feed.

Jefferson, the naturalist, also had a keen interest in the plants and animals of the western terra incognito. With the addition of the Louisiana Territory, the country he governed had doubled in size overnight. What was out there? He wanted the corps' leader to have a firm knowledge of botany, natural history, mineralogy, and astronomy. The president handpicked Captain Meriwether Lewis and saw to his training before the journey began, opening his own vast library for his perusal. Lewis was instructed to take detailed notes, create maps, and bring back souvenirs. In part, Jefferson, an amateur paleontologist, hoped that the corps might find some giant ground sloths or other Pleistocene mammal that had somehow survived to the early 1800s. The third president, a true Renaissance man, was fascinated with the giant sloths, also known as Jefferson's ground sloth. He had brought their fossilized bones to the White House and had given the creatures their first scientific generic name, *Megalonyx*, as part of a 1797 presentation to the American Philosophical Society. The name rooted in Greek is a reference to the long claws found on the giant mammal's hind feet. Later a specific name was added to honor the president's interest. *Megalonyx jeffersonii* was bigger than bear-sized, standing over six feet tall. Regrettably, the corps found none to return to the White House, which would have been a memorable sight.

In addition to Lewis, the expedition's "Permanent Party" was made up of Captain William Clark and thirty-one other people, including the young Shoshone interpreter Sacagawea and her infant, Jean Baptiste, whom she carried on her back. Also of note was Lewis's Newfoundland dog, Seaman. In all, it was a much smaller ensemble than the one that followed de Soto, but like the conquistadors, the troop was to largely find its food along the way.

After more than 540 days and an estimated 4,118 miles, the troop reached the West Coast. On November 7, 1805, Clark wrote: "Great joy in camp we are in View of the Ocian, this great Pacific Octean which we been So long anxious to See. . . . Ocian in View! O! the joy."

Their joy would last for three and a half months. The corps set up camp in the Columbia River estuary not far from the coast, and they over-wintered there before starting their long trip home on March 23. By September 1806 the expedition, homeward bound, was virtually out of food. We can imagine that they were also road-weary and homesick after the miles of mountains, prairies, and whitewater rapids they had overcome. The outside world had given them up for lost; with no communiqués from the field, they all were believed to be dead, swallowed up in the vast unknown. In Washington, however, President Jefferson kept the faith, still hoping they would return.

On Monday, September 15, the expedition was on the Missouri River near today's Kansas City and out of fresh meat. The elk they had killed eight days earlier had spoiled. William Clark wrote: "we landed one time only to let the men geather Pappaws or the Custard apple of which this Country abounds, and the men are very fond of." On Wednesday, September 17, Sergeant Patrick Gass scribed: "We got a great many papaws on our way to-day: a kind of fruit in great abundance on the Missouri from the river Platte to its mouth; and also down the Mississippi." The following day, in Chariton County, Missouri, with game still scarce, Clark recorded:

> we have nothing but a fiew Buisquit to eate and are partly compelled to eate poppows which we find in great quantites on the Shores. . . . our party entirely out of provisions Subsisting on poppows. we divide the buiskit which amounted to nearly one buisket per man, this in addition to the poppaws is to last us down to the Settlement's which is 150 miles. the party appear perfectly contented and tell us that they can live very well on the pappaws.

Luckily for the weary party, it was September, and pawpaws were ripe. Poet Riley's "lumps o' raw gold" sustained the troop on the last leg of its monumental journey. On September 23, 1806, after more than 860 days of travel, the Lewis and Clark Expedition officially came to an end in St. Louis. During their twenty-eight-month journey, only one man, Sergeant Charles Floyd, had died, apparently of a ruptured appendix. The only bloodshed occurred when Pierre

Cruzatte, a half-blind private, mistook Lewis for an elk and shot him in the leg. Luckily for the corps' leader, the wound healed quickly. There was sickness, however. In the closing days of the expedition, several men developed a mystery illness that included swollen, puffy eyes. Lewis and Clark had never seen anything like it and were clueless about its cause. Modern researchers speculate that the men may have suffered allergic reactions to the chemically active pawpaws they were eating.

The Lewis and Clark expedition was one of the defining moments in U.S. history and established the pair as the quintessential American explorers. The expedition made numerous natural history discoveries, met many Native Americans, and proved once and for all that there was no easy Northwest Passage. In many ways, writes historian Gary Moulton, they established the lay of our land: great plains in the middle, rugged seacoast on the west, and towering, virtually impassable mountains in between.

To a naturalist, it's pleasing that the lumps of golden fruit played a small part in Lewis and Clark's journey of discovery. To commemorate their expedition, I sought an adventure of my own. On September 15, 2003 (also a Monday), exactly 197 years after Lewis and Clark found their first ripe pawpaws on the Missouri, I set out to locate a new patch of my own. On a map I discovered a stream in Roane County named Pawpaw Creek; it seemed like a good place to start. It was sunny with swelling cumulus clouds drifting over like languid sheep. The late summer day felt more like early autumn. Goldenrod and ironweed were in bloom, but the dominant meadow wildflowers were yellow crown-beard and white tickweed.

Pawpaw Creek is a small stream that flows north into Clinch River down current from Melton Hill Dam. It gently meanders alongside a narrow country road. Parking in front of Paw Paw Plains Baptist Church, I walked the short distance to the stream. The ripe berries of spicebush glowed bright red along the way, and I gathered a handful to dry on the windowsill later. A solo white-eyed vireo sang from a thicket nearby; its song is jerky like a series of hiccups. In surprisingly short order I came to a pawpaw patch and quickly found eighteen ripe pawpaws of various sizes on the ground. A shake of the larger trees brought down several more, one falling remarkably close to a startled box turtle.

Three of the recovered treasures were so ripe and squishy I ate them on the spot, using the back of my right thumb to scoop out the custardy golden pulp. The taste is always a jolt—like tropical bubble gum with an aftertaste that can be a bit unpleasant. My hands and fingers soon became sticky from the yellow mush. My thoughts ran back to the men with Lewis and Clark. They probably gobbled up their finds just as quickly. It's difficult to imagine a diet made up solely of pawpaws, since they seem far too rich, but it's equally difficult to imagine being as hungry as they must have been.

It's a long way from the rare puddings John Lawson wrote about in 1709 to the Seelbach's Pawpaws Foster; a lot of human history can happen in three hundred years. Yet, we imagine that pawpaws have been growing on Pawpaw Creek quietly and generally unnoticed since long before de Soto. Like human history, nature is dynamic, but it's also remarkably consistent. If I were a philosopher, I'd call it the "Doctrine of the Reassuring Constant." It's somehow calming to know that in a rapidly changing world, no matter what mean-spirited things we do to ourselves or to nature itself, somehow, some things do remain comfortably constant.

Opossum
Didelphis virginiana

Raccoon has a bushy tail,
Possum's tail is bare.
Rabbit has no tail at all, 'cept a little bunch of hair.

"Boil Them Cabbage Down,"
traditional folk ballad, author unknown

Tall and willowy, Rachel Wahlert moves with a dancer's even flow. She's mature beyond her years—a natural beauty with a genuine, wide smile and blonde tresses that fall down over her eyes as she talks. In the summer of 2003, she was sixteen years old and rode her bike every day to the nature center to help with summer camp. One particular morning on Island Home Avenue, just before reaching the center's entrance, she came upon a dead opossum in the road. As she passed, she sensed something wasn't right. Recalling that female opossums are sometimes killed with babies still in their pouches, she turned back to take a closer look. This wasn't easy because the poor wild thing had suffered a severe head trauma. "Flattened," she recalled with a grimace. As Rachel approached, she heard "squeaky" noises, and peaking inside the opossum's fur-lined pouch, she found five babies, still pink with new life. Rachel literally had to pry them off their dead mother's teats. (Baby opossums don't suckle. Their mother's nipples extend down their throats; it's more like a slow intravenous drip.)

Removing the inner bag from a large box of raisins Rachel had with her, she used the pasteboard container to carry the "pinkies" on to Ijams. The tiny newborns were sent to UT's Veterinary Teaching Hospital and then to a local mammal rehabilitator.

Long before Rachel made her roadside discovery, opossums have had a natural propensity for drawing attention to themselves, mostly because of their peculiarity, although most naturalists would say it's really a result of their innate charm. Slow moving and simple, sloth-like and somewhat odd-looking, it's hard for them to escape the overall strangeness of their ragbag assemblage. In 1492 Vincete Yáñez Pinzón, the commander of Christopher Columbus's ship *Niña*, captured a female South American opossum with three young. The description of his find appeared in print a few years later: "Between these Trees he saw as strange a Monster, the foremost parts resembling a Fox, the hinder a Monkey, the feet were like a Mans, with Ears like an Owl; under whose Belly hung a great Bag, in which it carry'd the Young, which they drop not, nor forsake till they can feed themselves."

Such sensational copy only served to whet the European appetite for more news of the strange beast, since nothing that lived in the Old World could compare. (Indeed, Europe has no marsupials—animals that carry their babies in pouches—native to the continent.) Although the three young died on the return voyage to Spain, Pinzón sent his captured mother opossum to King Ferdinand, who took particular delight in the furry treasure, and for the next three hundred years, Europeans lined up to see it and other opossums that followed from the New World. In an era in which cabinets of curiosities filled with nature's oddities—both dried or pickled in jars—were popular, the living, breathing marsupials became the talk of the town. They were poked at, discussed, and debated by the Old World's leading thinkers. Artists and engravers created illustrations of the strange creatures; one from 1671, drawn by London mapmaker John Ogilby, depicts the men of Columbus's expedition with a rope and muskets sneaking up on the fearsome beast, which, of course, was depicted much larger than life. Known as "simivulpa," or fox-ape, in some early accounts, the strange creature fit the Old World's notion of the monstrous: creatures made up of parts from other animals and even humans.

The word opossum is attributed to Captain John Smith of Jamestown. It's derived from the Algonquian word "apasum," which means white animal. Captain Smith published the first complete description of the Jamestown experience, *A Map of Virginia: With a Description of the Countrey, the Commodities, People, Government and Religion,* after he returned to England. In it he too described North America's only marsupial as a hodgepodge of mismatched parts: "An *Opassom* hath an head like a Swine, and a taile like a Rat, and is of the bignes of a Cat. Under her belly shee hath a bagge, wherein shee lodgeth, carrieth, and sucketh her young."

In the early days of European exploration, opossums became a symbol of everything that was mysterious in the New World, much the way another marsupial, the koala, symbolizes Australia today. The Old World was hungry for the exotic, for it was emblematic of the new paradise that existed elsewhere. It's basic human nature, particularly when you're going through dark times, to dream of a utopia that exists somewhere else, for if a monstrous misfit with a pouch for babies can exist in this new paradise, then surely there's a place for me. Yet, the disheveled opossum proved to be no monster. In 1698 Edward Tyson, a fellow of the Royal Society produced a sixty-page dissertation on the anatomy of a female opossum collected in Virginia. He declared it no "Chimerical Monster," and although odd, its eccentricities could be explained. The opossum arrived in Europe at an opportune moment. The Age of Enlightenment was in its infancy, and Baconian science, the forerunner to today's scientific method, was about to change the way nature was viewed and studied: through careful observation and experiment. The term "scientist" had not yet come into play. A man of science (in those days they were all male) was known as a curioso, virtuoso, natural philosopher, natural historian, or simply, in the term I prefer, a naturalist. Opossums offered these early naturalists a peek into the previously unknown world of a developing embryo, pink and neoteric inside the mother's pouch.

The opossum's obvious maternal qualities and ability to produce copious young became a symbol of the fertileness of the New World. Yet, this fecundity proved to be its public relations undoing. Once in America, the Europeans quickly discovered that opossums were so prolific as to be common, and that banality lowered their significance. They also aren't the fearsome beasts that had been depicted in early illustrations but were rather lowly and slobbery. Killing a bear gave a hunter a story he could tell over and over, but beating a possum to death with a stick left little room for embellishment.

In his *A New Voyage to Carolina*, John Lawson wrote still further of the creature's disparateness:

> The *Possum* is found no where but in *America*. He is the Wonder of all the Land-Animals, being the size of a Badger, and near that Colour. The Male's Pizzle is placed retrograde; and in time of Coition, they differ from all other Animals, turning Tail to Tail, as Dog and Bitch when ty'd. The Female, doubtless, breeds her Young at her Teats; for I have seen them stick fast thereto, when they have been no bigger than a small Rasberry, and seemingly inanimate. She has a Paunch, or false Belly, wherein

she carries her Young, after they are from those Teats, till they can shift for themselves. Their Food is Roots, Poultry, or wild Fruits. They have no Hair on their Tails, but a sort of a Scale, or hard Crust, as the Bevers have. If a Cat has nine Lives, this Creature surely has nineteen; for if you break every Bone in their Skin, and mash their Skull, leaving them for Dead, you may come an hour after, and they will be gone quite away, or perhaps you meet them creeping away. They are a very stupid Creature, utterly neglecting their Safety. They are most like Rats of any thing. I have, for Necessity in the Wilderness, eaten of them. Their Flesh is very white, and well tasted; but their ugly Tails put me out of Conceit with that Fare. They climb Trees, as the Raccoons do. Their Fur is not esteem'd nor used, save that the *Indians* spin it into Girdles and Garters.

Early on, very little gold and silver were discovered in America, but there were other valuable commodities like trees and animals. And furs were as good as money, but an opossum's pelt was lightly regarded and even deemed worthless. This valuation sent a shock wave through an unlikely place, a fledgling democracy now known as the Lost State of Franklin, in the upper reaches of the Tennessee Valley.

In April 1784 the Revolutionary War with the British had just ended, but it still had to be paid for. Each of the original thirteen colonies owed considerable war debt to the new central federal government. North Carolina decided to cede all of its "overhill" western lands, located across the Appalachians, to the new union to pay off part of its indebtedness. The few Wataugan settlements that existed in this region were under the leadership of John Sevier, a soldier and land speculator of French Huguenot extraction originally from Virginia. When news of North Carolina's willingness to cast off this wilderness arrived over the hills, sentiment among its settlers turned to forming their own independent state. Cut loose, they were tired of being governed by officials living miles away who took little interest in them in the first place. In August 1784 delegates met in Jonesborough and proclaimed the counties of Washington, Sullivan, and Greene to be independent. In December a constitutional convention was called, and it officially created the State of Franklin, named after statesman and sage Benjamin Franklin, who apparently never sent thanks, acknowledged, or even recognized the honor.

The new state was the first created outside of the original thirteen. The following November, a constitution was approved, and the town of Greeneville was formally declared Franklin's capital. John Sevier was named its new governor, and he promptly granted a two-year reprieve on paying any sort of taxes. It was a popular thing to do, and times were good, but things soon became complicated. Sevier was an ambitious man who had moved to the Nolichucky watershed and was nicknamed Nolichucky Jack, or simply Chucky Jack, by his loyal followers. It was boasted that he had fought thirty-five Indian battles and had won all thirty-five, but President Washington had criticized his "murder of Indians." Some saw the energetic Sevier as the aggressor. Needless to say, a governorship suited him just fine.

As it turned out, the new federal government had never accepted the western lands ceded by North Carolina, so the Tarheel State quickly repealed its act of cession. Governor Sevier sent official notice to the governor of North Carolina that Franklin was now an independent state, which forced Governor Martin to immediately call a meeting of his council. After three days of deliberation, a proclamation was issued announcing the "revolt in the west," and the state's legislature was summoned to meet in Newbern to discuss the alleged separation of the Franklinites. At length, the august body released a manifesto strongly urging the State of Franklin to reconsider or,

> The State will be *driven to arms;* it will be the last alternative to *imbrue her hands in the blood of her citizens;* but if no other ways or means are found to save *her honor* and reclaim her headstrong, refractory citizens but this last sad expedient, her resources are not yet so exhausted or her spirits damped but she may take satisfaction for this great injury received, and regain her government over the revolted territory, or render it not worth possessing.

These were strong words, considering that North Carolina had only recently tried to cede the territory away to pay off a debt. The manifesto got one thing right, the Franklinites were headstrong, and for the most part its citizens decided they would keep their independence and began to create new counties in the region and recruit settlements in southwest Virginia to join their new state. They also petitioned the new U.S. Congress for statehood, which was ultimately denied. To make matters worse, the Cherokee, Chickamauga, and Chickasaw nations collectively declared war on the Franklinites, who had now cut themselves off from the outside world. The new Franklin settlements were violating established treaties, encroaching on Indian lands, and the Native Americans didn't know to which government they should take their grievances: North Carolina, Franklin, the new federal government, or the King of England.

Commerce also became an issue. What possible currency could be used in Franklin? At first, this problem seemed easy enough to solve. State officials' salaries were to be paid with animal furs. Governor Sevier was to receive 1,000 deerskins; the state treasurer, 500 deerskins; the governor's secretary, 450 otter skins; every county clerk, 500 raccoon skins; and each constable serving a warrant, a single mink skin. A monetary value was established in Franklin to encourage trade: good flax linen was valued at three shillings sixpence per yard; a good clean beaver skin was valued at six shillings; raccoon and fox skins were valued at one shilling threepence each; deerskins and otter skins were worth six shillings each; well-cured bacon was valued at sixpence a pound; and good distilled rye whisky was worth two shillings sixpence a gallon.

This system of currency was accepted by all with little concern of fluctuation or depreciation until counterfeiters figured out a way to corrupt it. Under the system, opossum skins were virtually worthless, but unscrupulous men began to sew raccoon tails to possum skins and pass them off as genuine 'coon worth one shilling, threepence, each. Faith in the State of Franklin's entire economic system was severely shaken. If you could fake a raccoon skin, could you do the same with an otter? And just how good did a distilled rye whisky have to be before it was worth two shillings sixpence a gallon? Could you mix three quarts of whisky with one quart of water and pass it off as a gallon worth two shillings sixpence?

Confidence in the new state began to fizzle. Many urged a return to the security of North Carolina sovereignty. Wasn't life easier back then? John Tipton led the "union men" wanting a return to Tarheel rule, and by early 1786 Franklin was a deeply divided state. North Carolina finally took interest in the region, sending judges to its upstart revolting communities. For a time both states held court in the same counties, and both states levied taxes on the same set of citizens. The last time the Franklin legislature met in September 1787, it failed to elect a council, and Governor Sevier was left alone. The short-lived independent state was dying of "political marasmus," or, in the parlance of a gardener, it was withering on the vine.

Tensions soon came to a boil. Sevier was watching his new state crumble around him. In 1788 Sheriff Jonathan Pugh was ordered to confiscate a number of Governor Sevier's slaves and livestock to cover four years of back taxes owed to North Carolina, a state Nolichucky Jack no longer believed he lived in. In return, Sevier rounded up 150 of his Franklin militia and laid siege on the home of rival and North Carolina loyalist John Tipton, where his belongings had been taken. When Governor Sevier appeared and demanded his things, only fifteen men accompanied Tipton, who sent word back to Sevier, "fire and be damned." In time, reinforcements for Tipton arrived under the command of a Colonel Maxwell. This surprising development sent Sevier's forces scrambling in all directions. Two men died, and several of the governor's men were taken prisoner, including two of Sevier's sons, whom Tipton vowed to hang on the spot. Friends of both parties stepped in to resolve the issue, and John Sevier escaped to govern another day. The "battle" at Tipton's home, fought in the closing days of February 1788, was the deathblow to the nascent backwoods state named for Poor Richard.

Consider then the poor beleaguered Franklinite, who was being taxed by two governments, living under two sets of jurisprudence, and under attack, every so often, by the Cherokees, Chickamaugans, and Chickasaws. He also worried that the raccoon skin he traded a week's labor for might be, in truth, a worthless possum hide; for him, independence was a bitter pill. After four years of conflict and confusion, Governor Sevier's term expired, and the Lost State of Franklin mercifully faded away.

There is a dark footnote to the Lost State of Franklin. Even though the commonwealth evaporated, its influence lingered. By its very existence, it encouraged settlement west of the mountains in the Tennessee Valley, on land that by treaty still belonged to the Cherokee. White settlements began to work their way down the foothills into territory as far south as the Little Tennessee River, all the way to the beloved Overhill capital of Chota. Homesteads were being sold by a Franklin land office for forty shillings per one hundred acres, land it had no right to sell. Under the Treaty of Hopewell, the first negotiated with the new United States, all Cherokees were placed under the "protection" of the federal government. However, the treaty signed in Hopewell, South Carolina, failed to resolve the primary bone of contention: white settlement on Cherokee lands and conflicts between frontier whites and the Native Americans continued. In September 1787 Cherokee chief Old Tassel wrote a letter from Chota to the governors of Virginia and North Carolina, pleading for disorderly whites to be removed from lands within sight of Cherokee towns. Tassel was noted for his peaceful negotiations with the whites. He was a man of integrity, intelligence, and reason; yet, despite his requests, the settlers continued to come.

By the summer of 1788, two very different cultures were colliding, and there simply wasn't room for both. Tensions flared; it was a violent time. A group of whites killed an old Indian woman, injured two children, and plundered a Cherokee town. Today, this act would be classified as a hate crime. Meanwhile, still stinging from his loss to rival John Tipton and the disintegration of the state he governed, Franklin's John Sevier journeyed down the Tennessee River with 150 supporters. It's difficult to look back over three hundred years and understand the motivations of a single man, but it does seem that Sevier had a personal vendetta to clear the valley of Native Americans. He also perhaps sought a return to glory. His militia raided and burned several undefended Upper Towns—Talassee, Chota, Chilhowie, Tellico, Settico, Coyatee, Hiwassee, Big Island—killing many Cherokees and sending scores of women and children fleeing to the mountains. A bloody time was becoming even bloodier. In response, Slim Tom and a group of Cherokee warriors visited the homestead of John Kirk on Little River, located roughly twelve miles southwest of my Chapman Ridge home. Finding Kirk and one son away, the party massacred the remaining eleven members of the family and left their bodies lying around the homesite.

Under a white flag of truce, a council was arranged by the whites at the home of Chief Abram. Several other respected peace chiefs, including Old Tassel, were also invited to attend, which they did. Once inside the cabin, Sevier's moblike militia surrounded it. To avenge the loss of his family, John Kirk Jr. then entered the building with a tomahawk and beat to death five unarmed men—Tassel, his son, Long Fellow, Abram, and Fool Warrior—most of them older men and all of them men of peace who were there under a flag of truce. It is reported that Tassel, realizing his fate, simply lowered his head to accept the deathblow. The political assassination of Old Tassel sent shock waves throughout the frontier, for he was highly revered by both sides as an elder statesman of profound honesty.

Mortified, the *Maryland Gazette* angrily reported on the incident: "they came under the protection of a flag of truce, a protection inviolable even amongst the most barbarous people, sacred by the law and custom of nations, and by the consent of mankind in every age: But under this character, and with the sacred protection of a flag, they were attacked and murdered."

John Sevier was not actually present at the time, but he was held responsible because he had left vengeful men in charge of a volatile situation. North Carolina charged him with treason, issuing a warrant for his arrest. His old nemesis, John Tipton, took him into custody, and the former governor of Franklin, Nolichucky Jack, was taken across the mountains to a North Carolina jail. A group of Sevier's supporters followed and arranged bail; the party then quietly rode back across the mountains. In time, charges against Sevier lapsed. When Tennessee became a state in 1796, he was elected its first governor. He eventually served six terms.

In the Lost State of Franklin, opossums may have had little value—although I suspect they were always welcomed at the dinner table. By the time of the Great Depression, 150 years later, possum pelts were held in a little higher esteem, largely because there were very few furbearing animals left. My uncle Joe and his brothers grew up on a farm in Sevier County (named for the same John Sevier). During the hard times of the 1930s, they trapped possums and sold the cured hides to Sears and Roebuck to make trimming for coats. The complete lack of more valuable skins such as beaver, mink, and otter had raised the value of the marsupial's hide. A good skin could bring one dollar to a family that had very little way of making money.

The lack of other game animals also meant that possums were still valued as a food item. Marielle Robertson grew up in Kentucky and remembers a folk song from her elementary school music book:

> Possum sittin' on a hickory branch,
> Hie away hie away home,
> We will make short work of him,
> Hie away hie away home.
> Put 'im in a pan an' cook 'im sweet,
> He'll be fit for a king to eat,
> Possum gravy can't be beat,
> Hie away hie away home.

Today, few give an opossum a second thought, but as a living, breathing part of the Tennessee Valley, they're a wonderment. Mammals are divided into two main groups: placental and marsupial. (The monotremes, a third, obscure group of mammals, actually lay eggs.) You and I, our cats and dogs, and all other mammals in North America, save one, fall into the first group. Our mothers carried us until we were more or less fully developed, nourished by temporary organs called placentas, which they produced inside their uteruses. Attached to the mother's bloodstream, the placenta carries nourishment to the developing embryo and removes wastes.

Marsupials operate a little differently. Back in 1492, when Pinzón returned to Spain with his captured opossum, the king and queen were encouraged to put their fingers inside the animal's pouch. At the time, no one in the enlightened world had ever seen such a novelty. Naturalists gave the pouch a name: marsupium, which means "little bag." Nearly all marsupials are found in Australia (about 140 species) and South America (three types of marsupials, including 72 species of opossum), so they are found almost exclusively in the Southern Hemisphere. Early on, people were clueless about how the babies got into the marsupium, and it was believed by many that during mating the male and female opossum simply rubbed noses. The young were thus conceived inside the mother's snout, and at some later point the female simply sneezed the embryos into her pouch. The long-standing notion was, or is, deeply ingrained in rural communities in the South. It was a plausible explanation, considering that the female is often seen with her snout in her little bag just prior to the arrival of her litter. In truth, she spends a lot of time licking the inside of the pouch, cleaning it for the arrival of her litter.

Opossum mating does in fact have a somewhat quaint aspect, although to them it's routine. A female opossum is in estrus about thirty-six hours, but the first twelve are usually when successful fertilization occurs. When the male and female find each other, they indeed nuzzle and rub noses. If she is receptive, he bites the fur on her neck and climbs on her back. They then topple over to the right; the direction is a key because if they remain standing, or topple to the left, their union is less likely to be fruitful.

The scientific name for the North American opossum is *Didelphis virginiana*. The genus name comes from the Greek *di* and *delphys*, which means "two wombs" and refers to its paired reproductive tract; the species name, *virginiana*, is Latin for "of Virginia." The female has two vaginas and two uteruses, and the male's penis is bifurcate, or forked, so the mating pair have to line up perfectly. If they are successful, gestation only lasts twelve to thirteen days, a remarkably short time. During the ten-minute birth of her tiny young (each a quarter of an inch long), the mother sits upright and the pink newborns have to crawl through the fur of her belly and find their way into her pouch. Once inside, each must find a nipple and latch onto it, where the developing pup, called a joey, remains for two months. After this period they may leave the pouch for brief excursions to ride on their mother's back but still return periodically to nurse. In another two weeks the young are weaned, and in roughly four more they become independent. The whole process only takes about three and a half months. By the time they are only six months old, the females in the litter have become sexually mature. Thus, in theory, two generations of opossums can be produced in one year, while each female can have three litters in the same amount of time. Since a female has thirteen nipples—an odd number and no one knows why—the maximum litter size is therefore thirteen, but it's usually six to ten. If a mother happens to birth more than thirteen, the ones that do not find a teat soon die.

The real surprise is that a wild opossum rarely lives two years, but during that time the females are baby-making machines. Their remarkable fecundity helps make the species successful. If giant pandas could reproduce with such gusto, the world would be overrun with them. The giant white-and-black Chinese bear (some believe they're actually in the raccoon family) is also a finicky eater, existing primarily on bamboo, another poor survival strategy. Opossums are plentiful in part because they'll eat just about anything. In nature, if you produce a lot of young and aren't too picky about your diet, there's a good chance your species will flourish. Omnivores fare better simply because they can usually find something edible. Opossums have fifty teeth, highly unusually for a mammal, and they put them to good use. They routinely eat eggs, snails, slugs, mice, moles, shrews, earthworms, insects, fruit, nuts, green vegetation, toads, frogs, small snakes, grains, garbage, carrion, and the maggots they find on it. I once helped care for an injured, non-releasable opossum that had lost several body parts in a fight. She had become an education animal at the nature center, traveled to area schools, and had an extreme fondness for green grapes, which she chewed with great zeal.

To round out the opossum's grab bag of distinguishing features, there are the humanlike hands located on the hind legs. They look like hands because of an opposable big toe that, like our own thumbs, allows the possum great dexterity. They're skilled at picking things up and climbing trees. They also have a prehensile tail that can grasp and even carry items such as bedding. The notion that they can suspend themselves by their tails from trees, so often repeated in old accounts, is somewhat exaggerated. True, a young possum can do this, but by the time they are older and have reached their adult weight, they are too heavy to hang like Christmas ornaments.

It has been widely believed that marsupials are a more primitive mammal that generally lost out in head-to-head competitions with the highly advanced placentals. New fossil evidence seems to indicate otherwise. "Marsupials aren't physiologically inferior in any way," reported Marilyn Renfree, a biologist at the University of Melbourne. In a 2004 *Discover* magazine article, Renfree points out that a marsupial mother is better suited to survive in a changeable environment. Placental mothers have to carry their unborns to full term. Should habitat conditions worsen and food and water become scarce, the mother's life is at risk because of the drain on her energy. During hard times a marsupial mother stops the production of milk, and while the young inside her pouch die, the mother survives to reproduce another day.

Survival often needs a bit on innate trickery. For some early naturalists, "playing possum" was supportive evidence that at least some mammals—that is, our own native marsupial—had the ability to plan and reason. They even gave the behavior a name "letusimulation," from *letum*, death, and *simulare*, to feign. As one unnamed naturalist wrote in 1894, "The feigning of death by certain animals, for the purpose of deceiving their enemies, and thus securing immunity, is one of the greatest of the many evidences of their intelligent ratiocination. . . . The most noted and best known letusimulant among mammals is the opossum. I have seen this animal look as if dead for hours at a time. It can be thrown down any way, and its body and limbs will remain in position assigned to them by gravity. It presents a perfect picture of death." Mercifully, the cumbersome word letusimulation has been dropped from our lexicon, but the figure of speech "playing possum" is synonymous with pretending to be dead.

Although the word play suggests that it's a conscious act, it isn't. When startled, an opossum will hiss, lunge at, or try to scurry away from trouble. If backed into a corner, the frightened creature may instinctively fall down, with its mouth slightly open. It also may defecate, drool, and give off a foul odor. These unappealing actions, designed to discourage predators, may last only a few minutes or can linger for several hours. When the seizure-like trance passes, the possum hops up and waddles away, but the entire fake death is involuntary and can't be controlled by the frightened marsupial. If this should happen on one of our highways, it spells doom for the poor animal; the pseudo-death becomes a real one. The discovery Rachel made while riding her bike to Ijams is not unusual. The Humane Society estimates that one million animals are struck and killed every day on our country's roads. Some die outright on the highway, while others crawl to the bushes. We can only assume that many of these traffic victims are also mothers, and whereas opossum pups ride with their mothers in fur-lined pouches, non-marsupial litters are hidden somewhere safe while the mothers forage. Given the roadkill statistics, this means that a lot of orphans are left quietly waiting for mothers that never return. Rachel's recovered orphans ended up at a mammal rehabilitator, but the sad truth is that there are not enough of these caregivers on the planet to nurture all the waifs.

Each year rehabbers are overwhelmed with injured and orphaned animals. Lynne McCoy, an East Tennessee animal rehabilitator for thirty years, raised 507 animal babies in 2003—everything from rabbits to hawks. Over a two-year period, 2002–03, she cared for 162 baby opossums, probably 90 percent from roadkill victims. Rehabilitators can put in sixteen-hour days in May and June, the height of baby season, and the hours are long with no financial reward.

As cities sprawl, animal habitat decreases. Roadways are civilization's spreading tendrils that fragment wild places, crossing existing animal trails as they push development outward. The Natural Resources Inventory estimates that 2.2 million acres of natural habitat is lost to development each year in America. Urbanization jeopardizes more plants and animals protected by the Endangered Species Act than any other cause.

High roadkill totals are also turning up in unlikely places, even deserts. A report released in May 2005 by the Center of North American Herpetology states that over 50,000 wild animals—27,000 reptiles, 17,000 amphibians, 6,000 mammals and 1,000 birds—are run over and killed annually in and around Saquaro National Park in Arizona. Merritt Clifton, editor of the online *Animal People Newspaper*, estimates that nationwide, 41 million squirrels, 19 million opossums, and 15 million raccoons are being killed each year by motor vehicles. (His compilation also reports that 26 million cats and 6 million dogs are killed on the nation's highways.)

Although squirrels, opossums, and raccoons seem to be the most common roadkill, Fran Nichols of the Knoxville Public Safety Department reports that even fox and deer turn up dead on city streets. In addition to mammals, amphibians, and reptiles, hit-and-run drivers also kill even birds. Screech owls are often struck, and the most unexpected roadkill I've investigated in the past few years was a yellow-billed cuckoo near my home. The surprise, as any birding enthusiast will tell you, is that cuckoos are canopy birds. They live high in the trees and are rarely seen on the ground.

What can you do as a concerned citizen? Slow down! Often, secondary two-lane roads are the most hazardous to wildlife because of narrow right-of-ways with little visibility around curves for both the driver and the animal approaching the road. The peak season for roadkill is the period from late summer to early fall. As mammal litters mature, they leave their mother's territory to find a home of their own, which may put them in harm's way. Most mammals forage at night. As summer gives way to autumn and daylight hours shorten, nights are longer. More cars are on the roads at dusk just when animals are beginning their nightly activities.

Second, do not throw foodstuffs out of the car. Apple cores and banana peels may be biodegradable, but they attract wild animals to the roadside. Owls are often hit because they are after mice lured to grassy curbs by the smell of trash.

Also take note of where animals are usually hit. These places are probably the intersections where their trails cross our roads. Pay particular attention as you approach these locations, slow down, scan the roadsides, and be prepared to brake. If problems continue, petition local officials to post "animal crossing" signs. You can also donate money or food to animal rehabbers like McCoy. They receive no funding and are forced to pay for everything out of their own pockets.

Rachel's rescue of the pink opossum babies was heartwarming and took considerable moxie. But an injured wild animal should be approached carefully, if at all. McCoy warns to use "common sense and proper precaution." If you can safely pull over, drag the victim out of the road with a stick. Even cute animal orphans can carry distemper or rabies, so use heavy gloves or, better yet, call the animal control office in your area, and let a trained professional handle the situation.

Sadly, there's a good chance that the opossum pups Rachel rescued did not survive. McCoy says, "Less than twenty-five grams is the equivalent of four-month-old premature humans. They're just too young." That being the case, we're left with roadkill as a metaphor for all endangered species—that is, of lives so small and insignificant that they are hardly noticed by a society moving too fast to care, unless, of course, you're a good-hearted young woman on a bike.

Fall

Wild Turkey
Meleagris gallopavo

Presents were made to them, "which are symbols of peace in all
those countries." Their hosts carried them to see a nation living
farther back, called the Taensa, (Tennessee?) by whom they were
received with great ceremony. The chief wore a white gown made
of bark, woven and spun by the women.

Father Hennepin
"Early American Travels," 1839

Her dark fingers worked nimbly with the innate accuracy that can only be
achieved by doing the same highly skilled task over and over. Or perhaps it was
cultural knowledge, and her hands simply knew what to do. Beside her lay a pile
of soft and wide contour feathers. A closer inspection of the heap would have
also revealed a multitude of earth tones: tawny, gold, amber, rust, umber, copper,
terra cotta—colors that looked good against the Native American's bronze skin.

Using strands of tree bark, she lashed the lower shaft of each feather—known
as the *calamus*—to a network of plant fibers, an interwoven foundation that in
itself took hours to weave. The feathers, attached one at a time, were laid down
side by side with the vanes pointing downward, overlapping like the shingles on
a roof, thus providing a means for water to run off and not pool to soak inward.
In many ways the native seamstress emulated nature's design, using the feathers
to create an interlocking layer that was lightweight and durable.

Several of these contiguous assemblages could be stitched together to create a garment. In the end, she stood up and wrapped her creation around her
shoulders, checking its length. She was pleased. It hung, long and cascading,

well below her waist and would be ample protection from the wind and rain; besides, it looked stunning and gave her the sensual appearance of a tall, graceful bird.

Among the Five Civilized Tribes of the Southeast, wild turkeys were hunted either for their meat or their gloriously golden-brown feathers. Some refused to eat the game bird because they considered it "stupid," and they did not want that trait passed on to themselves through its consumption. But turkey feathers—that was a different story. They were a highly desired natural resource. For clothing the Cherokee wove turkey feathers into elaborate auburn robes or shoulder mantles. The garments, made from the long contour feathers, were warm but not heavy like clothes made from deerskin. Naturally water-repellent, the feathered match-coats would have been like modern-day windbreakers. The women also made skirts from feathers that they wore with the mantles draped around their upper bodies. As the English and French traders would later discover, the Cherokees took great pride in their appearance.

The bones of the large birds were also made into tools. Archaeological digs on Hiwassee Island in Meigs County have turned up 633 identifiable turkey bones. Frequently, these had been made into awls—pointed, gouging tools for making holes in leather and wood.

Tribes in the American Northeast were also reported to wear robes or capes made from turkey feathers knitted together with natural strings. The feathers flowed over the wearer's shoulders and resembled a bird's back. In 1637 outcast Thomas Morton of Merrymount, a non-Puritan deported from the very Puritan Plymouth Plantation, described the article of apparel: "They make likewise some coats of the feathers of turkeys, which they weave together with twine of their own making very prittily. These garments they wear like mantles knit over their shoulders, and put under their arm."

Collectively, a bird's feathers interlock to cover and give the winged creature its overall form. The individual adornments are made from the same tough substance as our fingernails—keratin—and like our own nails they're dead and contain no living tissue. They are also very resilient. Native Americans wore feathers as decorative accessories in a variety of ways. Single large feathers from turkeys or birds of prey were secured with leather, thread, or animal hair and then tied to a lock of their own hair. The feather or feathers dangled from the side of the head, adding a splash of color, individuality, or authority to the wearer. Feathers were also attached to caps, headbands, or clothing. Some tribes used clusters of feathers that were fanned into artistic accents or dance-bustles.

Farther west, turkeys were revered, even cared for and fed. The Pueblo Indians of the American Southwest raised turkeys, giving the honored guests their own rooms in their large adobe pueblos. The birds were kept not necessarily for their meat but for their feathers, which were used as ceremonial offerings to their gods. Archaeological digs at Pueblo Bonito in New Mexico have turned up large numbers of turkey bones. Pueblo Bonito was a village of the Anasazi, the so-called ancient ones, who predated the present-day Pueblo people. Anasazi petroglyphs and pictographs painted on rock walls seem to depict turkeys as being part of their everyday life.

Wild turkeys have an instinctive wariness of humans. But newborn poults that are brooded and talked to in their first three days of life will imprint on people and lose all fear of humans in general. They are, in effect, tamed. When the Spaniards first came to the Americas in the 1500s, they discovered wild turkeys being domesticated by the natives in Mexico. The Maya served turkey meat to their society's elite. Nearby, the Aztecs called the bird *huexolotlin* and valued the royal animal so highly that they held a religious festival in its honor every two hundred days. To begin the celebration, villagers got up before dawn to scatter crumbled turkey eggshells on the streets to glorify the god that had given them such an excellent food source.

The Aztec ruler Montezuma required his subjects to pay him one turkey every twenty days in tribute. Assuming that the children were not asked to ante up, that still works out to around fifty-four thousand turkeys a year. The turkeys were not only eaten by Montezuma and his large household but were also used to feed a menagerie of animals the ruler kept; a single pet eagle required one turkey a day.

In 1519 the Spanish Conqueror Hernando Cortés encountered domesticated turkeys all along the Central American coast from Cozemel to Veracruz. Inland, his expedition discovered the Aztecs and their vaulted *huexolotlin*. Initially, Montezuma openly welcomed the Spaniards because he feared them. As a guest, Cortés perhaps was served two traditional Aztec recipes: guacamole and "turkey mole poblano," a dish of turkey in a thick, dark sauce made with chili and chocolate. Cortés requested that an estate be built for himself, and the Aztec ruler complied, giving the Spaniard four houses and fifteen hundred turkeys. But the ruthless conquistador ignored Montezuma's hospitality and took the Aztec leader prisoner to gain control of his people. In time, warfare broke out, and the Aztec were soon conquered.

The Spaniards, anxious to prove the worth of the New World, ferried turkeys along with the gold and silver they looted back to Europe. The King of Spain was so delighted with the bird that he ordered every ship returning from the New World to bring along ten turkeys: five males and five females. In time, the American game bird became a big hit on dining tables across the continent.

Turkey soon replaced the European peacock at banquets, and raising domesticated turkeys quickly spread from country to country.

It was during this time that the turkey acquired its familiar name. The Native American tribes that had tamed the bird had a host of names for it: *toú, urút, chiqui, cuvis, tshiví, siwí,* and, of course, *huexolotlin.* How the turkey acquired its familiar moniker is a matter much debated. Confusion over its origin played a role in the naming. It has been cited that its common name came from Christopher Columbus himself, who, believing initially he was in Asia, called the large birds he saw there *tuka,* which means peacock in India. Another theory holds that Luis de Torres, a physician working for Columbus, named the bird *tukki,* Hebrew for "big bird." At the time of conquest, the Spaniards called the New World the "Spanish Indies" or "New Indies," and the bird was referred to as "Indian fowl" or "Bird of India." After all, the native peoples who were raising the popular fowl had been labeled Indians by their conquerors.

As the domesticated banquet bird spread through Europe, its origins became even more obscure. Some believed that the bronze fowl came from Guinea through the country of Turkey, so they called it "guinea fowl." This even fooled Carolus Linnaeus, the popularizer of the modern scientific classification system. Using binomial nomenclature, the Swedish botanist gave the bird its Latinized name *Meleagris gallopavo—Meleagris* stands for guinea fowl, while *gallus* means cock and *pavo* means peafowl. Guinea is located in Africa, and peafowl are originally from Asia. The turkey's American roots had been all but forgotten.

In 1530 the British apparently acquired the bird on trading expeditions to the Levant, part of the Turkish Empire in the eastern Mediterranean. Returning to England, they called the prize "Turkey Bird." The English took to the succulent fowl in a big way. Turkey farmers once marched their flocks to market in London very much the same way the cattle herds were driven to market years later in the American West.

When the first English settlers came to the New World, they found the same birds in the woods for free that they had been buying in open-air markets back in the Old World. They must have been elated. Thomas Morton recorded in his *New English Canaan* of 1637:

> Turkeys there are, which diverse times in great flocks have sallied by our doors; and then a gun (being commonly in a readiness) salutes them with such a courtesy as makes them take a turn in the cook-room, they dance by the door so well. Of these there hath been killed that have weighed forty-eight pound apiece. They are by many degrees sweeter than the tame Turkeys of England, feed them how you can. I had a Savage who

hath taken out his boy in a morning, and they have brought home their loads about noon. I have asked them what number they found in the woods, who have answered *Neent Metawna,* which is a thousand that day; the plenty of them is such in those parts.

It was at this time that the bountiful turkey became an integral part of an American holiday—Thanksgiving. The Pilgrims of Plymouth Rock celebrated their festival of thanks only one time, sometime between September 21 and November 9 in 1621. Historians believe that it was probably in early October, after their first harvest and before winter set in. It was President Abraham Lincoln who made Thanksgiving an annual national holiday in 1863, and it wasn't until 1939, during the administration of Franklin Roosevelt, that the date was permanently set as the fourth Thursday in November.

Reports of the menu for the first Thanksgiving the Pilgrims celebrated with the Wampanoags and their chief Massasoit are a bit sketchy. Only two written accounts survive, one a letter written by Edward Winslow dated December 11, 1621, and the other, William Bradford's *History of Plymouth Plantation* written twenty years later. The foods the men mentioned were corn, Indian corn (ground into cornmeal), barley (mainly used to make beer), peas (but only a few because the first crop hadn't done well), fowl (probably ducks, geese, swans, and cranes), fish (mostly bass and cod), venison (the Wampanoags brought five deer), and wild turkey.

Winslow noted that Massasoit came with "some ninety men, whom for three days we entertained and feasted." Bradford records that "there was a great store of wild turkeys, of which they took many." Historians know the other foods that were available for the feast included mussels, raspberries, strawberries, grapes, cherries, blueberries, squashes, beans, pumpkins, walnuts, chestnuts, acorns, and hickory nuts. The pumpkin was probably stewed in maple sap, and the beans and corn cooked together in a traditional Native American dish called succotash.

As difficult as it is to imagine, it's even possible they ate eagle. Winslow mentioned the bird in a written account two years later and said that it "tasted like mutton." Thankfully, though, because they were so abundant in the woods then and so easy to domesticate, turkeys became the traditional Thanksgiving entrée.

The eminent American naturalist William Bartram penned one of the best early descriptions of a wild turkey during his historic travels into the Southeast from 1773 to 1778: "I saw here a remarkably large turkey of the native wild breed; his head was above three feet from the ground when he stood erect; he was a stately beautiful bird, of a very dark dusky brown colour, the tips of the feathers of his neck, breast, back, and shoulders, edged with a copper colour, which in a certain exposure looked like burnished gold, and he seemed not insensible of the splendid appearance he made."

The feathers edged with burnished gold give us a sense of what the robes made by the Native Americans must have looked like. A short time later in his travels, Bartram, a botanist by trade, also gives us a vivid description of the monumental presence of the courtly fowl:

> Having rested very well during the night, I was awakened in the morning early, by the cheering converse of the wild turkey-cocks (Meleagris occidentalis) saluting each other, from the sun-brightened tops of the lofty Cupressus disticha [bald cypress] and Magnolia grandiflora [southern magnolia]. They begin at early dawn, and continue till sun-rise, from March to the last of April. The high forests ring with the noise, like the crowing of the domestic cock, of these social centinels; the watch-word being caught and repeated, from one to another, for hundreds of miles around; insomuch that the whole country is for an hour or more in an universal shout. A little after sun-rise, their crowing gradually ceases, they quit their high lodging-places, and alight on the earth, where expanding their silver bordered train, they strut and dance round about the coy female, while the deep forests seem to tremble with their shrill noise.

After helping the colonists defeat the British, the French were still feeling somewhat jubilant in 1785, but their overburdened treasury was exhausted. Their national forests were also depleted from years of shipbuilding after their long struggle with the English over control of the high seas. King Louis XVI resolved to send French naturalists around the world to collect plants that might help stimulate the country's agriculture, commerce, and industry. As seen in the growing gardens around his palace at Versailles, the king was fond of plants. His ambition of bringing "all the trees and forest plants which nature has given, up to the present time, only to foreign lands" to France was a lofty dream. To this end, on July 18, 1785, His Majesty appointed André Michaux as his official botanist and promptly sent him to America to collect interesting and previously unknown plants. Michaux sailed to Charleston and began his many years of exploration in the New World. In April 1795 Michaux journeyed inland to search for plants in the mountains of western North Carolina. His plans were to cross the highlands into the little-known "Western Territories." Consequently, Michaux became the first trained European naturalist to visit the Tennessee Valley. Generally referred to as a botanist, the intelligent Frenchman was also an explorer, artist, naturalist, and linguist. The footloose "student of the world" had mastered English, Greek, Latin, and even Cherokee after only a few weeks. Coming down out of the mountains, Michaux came to Tennessee's oldest city, Jonesborough in Washington County, and traveled southwest to "the newly settled village of Knoxville," where he searched the countryside for several days while awaiting passage west to Nashville. Along the way he collected plants and animals for his trip back to France. On June 21 Michaux noted in his journal a list of the birds he had seen in the state. Wild turkey was listed. (On his way home, the Frenchman's ship was wrecked in a storm. Michaux and his botanical collection survived, but his bird and animal specimens were lost at sea.)

Albert F. Ganier writes that the early settlers in Tennessee found turkeys to be common all over the state and that a full grown gobbler could weigh as much as twenty-five pounds. In a letter dated October 12, 1723, a Jesuit missionary named Père Sébastien Rasles also reported on the abundance of the birds in Illinois: "We can hardly travel a league without meeting a prodigious multitude of Turkeys, which go in troops, sometimes to the number of 200. They are larger than those that are seen in France. I had the curiosity to weigh one of them, and it weighed thirty-six livres. They have a sort of hairy beard at the neck, which is half a foot long."

In 1784 J. F. D. Smyth wrote that the turkeys were countless in the Ohio Valley, sometimes as many as five thousand in a flock. An observation published in 1825 in *American Ornithology* was probably provided by John J. Audubon himself. It reported on massive movements of turkeys in the fall:

> When an unusually profuse crop of acorns is produced in a particular section of country, great numbers of Turkeys are enticed from their ordinary haunts in the surrounding districts. About the beginning of October, while the mast still remains on the trees, they assemble in flocks, and direct their course to the rich bottom lands. At this season, they are observed, in great numbers, on the Ohio and Mississippi. The time of this irruption is known to the Indians by the name of *Turkey month.*

These firsthand observations are vivid accounts recorded when wild turkeys were widespread and dominated their environs. The population's "universal shout" recorded by Bartram was heard across hundreds of miles. It must have been overwhelming. But the turkey's presence in aboriginal America was to slowly fade. As wave after wave of European settlers began to permeate the unsettled reaches of the New World, deer and turkey became dinner-table mainstays. The large ground birds were easy targets for skilled gunmen. A good, well-placed marksman could bring down several with a single shot. Turkeys

supplied meat, both for the settler's hungry family and for professional hunters, who shipped their kills to buyers in the big cities. In 1730 one could go to
market in the city and buy a dressed and ready-to-roast turkey for ten cents.
Turkeys were expatriated from most of their home range soon after the new
Americans arrived.

Turkeys also suffered another fabled defeat on a national level early in the history of the United States. Shortly after the Revolutionary War made the country
an independent nation, the new republic was struggling to establish an identity.
The Founding Fathers determined that an "official seal"—an emblem announcing to the world what America represented—was needed. A heavyweight committee made up of Thomas Jefferson, John Adams, and Benjamin Franklin was
formed to ponder the matter, and their ideas were presented to Congress. Ultimately, despite the weighty esteem the three brought to the table, the Second
Continental Congress, made up of representatives from the thirteen original
colonies, accepted only the trio's motto, *E pluribus unum*, "Out of many, one."
But the process had been started. Even back then it seems that Congress didn't
move that harmoniously or quickly.

On June 20, 1782—two committees and six years later—an overall design
was finally approved for a "Great Seal." On one side is an unfinished pyramid
with an all-seeing eye at the zenith. Over the eye is the Latin phrase *Annuit
Coeptis*, "Providence has favored our undertakings." Below the pyramid is the
motto *Novus Ordo Seclorum*, "A new order for the ages." The Founding Fathers
needed something of equal weight for the flip side. They eventually chose a bald
eagle holding a bundle of arrows in one foot and an olive branch in the other.
The bird's breast was protected with a shield of red and white stripes. Thirteen
stars arched over the eagle's head, and in its bill was a banner with Jefferson's
suggested motto, *E pluribus unum*. The eagle also became the national symbol,
although the bird had not been everyone's first choice.

In a letter dated January 26, 1784, and sent to his daughter Sally from France,
Ambassador Benjamin Franklin wrote:

> I wish the bald eagle had not been chosen as the representative of our
> country; he is a bird of bad moral character, he does not get his living
> honestly; you may have seen him perched on some dead tree, near the
> river where, too lazy to fish for himself, he watches the labors of the
> fishing hawk. . . . The turkey is, in comparison, a much more respectable

bird, and a true original native of America. . . . He is (though a little vain and silly, it is true, but not the worse emblem for that) a bird of courage, and would not hesitate to attack a grenadier of the British guards.

Franklin's true feelings about the turkey as national symbol have been debated for years. Some believe he only championed the game bird in jest while others feel the creator of *Poor Richard's Almanac* desired that his new country be built on middle-class, anti-elitist virtues and perhaps, as the letter to his daughter seems to indicate, felt that the utilitarian turkey-bird was a more practical symbol of the working class.

In terms of natural history, it can be hard to comprehend vast passages of time, what geologists call "deep time." Imagining what life was like for the Cherokee is difficult, but that was just a few hundred years ago. The wild turkey's roots actually go much further back in Tennessee history than Michaux or even Montezuma. The upper portion of a turkey tarsometatarus, the lower leg bone to which the toes attach, was recently unearthed at the Gray Fossil Site in Washington County near Johnson City. The location, discovered in 2000 during the construction of a highway, has proven to be one of the most significant fossil repositories ever found in the East. The Gray site is believed to have once been a large water-filled sinkhole or natural basin. The paleontological dig has yielded many surprises, including fossilized remains of alligators, tapirs, and rhinoceroses, three animals you don't normally associate with the Volunteer State. All of the fossils, including the ancestral turkey, have been dated to the Late Miocene or Early Pliocene Period (somewhere between 4 or $5^{1}/_{2}$-million years ago). That's a truly old turkey, and, in truth, the familiar bird has changed very little since then. The turkey's fossilized leg bone is on display at the Frank H. McClung Museum on the campus of the University of Tennessee.

Several million years after that primitive turkey died at Gray, the recorded range of its descendants stretched from New England to Mexico. Today there are five separate subspecies of the bird: the Florida wild turkey (*Meleagris gallopavo osceola*), found in the Sunshine State; the Rio Grande wild turkey (*Meleagris gallopavo intermedia*), located in the American Southwest and northeastern Mexico; Merriam's wild turkey (*Meleagris gallopavo merriami*) of the Rocky Mountain foothills; Gould's wild turkey (*Meleagris gallopavo mexican*), found in isolated locations along the Mexican border with the United States; and the Eastern wild turkey (*Meleagris gallopavo silvestris*), found throughout the eastern part of the country. Each has subtle color and physical differences from the other. A sixth subspecies of southern Mexico, which is believed to be the progenitor of today's domestic turkey, is now extinct in the wild. Estimates of the entire wild turkey population before Columbus run as high as 10 million birds. According to A. W. Schorger, Tennessee probably had more than 334,000, or about 8 per square mile. The national turkey hunt that began with the Pilgrims lasted about three hundred years or until the early 1900s, when there were very few left. In time, the small turkey populations that survived were hidden in mountainous, swampy, or heavily wooded areas. The last reported observations of a wild turkey in Connecticut came in 1813, in Vermont in 1842, in Massachusetts in 1851, in Ohio in 1878, and in Michigan in 1897. The flocks that once numbered in the thousands were disappearing.

Early wildlife conservation efforts of the late 1800s were merely efforts to see that the dwindling flocks were fairly divided. Little thought was given to actually saving the species from extinction until groups like the Boone and Crockett Club were formed to lobby for better conservation laws. In 1905 Tennessee gave its remaining turkeys full protection of a regulated hunting season. Early in that century Alexander Wetmore wrote about a hunt in East Tennessee that he had witnessed. It was a scene that must have been repeated thousands of times there and at other misty, early morning locations throughout the bird's dwindling range. Westmore wrote:

> Through dawn was approaching, the blackness of night still lay over the wooded mountains of eastern Tennessee. With a mountaineer companion, I came quietly along a little path where near-by trees and bowlders were mere shadows against the sky, to the shelter of a windfall beside an opening in the forest.
>
> We seemed so isolated from familiar things that my hand, resting on the rough bark of our sheltering log, brought a reassuring touch of reality in a world hidden in dim obscurity. The air was cold with the damp, penetrating chill of early spring. . . . At that moment we heard low calls and then a rapid gobbling that made me quicken with tense excitement. Wild turkeys, traced to their roosting trees the night before, were coming to the ground.
>
> My friend, skilled in woodland lore, with his turkey call began low notes to answer. As the birds continued, his imitations became louder and more varied, their invitation more urgent. . . .
>
> Soon dark shapes came walking quietly over the open ground before us. A little group of hen turkeys was approaching, pecking at the ground,

and stopping constantly to look about with vigilant eye. The intermittent gobbling of the cock was louder, and in another instant he appeared.

With spread tail, head drawn back, feathers erect, wings drooped, and body swollen, he strutted proudly before the seemingly indifferent hens. Light shone from the bronzed feathers of his back and breast. The bare, wattled skin of his head was red and purple, and his tail was tipped with brown. Truly he was a magnificent creature.

So intent had I become on the great birds that I had forgotten my hunter companion entirely, and the roar of his gun startled me almost as much as it did the turkeys. The hens disappeared instantly, running and flying among the trees, but the splendid gobbler lay prostrate where he had fallen at the shot.

What Wetmore witnessed before the gunshot shattered the predawn morning was the mating ritual of a male gobbler, or tom (juvenile males less than two years old are called jakes), strutting his "puffed-up" stuff in front of the indifferent hens (juvenile females are called jennies). The dominant toms have won the right to court the hens through combat with other males during the preceding months. Pecking orders are established both within the male population and the female. In some cases, a dominant male will have a subordinate male follow him to serve as a bodyguard. The gobblers are polygamous and will mate with as many females as they can during spring. The males play no part in nesting or the raising of the young. Most of the gobbling occurs before dawn, and it's the tom's way of telling the hens where he is located. It usually starts as Wetmore observed—while the male is still high in its roosting tree.

A fully mature male turkey is a striking creature. His naked head is featherless. The bare skin bumps and lumps on the head and neck wattle are called "caruncles"; the single fold of skin under the throat is known as the "dewlap"; and a slender appendage called a "snood" dangles from the center of the face down over the bill. During most of the year, the male's head is a neutral pink, but during mating or fighting, it flushes with bright colors: reds, whites, blues, and even purple. There is some evidence that the females prefer the toms with the longest snoods.

Courtship takes a while and is a kind of extended foreplay before the hens are receptive. The length of daylight has more to do with her timing than the tom's strutting. Once mated, a hen leaves the protection of her flock to become a solitary creature, seeking out cover to lay and incubate her eggs. She doesn't build a nest beforehand but rather scratches out a bare spot on the ground. When it's time to forage, she'll cover the eggs with dried leaves she finds around the nest. All the eggs aren't laid at once but come over a period of several days. Incubation doesn't really start until she's laid the fifth egg. The clutches, usually eight to twelve eggs, hatch after about twenty-five days of continuous incubation.

The hatchlings are fairly mobile from the start, but it takes two weeks before the wing feathers and the necessary muscles to control them are mature enough for poults to fly. During that time they roost on the ground and consequently are quite vulnerable to predators.

Except for mating season, when the toms strike out on their own, and nesting time, when the hens live solitary lives, turkeys are highly social. For most of the year, four types of flocks can be found. Biologist and turkey expert Lovett Williams identifies these as (1) family flocks with a hen and her young, (2) adult hen flocks made up of the mature females that did not successfully hatch poults, (3) adult tom flocks made up of the mature gobblers that regroup after mating, and (4) immature male flocks that form in late fall after they leave their mothers. It's in the mature male and female flocks that dominance hierarchies are worked out.

Turkeys are ground feeders that eat a range of insects and hard mast: acorns, beechnuts, hickory nuts, chestnuts, and other tree fruits and nuts. They have neck pouches in their upper esophagus called craws that are able to store large amounts of hard-shelled seeds as they forage. These items slowly pass down into their stomach, a muscular gizzard, that grinds and cracks open the hard shells. Like many other seed-eating birds, a turkey ingests small amounts of gravel to be used as grit to help the gizzard pulverize the feed into a pulp. The disappearance of the once dominant American chestnut tree in the early 1900s also had a profound effect on wild turkey populations.

By the 1930s wildlife conservation efforts intensified. State agencies began to operate more efficiently and, with stronger public support, began to approach wildlife management more seriously. It's safe to say that without turkey hunters there would perhaps be no more turkeys, and although that sounds like a nonsensical statement, it's true. In 1937, during the administration of Franklin Roosevelt, the Federal Aid in Wildlife Restoration Act (Pittman-Robertson Act) was passed. It placed an excise tax on firearms, ammunition, and other hunting equipment. Millions of dollars raised by the legislation were set aside to rebuild the turkey population. In Tennessee turkey hunting was prohibited between 1923 and 1929 and between 1941 and 1951. But despite the state's best efforts at protecting and restoring wild turkeys, populations continued to decline through the 1940s. By then, it is believed, they could only be found in small numbers in about 12 percent of their former national range. The 1945 Audubon Christmas Bird Count (CBC) in Tennessee turned up only four turkeys: two in Elizabethton and two in the Smokies. The state's CBCs, for the nine years between 1948 and 1956, found none. The bronze fowl finally showed up again in the CBC of 1957, when five were located in the Great Smoky Mountains.

Initially, restocking attempts were made with turkeys that were semidomesticated. In Tennessee a game farm in the Cheatham County area produced several hundred turkeys that were released between 1941 and 1950. The breeding stock came from Maryland and Mississippi. These birds were doomed to fail because they weren't suited for life in the wild. It was in the 1950s that a new technique for restoration was tried in the Volunteer State: members of wild flocks were live-trapped in one area and moved to another. In Tennessee, between 1951 and 1970, a total of 390 were trapped and moved to suitable habitat. In 1962 the estimated statewide turkey population totaled 3,700. By artificially thinning and spreading the flocks, eventually all ninety-five counties in the state had turkeys once again. By 1993 the Tennessee Wildlife Resources Agency had stocked approximately 6,400 wild turkeys statewide. By then it was believed that the state's total turkey population was around 75,000, quite an improvement in just forty years.

In 1973, the nonprofit National Wild Turkey Federation (NWTF) was founded in Fredericksburg, Virginia. (It later moved to South Carolina.) The group supports scientific management of wildlife and promotes wild turkey hunting as a traditional North American sport. NWTF volunteers and partners work with federal, state, and provincial wildlife agencies. Since 1985 more than $202 million has been spent on more than thirty-one thousand projects, all to the betterment of wild turkeys and other game and nongame animal populations throughout North America. Today, the recovery of wild turkeys represents one of the biggest success stories of conservation in the United States. Because of careful management, creation of refuges, regrowth of mature forests, and reintroduction of new wild flocks by wildlife agencies, the familiar bird has made a vigorous comeback. NWTF estimates that there are about 7 million turkeys in North America, close to the estimated 10 million that lived here before the arrival of Columbus. With an estimated 3 million turkey hunters, NWTF reports that the outdoor sport is the fastest-growing form of hunting in the country.

In Tennessee, for two decades beginning in the early 1980s, turkey hunters set records with each passing year. The total number of bagged turkeys topped 1,000 for the first time in 1984; it climbed to over 10,000 birds in 1995 and reached 30,000 by 2002. In 2004, a record 34,000 turkeys were bagged during the regulated hunting season, another sign that the game bird's population had rebounded. In 2005 the hunt totaled 33,419, which represented a decline in turkeys killed for the first time in twenty years, a possible indication that the population was leveling off. With those numbers, you might think that hunters were blasting away and filling their trucks with dead turkeys. But it was reported that in 2005, it took a hunter an average of 22.7 days to get one bird. So that's still a lot of hunting and not so much finding.

During the 2003 Fall Bird Count, the Knoxville Chapter of the Tennessee Ornithological Society counted forty wild turkeys in Knox County in one day—a new record for that sampling.

For most of my life, the only place you might see wild turkeys in East Tennessee was in Cades Cove in the Great Smoky Mountains. If you were diligent, you could find the shy creatures foraging the edges of fields in the shadow of the woods. After the turn of the millennium, reports began to circulate that flocks were becoming more widespread in the valley. Despite my best efforts, I saw none until November 2000. It was in Anderson County, only a short distance from Oak Ridge at the University of Tennessee Arboretum. The 250-acre research facility is a project of the University of Tennessee Forest Resources and Research and Education Center with trails open daily to the public. It was a blue-sky, somewhat crisp day in late autumn. The gold- and melon-colored leaves that still clung to the trees made the scene feel festive. As I climbed the gentle slope of the Forest Loop Road—a primitive, gravel roadway that's more trail than road—I encountered a flock of about thirty wild turkeys. I watched stunned as the closely packed flock crossed in front of me like courtly lords and ladies dressed in autumnal robes of tawny brown. They were most assuredly elegant, and I felt like bowing in respect, not only for their beauty but also for their remarkable resilience.

If your mental picture of a turkey is crafted around the frozen, heavy lumps of meat bound up in the mesh bags you see at your local market, then you're working with flawed data. A wild turkey is a magnificent and regal creature. It's easy to see why the bronze beauties once called *huexolotlin* by the Aztecs were so admired by the Native Americans.

It seems that the wild turkey is currently faring much better than its domesticated cousin, as witnessed in an ABC News report. Each and every year since the early 1950s, a live farm-raised turkey has been presented to the president, who grants the bird a well-publicized presidential pardon. In 2003, just before Thanksgiving, President George W. Bush pardoned a turkey that had been named "Stars." Now, you might wonder what happens to all of those tame birds that have been spared the chopping block. Where are the Truman, Eisenhower,

Kennedy, Johnson, Nixon, Ford, Carter, Reagan, Bush-the-elder, Clinton, and Bush-the-younger birds? Do they go to some posh turkey ranch to roam and live out their days like retired racehorses?

In a word: no. In truth, the birds don't live very long. They die of natural causes. They're bred to be so fat that they can't fly. And their flesh has been encouraged to grow so quickly that their skeletons, hearts, and other organs can't keep up. They're coronaries waiting to happen. ABC News reported that two of the Clinton birds could barely even walk. The pardoned turkeys live very short lives, in some cases only a day or two. Some of the most popular breeds of domesticated turkey being propagated in the United States are the American bronze, white Holland, Narragansett, and the bourbon red. In 2002 the U.S. Census Bureau reported that a total of 270 million were raised in this country; most did not get presidential pardons. Their fate was altogether different.

A subtitle for this chapter might well be borrowed from J. R. R. Tolkien. In 1937 he published his tale of Bilbo Baggins, a furry-footed hobbit who went on a remarkable journey. The story of the hobbit's travels had the subtitle *Or There and Back Again*. The same might be said about "turkey-birds," for their odyssey to oblivion and back, from the New World to the Old, has been almost as miraculous as that of the heroic hobbit's trek through Middle Earth.

As the fossil leg bone discovered at Gray in upper East Tennessee attests, turkeys had been in this part of the world for over 4 million years, but they were virtually eliminated after the white settlers moved into the valley. And now after decades of active conservation programs, the turkey is back where it belongs— wild and free—while its farmyard cousins first domesticated by Native Americans centuries ago are caught up in a sort of Middle Earth purgatory all their own.

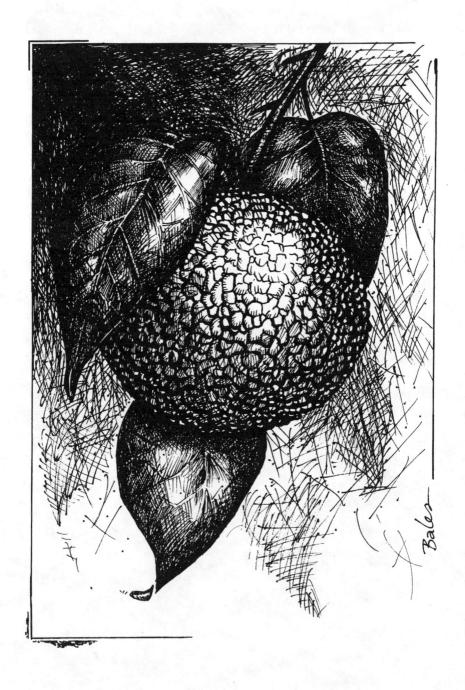

Osage Orange
Maclura pomifera

In science as in life, it is well known that a chain of events can have
a point of crisis that could magnify small changes. But chaos meant
that such points were everywhere. They were pervasive.

James Gleick
Chaos: Making a New Science, 1987

Some Saturdays are perfect. This one was warm and languid in late fall—a cloud-
less day you wanted to hold onto with both hands, relishing its sweetness. Call
it Indian summer; the crisp morning had morphed into a perfect afternoon.
We knew that gray winter was around the bend and that somehow we had been
granted a reprieve.

Our group was working a late-season creek cleanup, removing litter from
an urban stream in downtown Knoxville. The environmental project was being
carried out by Upward Bound, which was coordinated by Nancy Headlee of
the University of Tennessee's Math and Science Regional Center. The program
introduces high school students to a wide range of science-related activities and
community-service work. The six young people taking part that day were removing trash and other floatable litter from the lower portion of Second Creek, the
urban stream that flows through the former 1982 World's Fair site and empties
its contents into the Tennessee River just east of Neyland Stadium.

Wearing waders and gloves, we carefully high-stepped our way down the
shallow stream, slowly filling garbage bags with trash. Most of what we were
finding were typical big city throwaways: plastic beverage containers and dis-
posable coffee cups. A lot of the recovered debris was even more petite—pack-
ing peanuts and cigarette butts. Our peaceful, though tedious, work was jarred
to a halt by the excited shout of one of the exuberant teenagers.

"Green brain," cried Candace. "I found a green brain!"

Representing Ijams Nature Center, I was there to organize the work and assist in any way I could, which on this day meant identifying the "green brain." The site was near the university's Biology Annex, so it was possible that the verdant lump had somehow escaped from the lab. I've seen enough B-movies to know that this sort of thing routinely happens. But in this case our mysterious find wasn't an escaped cerebellum but rather a cast-off fruit. The wet, chartreuse sphere Candace was holding was about the size of a grapefruit, with dimples and bumpy ridges like a human brain. On closer inspection, several green brains were found along the stream bank and in the water. The imperfect, wrinkled orbs were what old timers called hedge-apples, the fruit of a tree—Osage orange.

Although widespread, Osage orange is not native to the Tennessee Valley; it's an invited guest, a riparian plant that did well because it likes bottomland and river shorelines. Its original range was limited to river valleys in a small region of Texas, Oklahoma, and Arkansas, principally centered along the Red River. Its common name comes from the Osage tribe, Native Americans who lived near the same area. Although today the trees are largely overlooked, for a time Osage orange was one of the most sought-after plants in America.

The wood from this broad, spreading tree has an orange tint and is extremely hard, yet flexible. Native Americans used it to make bows and war clubs. For this reason, early French explorers of the Louisiana Territory called the tree *bois-d'arc,* or wood of the bow, a term eventually corrupted to "bodark," another regional name for the tree. That combatant tradition survives today. Archery equipment and the billy clubs carried by police are made from the tough wood.

The range of Osage orange was dramatically expanded through human intervention. In the opening days of the Lewis and Clark exploration, Meriwether Lewis encountered Osage orange, a tree he had never seen. Lewis was handpicked and partially trained by President Jefferson. Part of his mission was to look for new plants and animals. On the expedition, he located and recorded 177 new plants. The very first plant, Osage orange, was collected in May 1804, even before the famed Corps of Discovery had left Camp Wood, their starting point. Captain Lewis, eager to please his benefactor, sent cuttings to the president. The sprigs came from trees transplanted near the fort from an Osage village three hundred miles farther west. Lewis noted at the time: "So much do the savages esteem the wood of this tree for the purpose of making their bows, that they travel many hundred of miles in quest of it."

Legend has it that one of the cuttings sent back by Lewis was planted at Red Hill in Virginia on the grounds of the home of Patrick Henry. That tree still grows today and is listed as the National Champion Osage orange—the largest and oldest in the country. Recent findings by dendrochronologist Carolyn Copenheaver of Virginia Tech has cast doubt on the often-repeated story. She fixes the tree's age at 330 years, much too old to be a byproduct of Lewis and Clark. But if this is true, how did the champion tree get to Red Hill in the first place? Whatever the facts, the Lewis and Clark notoriety did help introduce the tree to easterners.

If left unattended, Osage orange can become a stately member of the landscape, but when heavily pruned, its growth remains short and dense. In time, it became a favored hedgerow plant and was widely touted in publications in the mid-1800s.

As the Great Plains were being settled, hedgerows of Osage orange became the most widely used method of defining property and fencing in livestock. The hedges were said to be "pig tight, horse high and bull strong." Needless to say, they were formidable, a good way of keeping the wanted in and the unwanted out. The extensive gardens of Nicholas Longworth in Cincinnati, Ohio, were fenced with the thorny plant. In 1854 *Scientific American* reported: "It has proved to be an effectual barrier to intruders, who endeavored to plunder [Longworth's] choice fruits—grapes, peaches, etc, owing to its armor of large pointed thorns." Later, in October 1864, a J.T.D. of Springfield, Illinois, recorded: "There are hundreds of miles of Osage Orange hedge in the State of Illinois; and in ten years there will be thousands of miles of it."

J.T.D. added that one entrepreneur alone made ten thousand dollars selling Osage orange seeds to property owners eager to mark their boundaries. In 1850, a bushel of these seeds sold for fifty dollars, a sizable sum. Today, a good hedgerow is rarely the topic of discussion, but 150 years ago, as the nation was quickly expanding to the west, defining one's property was all-important, a proclamation of wealth like driving a Cadillac is in our time. New property owners took great pride in their hedges. In a sense, it defined status.

The *Southern Planter* also championed the thorny plant as a live fence: "Beyond all question, we think that the 'Osage orange' is better suited for hedges in this country than any and all other plants which have been offered to the public. Its superiority is seen in that it is a native of the country, it is of very rapid growth, and the number and size of its thorns render it a terror to all animals."

Osage orange quickly spread throughout the eastern half of the country. Although there was considerable debate about the cold-weather hardiness of the traditionally Red River tree, they made it as far north as Michigan. "My Grannie-poo had Osage oranges on their farm," recalled Alison Brucks with a smile. "We used to throw the little brains at each other when we were kids." Alison moved to the Tennessee Valley when she joined AmeriCorps. Her great-grandparents on her mother's side had lived near Decatur, Michigan, in Van Buren County, east of Lake Michigan. Although no longer growing in a hedge, the trees still marked the farm's property line.

It was probably introduced into Tennessee during the 1800s as well, from the valley up into the mountains. Remnant trees can be found in the immediate vicinity of former home sites in the lower elevations of the Great Smokies in the Sugarlands near Gatlinburg, and along Parsons Branch near Calderwood on the North Carolina side of the national park. The champion Osage orange in Tennessee is in Maury County, south of Nashville. Located near a private residence, it's 63 feet tall and has a trunk circumference of 276 inches.

It has been estimated that, at the height of its popularity, a quarter-million miles of Osage orange hedge grew in this country, enough to go around the entire planet over thirty-one times. In 1870 William Lodge described the peach orchards near Kenton, Delaware, southwest of Smyrna and Delaware Bay: "We pass orchard after orchard, walled in from the road by the impenetrable Osage orange hedge that here grows luxuriantly. The country is nearly level, and the roads so straight that we look before us away to where the lines of green converge to a point."

As a hedge, Osage orange needed to be trimmed often, encouraging it to produce suckers and dense growth. Within five years of its original planting, if properly maintained, the hedge was said to be impassable. In Texas it was recommended that the hedge be trimmed every three months, and a special cutting machine was designed for the purpose. The high maintenance of the quick-growing green fence probably led to its eventual decline in popularity. In 1874 barbed wire was invented and soon became the fencing medium of choice.

But barbed wire isn't very good at stopping the wind. Between the mid-1800s and 1948, an estimated 123,191 miles of windbreaks and shelterbelts were planted in the Great Plains. In Kansas alone 39,400 miles of Osage orange hedges were created. Windbreaks were used to protect exposed homes from strong winds, reducing the amount of energy needed to heat the structure. One experiment conducted in Nebraska proved that a house protected by a windbreak used 22.9 percent less fuel than one without such a barrier. Windbreaks planted on three sides of the house yielded 30 percent savings. Shelterbelts were planted by farmers and ranchers to protect their livestock from the same blowing wind and storms. Herds with protective shelterbelts needed to be fed less food and fared better through winter.

The resilient tree found a second commercial viability around the same time. Silk was a valuable commodity, but it had to be imported from overseas. For years entrepreneurs had been trying to establish a silk industry in this country. Various types of moth caterpillars were tried, each requiring different foliage for food. (Gypsy moths were introduced into America by Frenchman Étienne Léopold Trouvelot for this purpose, but they proved to be a poor silk producer and an environmental disaster.)

An exhibition held in Philadelphia in 1881 promoted sericulture—the production of raw silk by the raising of silkworms—as an excellent cottage industry for women at home. The *Century*, a popular quarterly journal, reported in 1884 that the qualities needed for the stay-at-home sericulturist were "neatness, carefulness, watchfulness and patience—precisely the qualities of a trained nurse." It added that the labor was not heavy, and the only really taxing portion of the work lasted only thirty-five days once a year, the time the caterpillars were active. All that was required was a light and airy room to raise the small livestock, a good supply of silkworm eggs, and plenty of fresh foliage to feed the hungry creatures, for caterpillars are literally eating machines. White mulberry leaves were recommended, but an acceptable substitute was the widespread, lush foliage of Osage orange, a close relative of mulberry. The practitioners of silk husbandry were advised to keep their larvae well supplied with food and the room clean and in a healthful condition. Once the caterpillars spun their cocoons, the silk worker had the tedious chore of unwinding the silk on to a reel. Some of the best cocoons were allowed to progress naturally, producing moths that served as breeding stock for the next year's eggs.

To promote the industry, competitions were held with prizes going to the sericulturists with the best cocoons. To entice would-be silkworm raisers, the journal pointed out: "Silk is like a diamond—worth money in any currency. . . . American silk has been raised, reeled, dyed, spun, and woven into ribbons and fabrics. American women have worn these fabrics and pronounced them as good as foreign silks."

In the United States the need for Osage orange as caterpillar fodder soon faded. Despite the unabashed promotion, sericulture never quite took off in this country. By the mid-1900s, although the United States had become the leading manufacturer of silk products, the raw material to make them did not come from American women raising moth larvae in their spare bedrooms. It was imported from Japan, China, France, Italy, and India.

Osage orange wood was also used for fence posts and railroad ties because it resists rotting and insect infestation. In fact, insects aren't nearly as fond of the plant as hedge growers were. The wrinkled fruit has a distinctive citrus smell. It's filled with a foul-tasting sticky white latex, a sap that looks like Elmer's Glue. Cut-up sections of the fruit were once used as a natural insect repellent. They contain the chemical 2,3,4,5-tetrahydroxystilbene, which has been proven to drive away household pests like cockroaches, ants, spiders, fleas, and crickets. It's reported that a single fruit placed under a sink or other problem area will last for up to two months and force the roaches to relocate. This is something I've not yet tested, but Donna Young, the greenway coordinator for the City of Knoxville, did put the fruit to the test. Donna has an interest in the folk uses of plants and reports that she didn't have any luck when she used Osage orange as an insect repellent.

Being America's favorite nineteenth-century hedge plant no doubt helped Osage orange expand its range. The male and female flowers occur on separate trees, and the close proximity of the intimate hedge plantings aided their reproduction. Botanists call this division of gender *dioecious,* from the Greek meaning "two in separate houses." For plants it can be a decided handicap because they can't exactly pull up stakes and move closer to a member of the opposite sex. The male plants generally compensate by producing copious amounts of wind-blown pollen, hoping that some find mature female flowers, but a solitary male or female Osage orange planted in an isolated location would be as generically marooned as Robinson Crusoe, with about as much chance at reproducing as Defoe's castaway.

Being the favorite fencing shrub of the 1800s put Osage orange into many unusual places. In Franklin, Tennessee, a hedgerow of the thorny tree planted just west of the Harpeth River placed it in the path of monstrous events and left an indelible mark on American history during a particularly tragic period: the Civil War.

Before sunrise on November 30, 1864, the Northern army under the command of General John M. Schofield arrived at Franklin after slipping past the Southern army at Spring Hill during the night. The Union troops were traveling north, and Schofield didn't want to fight in the small city. He wanted to move on to Nashville, but his advance was slowed because of damage to local bridges. The Federal infantry quickly began to repair the bridges and set up temporary breastworks for protection just in case they were engaged before they could cross the river. The breastworks were makeshift obstacles, curving in an arc east to west, stretched across the southern perimeter of the town. They were designed to slow the advancing Southerners. East of Columbia Pike, the Union army took advantage of an Osage orange hedge, entrenching themselves due north of the thorny barrier.

Following the Federals, General John Bell Hood and the Confederate Army of Tennessee were in hot pursuit. By this point in the war, Hood was a shadow of his former self, trying to regain a bit of the glory of his early days. The general, still suffering from the loss of a leg, a withered left arm, and other wounds received at Chickamauga and Gettysburg, was undoubtedly painfully crippled and mentally exhausted. Hood had moved his army into the Volunteer State, perhaps hoping to draw General William T. Sherman out of Georgia. Hood wanted to stir things up. But more than that, he was upset. The day before, Hood had had the superior position; yet, Schofield had evaded him at Spring Hill. Hood arrived at Franklin in early afternoon only to discover over a mile of open country between his troops and the army in blue, which was quickly trying to fortify its position. Against the wishes of his commanding officers, the beleaguered Hood foolishly ordered a full frontal assault, and his men obeyed.

"They came up fast, driven by Hood's fury, and when Hood saw the Federal battle line he ordered an immediate assault: a wild, reckless order, born of anger over the failure at Spring Hill," writes Pulitzer Prize–winning historian Bruce Catton in *Never Call Retreat*. Hood's order was suicidal. As Catton continues, "The Federal position here was as powerful as the one Meade held at Gettysburg against Pickett, and to attack it was to invite a repetition of Pickett's fate. But Hood had a score to settle."

By all accounts, it was a lovely Indian summer day, but the late afternoon calm was soon shattered by gunfire, Rebel yells, and the screams of dying men. Perhaps Hood felt that the Union Army, numbering 22,000 infantry and 13,500 cavalry, hadn't had enough time to completely dig in. It was a grave mistake. At 3:30 P.M. the Southern army, more than 20,000 strong, began their advance in three separate battle groups. When the recently completed breastworks were finally reached, hand-to-hand combat, like cats fighting, broke out.

The easternmost Confederate group, some 8,000 men, was commanded by A. P. Stewart. One of Stewart's commanding officers was General William "Old Blizzards" Loring, who had earned his colorful nickname at Vicksburg when he shouted above the roar of cannon fire, "Give them blizzards, boys! Give them blizzards!" His moniker was just as apropos at Franklin. During the fiercest part of the battle, Loring pushed ahead to attempt a flanking maneuver, hoping to get around the Northern fortification by the river and allowing the Southern army to spill in behind the breastworks from the east.

Surviving thunderous artillery fire that pounded the area from Fort Granger across the river and from two batteries of Federal troops located due north, Loring's men charged across the open fields of William Collins's farm and up a twenty-foot railroad embankment. Just past the tracks they became entangled in the Osage orange hedge that had been cut chest-high and fashioned into a continuous abatis in front of the Northern trenches. The "sharp and thick branches" of the impenetrable hedge blocked their path, halting their assault. The effort was made even more suicidal because Union General John Casement's division defending the section for the North was armed not with muskets but with new repeating rifles. Stanley Horn writes that "never before in the history of warfare had a command the size of Casement's killed and wounded so many in so short a time."

Joseph Thompson, a surviving member of Scott's Brigade with Loring that day, later wrote that "a wall of fire rose that swept our ranks like hail. Many fell then, but on we went up to them, and when we got to their works we found that we could not get to them on account of a Osage orange hedge in front of their works, so thick that we could not pull it away or cut it. Poor Capt. Steward, the last I saw of him . . . (he) was trying to cut a path through the hedge with his sword. He fell with four bullets in him."

J. P. Cannon of the 27th Alabama Infantry recorded: "They enfiladed us at every shot, but we pressed on until . . . our single line had become so thinned and nearly every officer, from General Scott down, killed or disabled, that it seemed like madness to attempt to go further."

James M'Neilly, the chaplain in Quarles' Brigade, reported that

> an Osage orange hedge had been cut down, and its thorny branches formed an impenetrable abatis. They had been repulsed with heavy loss. As they streamed back General Loring was riding among them trying to rally them. He turned his horse to face the enemy. He was in full uniform that glittered with golden adornments. His sword belt around him and the broad band across his shoulder and breast were gleaming in gold; his spurs were gilt; his sword and scabbard were polished to the utmost brightness; over his hat drooped a great dark plume of ostrich feather. . . . He sat perfectly motionless, with his sword . . . lifted high above his head and glittering in the light of the sinking sun. As the bullets hissed about him thick as hail, he seemed to court or defy death. His face had

the look of grief and of scorn . . . and he cried out in anguish: "Great God! Do I command cowards?"

Glistening and golden in the setting sun, Old Blizzards could not have been a better target; yet he seemed impervious to the Northern bullets. He sat motionless on horseback facing the onslaught as if by his will alone he could turn the tide. He couldn't. In late November nightfall comes early; still the fighting continued. The ground became carpeted with Confederate causalities, writhing and moaning. In the end, there was little they could do but fall back to the shelter of the railroad embankment and, under the cloak of darkness, crawl away over the dead and dying.

A successful push through the hedge might have turned the battle, but that didn't happen. By 9:00 P.M. the fighting was over, described as the bloodiest five hours of the entire war, certainly the bloodiest in Tennessee. The eastern flanking action had failed miserably; the Osage orange had held. As an impassable, impenetrable boundary, the hedge apple had stopped a battle group dead in its tracks. The troops caught in it were little more than rifle range targets—that is, all except for Old Blizzards himself. Historians James Lee McDonough and Thomas Connelly describe the Osage orange abatis as being "the *coup de grace* to any united effort." Loring's division suffered more dead than any other Southern division that day. In total, the Confederate Army of Tennessee had been beaten back, recording 1,750 killed, 3,800 wounded, and 702 captured—almost 6,000 casualties in just five hours. It was a staggering loss that virtually destroyed the army's effectiveness for the remainder of the war. The Southerners also lost a dozen generals: six killed and six wounded or captured. Old Blizzards survived to fight another day. The Union dead and wounded numbered 2,326, a comparatively light number of casualties.

Days after the battle Hood marched the remnant of his broken army to the state capital. On December 15 and 16, the remainder of the Confederate Army of Tennessee was smashed in the Battle of Nashville. Mercifully, the war ended four months later—April 9, 1865—when Lee surrendered to Grant at Appomattox Court House in Virginia.

The misty ceiling was so low that the rain didn't have that far to fall. It splashed on my windshield like exploding artillery shells. My drive to Franklin was slowed by the grayness. It was not the sort of day one normally chooses for travel: November 30, 2004, exactly 140 years after the North and South met in the farm fields just below the Tennessee city. The soppy day added to the solemn occasion. In 1864 Union commander Major General Schofield had arrived at the Branch Carter farmhouse outside Franklin at 1 A.M. Commandeering the home as his command post, he sent the entire Carter family to the safety of their basement. Fourteen decades later, as two school buses pulled away, I arrived at the same structure—now a registered historic landmark and museum. At the home built in 1830, I met Thomas Cartwright, the museum's director and historian. A tall man with a touch of gray in his beard, he spoke with passion about the war that had so marked his city.

The congenial Cartwright led me and seven others on a tour of the house and grounds, pointing out battle scars that still remain on the property. One outbuilding, the farm office, has 207 bullet holes piercing its red weatherboard exterior. It's recognized as the most battle-damaged building still standing from the entire war, a conflict that saw Americans killing Americans.

As the rain continued to fall, Cartwright spun a story so laced with detail and emotion it chilled my cold, wet frame. We stood on the covered back porch looking south into ground zero of the battle. Cartwright vividly described the events of that long-ago day, which was filled with screams and cries as the two armies shot, stabbed, punched, clawed, and eventually even threw dirt and sticks at each other. Soldiers of the Confederate Army of Tennessee had scratched their way toward the porch we were standing on. Hand-to-hand combat is horrific. At close range, bayonets are lethal. Soldiers swung their muskets like clubs, cracking open skulls, spilling their gray gelatinous contents. "Blood ran in rivulets along the ground that soon formed streams," said the landmark's director. One Union soldier fired from the back doorway, ducking inside to reload time and time again. Pits made by his bayonet can still be seen in the doorframe. The advancing Southern troops pushed on into the barrage of bullets that splashed with dull thuds like a driving rain—except these hailstones ripped and tore through flesh and muscle, bone and sinew. "Within a hundred paces of their main line, it seemed to me that hell itself had exploded in our faces," later wrote surviving C.S.A. general George W. Gordon.

The Confederates actually came within spitting distance of the back porch before their assault was forced to turn back. As our tour group walked through the restored and furnished rooms of the farmhouse, Cartwright described the day after the battle as wounded soldiers were carried to a makeshift hospital inside the historic site. The home's large dining table was used to treat wounds and perform amputations; severed arms and legs were tossed through a front window like chunks of firewood, piling up outside in a horrific heap, a macabre scene that was repeated far too often in this stubborn war. The floor of the spacious room was so blood-soaked that, after the war, it took years of scrubbing to remove the hellish stains. If the creaky old house is haunted, it would come as no surprise to anyone who knew the tale of its darkest day.

Hiding in the safety of their earthen basement, the twenty-plus members of the Branch Carter family had little inkling that they had a personal stake in the battle being fought above them. In the spring of 1861, Tod Carter, Branch's young son, had enlisted in the 20th Tennessee Volunteer Infantry. He worked his way up to the rank of captain and for a time served as a war correspondent, writing for the *Chattanooga Daily Rebel* under the pseudonym "Mint Julep." On that fateful evening he was with the Confederate Army advancing from the south. He knew the lay of the land; he had grown up there. The good captain was fighting for his birthright but was mortally wounded only two hundred yards from its backdoor. Young Carter was brought to his childhood home, where he died in one of the family beds two days later; for him the long nightmare was over.

The battlefield at Franklin is no longer intact. Like many other historic locations, developers have fragmented the site. Neighborhoods and small businesses now sit on locations that saw the fieriest fighting. To some it's hallowed ground; to others it's opportunity. "Those boys consecrated this ground with their blood," said Cartwright, "And on that ground we build Pizza Huts and parking lots." The modern-day struggle between commerce and preservation is more insidious than the war because it's not fought out in the open. Land is bought and sold quietly, bit by bit. For years the town fathers looked upon the battle as an embarrassment, the last gasp in a losing effort. Today, the Battle of Franklin is remembered piecemeal by a handful of scattered markers and plaques. The grandeur of the monumental struggle has been lost, perhaps forever. There is a modern-day effort to raise the necessary millions it will take to buy back some portions of the battlefield and restore their historical eminence. As local preservationist Robert Hicks concludes, "We need a battlefield where you can walk where men fought and died. People don't want to take their families to Franklin to see a parking lot."

After the tour of Carter Mansion, I asked Cartwright about the dense hedgerow that had played such a vital role on the eastern flank. "Does it still exist?" I wondered. "No," he replied, "but there are two very old Osage orange trees in the vicinity." On a damp, folded map I pulled from my pocket, he pointed out the section of railroad track where Loring's charge had been stopped. Leaving the grounds of the Carter house, I crossed Columbia Pike and walked past two pizzerias near the site of the family's former cotton gin building, the ultimate epicenter of the struggle. This location, now covered with asphalt, saw heavy fighting. Generals Adams, Cleburne, and Granbury were killed nearby along the deep ditches and breastworks that had been hastily built twenty yards to the south. Passing through a quiet neighborhood, I came to Lewisburg Pike, two antique shops, and the railroad line. Standing on the track, I looked across the remains of the Collins farmland, owned by the Carters' neighbors to the east and the site of Loring's eastern flanking attempt. The rain had slowed to drizzle as I gazed over the sodden section of field, imagining the noise and smoke of that day 140 years before. I turned to walk down the raised railroad embankment towards the Harpeth River.

Today the section of railroad track looks like any other in the South; there are no signs to suggest that hundreds had died trying to cross the embankment. My walk was unimpeded. The Osage orange hedge once planted north of the line is gone, replaced by invasive bush honeysuckle and privet. Immediately below the track are a few modest houses. As I turned to overlook the entire scene, a ghostly mist reminiscent of artillery smoke drifted in from the swollen river. The hackberry trees to the south had dropped their leaves and stood as dark skeletons in the haze. Isolated from the nearby city, not in distance but in thought, a shudder resonated through me, chilling my core. I shivered more from the poignancy than from the dampness of the day. A profound sorrow washed over me; I shook my head at the senselessness. The war had been winding down; the battle had meant little if anything, fought more for pride than substance.

The morning after the carnage, December 1, 1864, the full extinct of the tragedy had been revealed. As historians McDonough and Connelly later wrote:

> Along the narrow space between Lewisburg and Carter's Creek pikes lay almost 1,700 Confederate dead. Near the Columbia Pike, where the fighting had been the most severe, the outer ditch was in some places piled seven deep with corpses. The dead, many mangled and blackened by gunsmoke, lay in every grotesque, twisted fashion. Some Confederate dead were found standing upright, their rigid legs jammed between the bodies of comrades. . . . Through the cold dawn hours searchers moved through the grisly outer ditch. Some searched for personal friends, dead or alive. Stretcher bearers carried off hundreds of wounded who had suffered through the night. Franklin became one massive field hospital.

The remains of Hood's army regrouped the next morning to bury their dead, digging long trenches and marking each grave with a makeshift wooden headboard inscribed with whatever was known about the deceased. In some cases it was very little. It took two days to complete the grim task. During the cold winter that followed, the wooden markers were collected by local residents to burn in their stoves. The anonymous dead lay in unknown graves until April 1866, when Colonel John McGavock of nearby Carnton Mansion set aside two acres next to his family cemetery so that the Southern dead could have a proper grave- yard. Men were hired to find the burial trenches and move the remains. All of the dead were not found but ultimately 1,496 bodies, their identities unknown, were located and reinterred in the cemetery that now borders a country club where men play golf and speak of mutual funds.

The almost forgotten Battle of Franklin was a death knell. "This is where the Old South died," says preservationist Robert Hicks, "and we were reborn as a nation." Leaving Lewisburg Pike, I walked along the rain-soaked streets through a quiet neighborhood, soon finding the two aged Osage orange trees still grow- ing in the vicinity of the railroad line. Historian Cartwright had told me about the old trees just an hour before. Both were perhaps descendents of the hedge- row that had stopped Loring's charge and, as such, are living monuments. It was a circuitous chain of events that moved Osage orange from its native Red River home to this historic point of all-out chaos that long-ago November afternoon. But such is the way with dynamic systems; the fluttering of a single butterfly or planting of a lone seed can cause major ripples. Turn back the clock and replay the era, day by day, and it would not have unfolded in exactly the same way. Indeed, historians believe that if the Northern general George McClellan had pursued Lee after his defeat at Antietam in Maryland and crushed the retreating Southern army, the entire war might have ended two years sooner and the town of Franklin would have remained untouched by battle—inviolate and intact.

I paused just long enough to admire the towering presence of the elderly trees, and as the rain began to fall heavy once again, I zipped up my coat, turned, and walked away.

Eastern Sycamore
Platanus occidentalis

Upon this beautiful country through which we now wandered, the Indian lavished that wealth of affection which he always feels for nature and never for man. He gave to the hills and streams the soft poetic names of his expansive language. . . . The Cherokee names of Cowee and Cullowhee, of Watauga, of Tuckaseege, and Nantahela, have been retained; and some of the elder settlers still pronounce them with the charming Indian accent and inflection. . . . Now we stopped under a sycamore, while a barefooted girl brought a pitcher of buttermilk from a neighboring house.

Edward King
"The Great South," 1874

Call it coincidental. It was 1953, the year Edmund Hillary and his Nepalese Sherpa guide, Tensing Norgay, became the first humans to climb Mount Everest, the world's tallest mountain. The two reached the summit—more than twenty-nine thousand feet above sea level—on the morning of May 29, snapped a few photos, planted the flags of Britain, Nepal, India, and the United Nations and left after about fifteen minutes. It was a long way back down.

That same summer Stuart Roosa took a job as a smokejumper fighting wildfires in Oregon with the U.S. Forest Service. In addition to an affinity for heights, he soon developed a love of trees. Roosa's adventurous spirit eventually led him to become an Air Force test pilot, which caught the attention of NASA. In 1966 Roosa became an astronaut in training, a job that in time took him farther away from the Earth's tallest mountain than Sir Edmund and Tensing could have possibly imagined.

On January 31, 1971, Roosa, along with Alan Shepard and Ed Mitchell, was aboard Apollo 14 when it was launched from Cape Kennedy on its way to the moon. Tensions were high. It was the first mission since the near disaster of Apollo 13 the previous April, but this time, all went well. In those days, each NASA astronaut was allowed to take along a few personal items known as PPKs, Personal Preference Kits. Usually they were small mementos: stamps, coins, patches. On this flight Shepard took two famous golf balls that he smacked around the lunar surface. Because of Roosa's love for trees, he took a metal canister, six inches long and three inches wide, filled with hundreds of tree seeds. Working with the U.S. Forest Service's Stan Krugman, he had planned a simple experiment: Would seeds taken to the moon sprout back on earth? Would the weightless journey affect them? Would they reproduce and grow normally? The experiment was also a publicity stunt. The country's bicentennial was approaching; if the tree seeds grew, the young seedlings could be given away to celebrate America's first two hundred years. Krugman, staff director for forest genetics research in 1971, chose the seeds: redwood, loblolly pine, sycamore, Douglas fir, and sweet gum. They were all from trees that would grow well in many parts of the country.

In space, the seeds stayed with Rossa while he piloted the command module *Kitty Hawk*, which orbited the moon while Shepard and Mitchell took the lunar lander *Antares* down to the surface on February 5. They spent thirty-three hours on the moon collecting 42.9 kilograms (94.5 pounds) of rocks, and Shepard took a makeshift six-iron to a pair of golf balls. At the time, he was quoted as saying that his second shot went "miles and miles and miles." Roosa and the tree seeds made thirty-four trips around the moon and returned to earth when the trio were reunited. During decontamination the seed canister burst open, spilling its contents. Working by hand, Krugman carefully collected and separated the seeds by species and sent them to forestry labs in Mississippi and California, where, much to the delight of everyone involved, most of them germinated.

The hundreds of resulting seedlings were much in demand. Public officials all over the country wanted one of the Apollo trees to plant. One, a sycamore, made its way to Elizabethton, Tennessee, in Carter County. It became the Sycamore Shoals "Moon Tree" planted in 1976 by Governor Ray Blanton and other dignitaries to celebrate both the bicentennials of the country and Fort Watauga, a historic site that played a pivotal role in American history.

When the first white settlers began to trickle into the Tennessee Valley in and around the Appalachians, they looked for great stands of sycamores. In a low-lying area, these stately trees were an indication of rich bottomland, a good place for year-round water and a prime location in which to settle. They cleared sites near the massive trees and built their homes. It was the wise thing to do.

In 1769 they settled along the Watauga River at Sycamore Shoals in today's Elizabethton. Historically, it was the first permanent American settlement outside the now-defined boundaries of the original thirteen colonies. The community at Sycamore Shoals became the gateway to the American West as pioneers trickled in from the established colonies. Originally, the settlers thought they were in the British colony of Virginia, only to learn two years later that their home was part of North Carolina instead. They sought protection and were denied, probably because their wilderness home was too remote to be governed. To establish order, the group formed their own government, the Watauga Association, and drafted the first written constitution west of the Allegheny Mountains. In 1772, four years before the Declaration of Independence, the Wataugans became the first group of American-born settlers to create a free and independent community. The rest of the colonies were still under British rule.

In March 1775 the Transylvania Company led by Richard Henderson met with twelve hundred Cherokees at Sycamore Shoals to negotiate a land deal. After weeks of counsel and against the wishes of Chief Dragging Canoe, the Native Americans agreed to trade 20 million acres—the entire Cumberland River watershed and lands that extend all the way to the Kentucky River—for two thousand pounds sterling and other goods worth about eight thousand British pounds. The Transylvania Purchase, as it is known, is considered the largest private or corporate real estate transaction in U.S. history.

The following year the settlers built a stockade fort opposite the shoals. The land deal had not set well with Dragging Canoe. Tensions in the region were growing, and a band of warriors led by Old Abram attacked the settlers, who had sought refuge in the fort. After a two-week siege, the warriors gave up and left the area.

The original Watauga Association was short-lived. After the American Revolution, the area it covered became part of the ill-fated Lost State of Franklin, and finally, in 1796 the growing cluster of communities fell under the protection of the new state of Tennessee.

Today the restored Fort Watauga hosts "Living History" weekends once a month. It was a sunny, blue-sky day in winter when I visited. Venison stew was being cooked over an outside fire and a woman dressed in period attire was preparing a Dutch oven to bake scones. One of the reenactors, Dennis Voelker from Spruce Pine, was there as an eighteenth-century trader. He and his wife, Lorraine, specialize in crafting period trade goods, and Voelker was on hand to sell his wares. Being a writer, I bought a quill pen made from a turkey wing feather and a bag of red maple bark. Brewed like tea, the bark yields a "serviceable," light brown ink similar in color to maple syrup. I also bought a small measuring cup made from a deer's antler. The container, about twice as tall as a thimble, was made to hold one hundred grams of gunpowder, enough to fire a musket one time. Since I don't own a musket, I have yet to use the curio. But who knows? It's best to be prepared.

While at the site I walked down to the river to see if there were still any sycamores at Sycamore Shoals. As on any other riverbank in the valley, there were several. The largest one I located couldn't be measured because it leaned out over the water. From the two or three I was able to get a tape measure around, I'd estimate the big one to be over twelve feet in circumference. But these trees are anonymous; they grow quietly along the shoreline out of the limelight. If you ask anyone who works or volunteers at the state park, they'll tell you the most famous sycamore at the site is the thirty-year-old "Moon Tree" planted inside the stockade.

Sycamores had long been rallying points. Before the American Revolution, colonial patriots designated a large tree in each colony as a "Liberty Tree," a secret meeting place to gather and plot against the British. Many of these special sites were sycamores because in those early days they were giants. Their massive girth made them the largest deciduous hardwoods in North America. In 1802 François Michaux found an aged sycamore on the bank of the Ohio River, thirty-six miles from Marietta, Ohio, that measured an astonishing forty-seven feet in circumference. Michaux and his botanist father, André, traveled extensively throughout the East in the 1700s and early 1800s. They were studying and collecting items of natural history, particularly trees. In 1810 Michaux the younger published *Histoire des arbres forestiers de l'Amerique Septentrionale*. Originally produced in Paris in three volumes with 156 color plates, the amended English translation, *The North American Sylva, or a Description of the Forest Trees of the United States, Canada and Nova Scotia*, is considered the foundation of American forestry. What François and André learned about the American river bottomland tree was fascinating.

A sycamore, as it gets older, sometimes becomes completely hollow. This does not hurt the tree, for the innermost section of a growing tree trunk is dead anyway. The hollow sycamores of aboriginal America were so large that the early settlers would sometimes live inside them until their houses were built. The rebels in colonial America who rallied at sycamore Liberty Trees to discuss the British could have actually held their meetings inside the empty bole. A hollow sycamore recorded in Maryland had an inner cavity that measured eleven feet in diameter; twenty-one people were able to stand in a circle around its interior chamber. And in Ohio early settlers boasted of a tree that could hold forty men inside its cavity or fifteen on horseback. Today, all the old-growth sycamores that were present in the virginal forests of the Southeast are gone. Many of these were perhaps five hundred to six hundred years old. The ones we see today are second-, third- or even fourth-growth trees, several generations removed from their stately ancestors. (The champion sycamore still standing is in Montgomery County, Kentucky. It measures just over thirty-six feet in circumference.)

Once the early pioneers had finished with their temporary housing, they simply chopped the trees down. They cut the hollow trunks into sections and, putting bottoms and tops on them, used them as storage bins and as wooden silos for grain. The hollow wooden cylinders were also used to make cisterns, tubs, horse troughs, and lard pails. Native Americans used sections of the trunks as dugout canoes. It is reported that one of these was sixty-five feet long (the equivalent of four and a half Honda Civics parked end to end). It weighted nine thousand pounds or more than three Ford Escorts. It is even possible to tap into a sycamore and drain off its sap. The watery liquid was boiled down to make a sweet confection much like maple syrup, although it took huge amounts of sap and the results were often mediocre at best.

In the spring sycamores produce tiny flowers, both male and female ball-like clusters that hang from separate twigs. After pollination, the male flowers wither and fall away. The female flower produces a spherical fruit that slowly ripens. As a sycamore ages, it exfoliates. Its outer bark looks like torn wallpaper. It becomes brittle, cracks, and falls off in big flakes, revealing a smooth, mottled underbark with blotches of tan, yellow, cream, and greenish white, much like bleached bones. The tree is leafless in winter but not unadorned. Early settlers called sycamores buttonwood or buttonball trees for the ripening fruits that hang like forgotten Christmas ornaments from the bare branches. The button-balls are modest, compact spheres about the size of the buttons on a woman's coat. They are made up of tight clusters of nutlets surrounded by downy hairs. If you pick up one of the nutlets and separate it from the fibers around it, you'll find a seed shaped like a tadpole about a half-inch long. Each buttonball holds enough seeds to start a small grove of its own. The tree stubbornly holds on to its maturing fruit all winter, waiting to release the compact, ripe nutlets to the wind and rain of spring. Because the nutlets float in air or water, they can spread downstream to create new sycamore groves along the shore.

The massive trees are also highly competitive. Once they sprout, they hang on tight and fiercely defend their space. Like tulip trees, they're one of the first hardwoods to grow in an open area, and they must have full sun to be success-ful. To discourage other plants from invading their domain, sycamore leaves contain a natural herbicide. Every autumn these leaves fall to the ground and decompose, leaching out their toxins in the process. The resulting soil is not conducive to new, competing plants.

There is a character in Toni Morrison's novel *Beloved* named Baby Suggs. A former slave living in post–Civil War Ohio, Baby Suggs is "starved for color." Like you and me, Suggs is a visual creature with penetrating eyes designed to absorb, analyze, and relish the subtle nuance of a full color palette. Yet, she is cooped up, locked in a world that is slate-colored and earth brown. Freedom is a new concept for Suggs; overwhelmed, shrouded in sadness, her needs are more basic. She longs for something colorful and cheery to look at.

And here I am, living over a century after the time in which Morrison's novel is set, mired in gray winter, searching for ways to shake the cabin fever that's settled into my bones. I'm also starved for color. That's why, for me, sycamores stand out at this time of the year, and although their brilliance is more of contrast than hue, they are the stars of the drab winter forest—stark skeletons of the valley's bottomland, pale green and bone-colored. Despite their ashen austerity, Baby Suggs would have loved sycamores.

Sitting on the ground, looking into the heart of a modern sycamore as the wind blows the buttonballs back and forth, you can imagine a ghostly banquet. The Carolina parakeet was this country's only member of the parrot family. It loved to eat the nutlets from the buttonball trees. These native, wild parakeets traveled in huge flocks throughout sycamore country. This is why the color-starved Baby Suggs would have loved sycamores. Carolina parakeets were feathered rainbows: chartreuse green with bright saffron yellow heads, red-orange masks as vibrant as Van Gogh sunflowers, and bluish wings with hints of teal in the primary feathers; arguably they were the most colorful creatures ever to fly over our country. Like a box of freshly opened crayons, they exploded with color, rich and vibrant. Thousands and thousands of the tropical-looking birds once flocked together, chattering over the Southeast. The early sycamore groves would have attracted them to broad river bottomland. The decline of both the large trees and spirited parakeets began with the early settlers.

Louis Joliet was the son of a wagon maker born in Québec. At the local Jesuits' School he showed promise as an academic, especially in mathematics but fell under the spell of the adventurousness of the age. He began to explore the Canadian wilderness and trade with the region's indigenous tribes. In 1673 Canadian governor Louis Frontenac sent him on an expedition to map the Mississippi River and determine where it terminated. It was believed that it might empty into the Pacific Ocean. With Father Jacques Marquette and five other voyagers in birchbark canoes, Joliet left St. Ignace on the Straits of Mackinac on May 17. After paddling across Lake Michigan to Green Bay, the explorers traveled the Fox River, went overland to the Wisconsin River, and floated on to the Mississippi. Ultimately, Joliet's mission proved to be a success, with the first mapping of the Mississippi River by white men.

Somewhere along the way (the exact location is unclear), he noted: "Both shores of The river are bordered with lofty trees. The cottonwood, elm, and basswood trees, there are admirable for their height and thickness. . . . We killed a little parroquet, one half of whose head was red, The other half and The neck yellow, and The whole body green."

It is believed that the party was on the Tennessee border. If the bird was killed on the east side of the river, it would have been the first written record of any bird in the Volunteer State—a Carolina parakeet. Other travelers on the Mississippi reported the green birds. Estwick Evans observed "numerous paroquets occupy the trees on its banks" near New Madrid in 1818. And in 1820 John James Audubon noted that the "the woods were literally filled with Parokeets."

A few years later, in 1831, French statesman and philosopher Alexis de Tocqueville traveled extensively in the United States. His visit eventually led to his book *Democracy in America.* De Tocqueville's traveling companion was Gustave de Beaumont. On a trip along the Mississippi, the beautiful scenery wasn't enough to entertain the pair of adventurers, for Beaumont wrote:

> I think we should have died of boredom and despair if we had not had to sustain us our accustomed philosophy and each a *fusil de chasse* [flint-lock rifle]. We awaited *better times* wandering through the surrounding forests and exploring the shores of the Mississippi. Tocqueville and I killed a multitude of charming birds, among others some parrots of charming plumage; they were green, yellow and red. We killed four on the same hunt. The only difficulty is to kill just one, the death of the first makes all the others come; they perch on the head of the hunter and have themselves shot like ninnies.

And then later on the same trip in eastern Carroll County, between Memphis and Nashville, Beaumont noted: "This morning, I wanted to hunt a little; I walked through the woods for an hour or two; I saw a number of charming birds, notably some red and yellow parrots unequalled in their beauty. But, armed as I was, I couldn't kill a single one." (Isn't it odd that someone could find a colorful, charming bird and promptly want to kill it?)

Gunplay aside, these early accounts firmly establish the "charming birds" in West Tennessee and along the Mississippi River. Earlier, John Lawson had documented them in their namesake, the Carolinas. In his *A New Voyage to Carolina*, published in 1709, the gentleman naturalist writes:

> The Parrakeetos are of a green colour, and orange-colour'd half way their head. Of these and the Allegators there is none found to the Northward of this Province. They visit us first, when Mulberries are ripe, which Fruit they love extremely. They peck the Apples, to eat the Kernels, so that the Fruit rots and perishes. They are mischievous to Orchards. They are often taken alive, and will become familiar and tame in two days. They have their Nests in hollow Trees, in low, swampy Ground. They devour the Birch-Buds in April, and lie hidden when the Weather is frosty and hard.

Perhaps the most detailed eyewitness accounts of Carolina parakeets comes from Alexander Wilson. Born in Scotland in 1766, Wilson moved to America to escape the oppression he felt in his own country. Arriving in New Castle, Delaware, in 1794, the young Scot took up weaving to earn a living. He traveled about selling his woven goods, observing the birds and animals along the way. In 1802 he met William Bartram, who persuaded Wilson to take up the study of birds in America. This was no chance meeting, for it changed the course of the Scotsman's life. He spent the rest of his days studying and painting what he found, publishing his nine-volume *American Ornithology*, beginning in 1808. He is generally considered to be the "Father of American Ornithology." In Big Bone Lick, Kentucky, he observed the colorful parakeets:

> When they alighted on the ground, it appeared at a distance as if covered with a carpet of the richest green, orange and yellow: they afterwards settled, in one body, on a neighboring tree, which stood detached from any other, covering almost every twig of it, and the sun, shining strongly on their gay and glossy plumage, produced a very beautiful and splendid appearance. Here I had an opportunity of observing some very particular traits of their character: Having shot down a number, some of which were only wounded, the whole flock swept repeatedly around their prostrate companions, and again settled on a low tree, within twenty yards of the spot where I stood. At each successive discharge though showers of them fell, yet the affection of the survivors seemed rather to increase; for, after a few circuits around the place, they again alighted near me, looking down on their slaughtered companions with such manifest symptoms of sympathy and concern, as entirely disarmed me. I could not but take notice of the remarkable contrast between their

elegant manner of flight, and their lame and crawling gait among the branches. They fly very much like the Wild Pigeon, in close, compact bodies, and with great rapidity, making a loud and outrageous screaming, not unlike that of the Red-headed Woodpecker. Their flight is sometimes in a direct line; but most usually circuitous, making a great variety of elegant and easy serpentine meanders, as if for pleasure. They are particularly attached to the large sycamores, in the hollow of the trunks and branches of which they generally roost, thirty or forty, and sometimes more, entering at the same hole. Here they cling close to the sides of the tree, holding fast by the claws and also by the bills. They appear to be fond of sleep, and often retire to their holes during the day, probably to take their regular siesta. They are extremely sociable, and fond of each other, often scratching each other's heads and necks, and always, at night, nestling as close as possible to each other, preferring, at that time, a perpendicular position, supported by their bill and claws.

It's curious that even the Father of American Ornithology took a gun to the friendly green parakeets, but that's one of the ways birds were studied in the 1800s—up close, personal, and very much dead. Although no written accounts survive that place them any farther east in Tennessee than the Cumberland River, they occurred in the Carolinas, Georgia, Virginia, the Tennessee River floodplain of West Tennessee, and along the Mississippi River near Memphis, so it's reasonable to believe they were once found in the Tennessee Valley as well.

"They certainly should have been here," says Paul Parmalee, professor emeritus of zooarchaeology at the University of Tennessee. "The habitat was right, large sycamore trees, river bottomland. But we have found no archaeological evidence of them."

Carolina parakeets were the size of blue jays, about twice as large as the popular Australian budgerigar, the chirpy parakeet we're used to seeing in pet stores. Their preferred habitat was wooded creeks, "timbered rivers," riparian zones, and rich bottomlands, especially southern swamps with cypresses and woodlands with large stands of sycamores. They were birds of the Southeast that occasionally ventured as far north as New York and west into the Great Plains. Their range closely matched that of sycamores.

Almost an anomaly in the parrot family, the charming green parakeet had adapted to colder climates and brought rich, luxuriant color to drab winter days. They ate a wide variety of seeds and fruits: mulberries, wild grapes, maple seeds, bald cypress balls, beechnuts, hackberries, buttonballs, buds, and flowers. Their fondness for cocklebur was often documented. Like cedar waxwings, they traveled in groups from tree to tree or shrub to shrub, devouring whatever happened to be in season.

Unfortunately, as Lawson noted as far back as the 1700s, Carolina parakeets also had a taste for the young fruit of pear and apple trees, and they ate the ripening grain in a farmer's field. This made them pests that had to be killed. And as Alexander Wilson observed, the highly social parakeets were altruistic. They had the rather human quality of rushing to the aid of a wounded flock-mate. A single man with a gun could kill hundreds, as unwounded birds remained present to protect their fallen comrades. Hunters made piles of the lime green bodies, creating stacks as tall as a man.

Zoologist and ethologist Frans de Waal calls such animal actions as being *succorant behavior* and defines it as "helping, caregiving, or providing relief to distressed or endangered individuals other than progeny." De Waal compares it to human empathy.

But that alone probably did not doom the social bird. Habitat loss, the cutting of their large hollow sycamores, must have had a profound impact. Their range began to shrink as soon as European settlement began to spread. Carolina parakeet flocks roosted and nested in hollow trees. Chimney swifts did the same, but as the pioneer movement swept across the continent, cutting down the forests as it went, the swifts changed their behavior and began to build their nests in chimneys. The parakeets apparently could not adapt to life without large hollow trees. In nature, if you don't adapt to change, you don't survive.

According to Daniel McKinley, another possible agent that robbed the parakeets of their hollow homes was the introduction of European honeybees. Escaped bees took over many hollow trees. As the pioneers slowly moved west, the honeybee swarms advanced in front of the homesteaders as a vanguard of change. Native Americans knew the settlers were coming by what they called the "white man's flies" that preceded them. The last reliable sightings of Carolina parakeets in Virginia came in 1774, in North Carolina in 1791, in Alabama in 1838, in Kentucky in 1878, and in South Carolina and Arkansas in 1885. In Tennessee the last recorded sightings were reported by S. N. Rhoads, quoting Benjamin Miles: "In the early part of the 1850s a flock of paroquets came to our orchard and we chased them out and killed them with sticks and apples; saw a flock at Ashport (Lauderdale County) on the Mississippi River one hundred in number in 1874, and saw one killed alone, within five miles of Brownsville in 1876—the last I have ever heard of." After they beat them to death with sticks in the Volunteer State, the bird made a last stand in Florida. Unconfirmed accounts persisted until the 1920s, until finally there were none.

On Thursday, February 21, 1918, the last documented Carolina parakeet died in captivity at the Cincinnati Zoo. Its name was "Incas." At the time, it was living in the zoo's stone aviary, which ironically was the same place the last known passenger pigeon had died three and a half years earlier, on September 1, 1914. The zookeepers who cared for the "listless" Incas sincerely believed it died of grief since its mate of thirty-two years, "Lady Jane," had died the previous summer. The highly social parakeet couldn't bear to be alone; perhaps it also sensed it was the last of its kind.

In the summer of 2002, Lindalee and I visited Cincinnati, where we stopped by the zoo to pay our respects to the lost birds. A new aviary has been built. In the early 1970s the old stone aviary was scheduled to be razed to make room for an enlarged ape facility. Wildlife painter John Ruthven led a movement to raise money to have Incas's last home moved and renovated. On September 1, 1977, the relocated and refurbished limestone building—now listed on the National Register of Historic Places—was opened once again to the public. A bronze monument was also commissioned to commemorate the passing of both the last native North American parakeet and passenger pigeon. The building is smaller than you might think. It sits only fifty feet from its original location. As we walked around it, I tried to get some sense of the surroundings—the view from the caged windows where Incas had perched with Lady Jane. But, in the end, I was only filled with a profound regret. I had simply arrived on this earth too late to see the vibrant bird.

The present has a way of covering up the sins of the past. We become complacent, lulled into the false belief that this is the way things have always been. In the great lowlands of eastern America, Carolina parakeets and buttonball trees as round as houses were once the norm. They're all gone. The only reminders are the small stands of sycamores that exist today along local streams. Sometimes you have to search for the ghostly voices, the phantom past, but it's there. The bones of the great flocks of chartreuse parakeets have rotted away but at least the sycamores remain.

Walking along the shore at Sycamore Shoals, I encountered a buttonball on the ground. Picking it up, I held it in my hand, turning it over again and again, feeling its rough surface. The sphere was beginning to break apart; a few nutlets splayed out. I imagined some of the seeds on a trip to the moon and thought of the Wataugans settling into their new home just across the river. There are a lot of stories in small everyday things. I also see a bit of our lost natural history—a vibrant yellow-green bird, full of life, nibbling at the buttonball—and wonder: How can this be? Are we not lessened by the loss? I'm sure Baby Suggs would have agreed, for on a gray winter's day, she would have been starved for color.

Bald Eagle
Haliaeetus leucocephalus

I have learned much from this history and have realized, finally,
that sadness at loss is our best *first* response. It should not be our
only response. We know the world gives us life, beauty and solace.
We would be ungrateful if we failed to give that back.

Christopher Cokinos
Hope Is the Thing with Feathers, 2000

Soaring high overhead, riding aerial thermals as deftly as a sailboat glides across
a shimmering sea, a bald eagle in flight is undeniably one of the most inspiring
sights in the natural world. The magnificent bird of prey is the perfect balance
of grace and power, beauty and steely-eyed resolve.

Bald eagles are our national symbol, and I can think of no other feathered or
furry creature that commands such respect. Whether it's flying over a remote
lake or swooping into a crowded stadium before a World Series game, people
pause to watch in wide-eyed wonder, their hearts pounding in disbelief. They
cheer. They applaud. They jump up and down. Eagles have become one of the
most revered icons in our culture, but it hasn't always been that way.

In the late 1800s there was an odd tradition in this country that took place
among the menfolk around Christmas. The guys would gather outside, form
teams, and conduct "side hunts." For the afternoon each side would kill birds,
pile up their lifeless carcasses, and at the end of the day count the totals. The side
with the most dead birds won. It didn't matter what kind of bird, any that happened to fly by would do, whether it be an eagle, a chickadee, or a bobolink.

In 1900 the newly formed National Audubon Society suggested something
radical. They organized the first Christmas Bird Count (CBC). Instead of killing

them, why not simply count all the birds you could find? You still got out of the house and there was also an element of competition. Wouldn't that be easier on the birds? And think of the savings in ammunition. The hardened gamesmen must have been "under-whelmed," but luckily for the birds, they agreed and the concept caught on, spreading slowly throughout the country.

In Tennessee the first Audubon CBC happened two years later in Knoxville. According to the late J. B. Owen, the state's first bird count was made by Magnolia Woodward, who tallied birds around her home near Park Avenue (later changed to Magnolia Avenue). A visit to the Audubon Web site reveals that the count was made on December 1, 1902. In two hours that day the list of birds counted included eight flickers, six Carolina chickadees, three tufted titmice, one wren, and twelve goldfinches—typical backyard birds for then and now.

In 2002 I decided that the best way to commemorate the centennial of the state's first count was to go to the same location and inventory birds once again. A check with the McClung Historical Collection turned up a city directory for 1903. (The data would have been collected in 1902.) Miss Magnolia Woodward, a teacher at Girls High School, lived on Castle Avenue (today Castle Street) just off Park. That neighborhood was part of the Chilhowee Park Community, an early suburb of Knoxville.

On Sunday, December 1, 2002, exactly one hundred years after Magnolia inventoried birds there, I counted for two hours just as she had done. It was sunny but very cold. Today, east Knoxville is quieter; the city's growth of the last forty years has been towards the west. The bumper-to-bumper traffic you find on the west side doesn't occur on the east. The cars that passed that day slowed to look at me—their curiosity was piqued, since a man walking around a neighborhood with binoculars in our modern world is an odd thing—but they quickly moved on. Although I managed to count more birds than Woodward, including two hawks, 86 percent of what I saw were starlings and city pigeons, both introduced urban species that weren't around her neighborhood one hundred years ago. Otherwise, we counted many of the same species, and as with Magnolia, not a single bird died in the process.

The birds I saw that day were of sentimental value only. The neighborhood where Woodward and I counted one hundred years apart is today not in an official CBC circle. In the late 1950s the Knoxville circle was established in the western part of the county. At the time it was mostly old farms, woodlands, and lake shoreline because the city had not yet started to grow in that direction. The Knoxville circle is one of the twenty-nine formal CBC circles across the state. Like the more than fifteen hundred official circles located in the Americas, each of the statewide circles is fifteen miles in diameter. In 2002, a total of 155 species were located in Tennessee with a grand total of 1,058,874 individual birds counted, including 138 bald eagles. (That number is up considerably from the twelve bald eagles counted in 1962.) That's a huge leap from what Magnolia Woodward found in Knoxville in 1902; one can only assume that she would have smiled at the progress.

In Tennessee H. P. Ijams was such an avid early member of the local Audubon chapter that he allowed the group to build a clubhouse on his family's property. H.P. and his wife Alice lived on eighteen-plus acres in south Knoxville on Island Home Avenue. The young couple were devoted naturalists who slowly converted the rural property they had bought in 1910 into essentially a privately owned wildlife sanctuary that they willingly shared with the public. While the local Audubon organization was primarily concerned with the protection of birds, the interest of Ijams and friends Samuel Arthur Ogden and Brockway Crouch drifted more towards bird study. This difference in focus prompted the trio to form a separate local bird club. Following the lead of a group in Nashville that had founded the Tennessee Ornithological Society in 1915, the Knoxville group formed the East Tennessee Ornithological Society on January 13, 1924. They met in the Ijams home, and H.P. was elected the group's first president. As other club chapters began to spring up around the state, the organization changed its name to the Knoxville Chapter of the Tennessee Ornithological Society (KTOS). Some eighty years later, that club still meets the first Wednesday of every month.

The Audubon movement founded by two Boston socialites was nothing short of miraculous, for it represented a major paradigm shift in this country. The collective mindset slowly began to change. Wildlife was no longer to be thought of as an expendable commodity but, rather, as a precious national treasure. Many species benefited immediately. For some—heath hen, Labrador duck, great auk—it came a little too late, but for birds like the whooping crane, osprey, and this country's most iconic bird, the bald eagle, it was timely enough. Although all three still had a life-and-death struggle ahead of them, it gave them a fighting chance. At least they stopped ending up in a pile with other dead birds on Christmas Day.

Bald eagles once roamed the entire continent, and they had reigned for a long time. Fossilized eagle remains dating back eleven thousand to thirty-eight thousand years have been found in the Rancho La Brea Tar Pits in Los Angeles. They are one of the world's eight species of sea eagle: their scientific name *Haliaee-tus leucocephalus* means "white-headed sea eagle." Their common name comes from the Old English word "balde," which simply means white-headed. North America has two eagle species. Golden eagles are found in mountainous regions, while bald eagles live near water. The latter's tie to watery environs is reflected by their diet—their principal food is fish. Rarely do bald eagles nest more than two miles from a large body of water. It has been estimated that when the early colonists began to arrive in this country, there were probably between twenty-five thousand to seventy-five thousand bald eagles in the lower forty-eight contiguous states. They essentially lived along every large river and lake on the continent: from Alaska and Canada south to Baja California and east to Florida. If you include the numbers found in Canada and Alaska, their total population could have been as many as a half-million. In the East the Chesapeake was rich with eagles. One estimate believed that the bay's shoreline hosted one eagle nest every 2.4 miles, or about three thousand mated pairs. But with the arrival of the European settlers, the eagles' historic numbers soon began to fall. One early account, dated in 1668, reports that an "infinite number" of bald eagles were shot to feed hogs in Cumberland County, Maine. Pig food. As I write the words, my fingers tremble; anger rises to clog my throat. I can hardly believe what I have just read, but it's documented to be true.

In 1888 Barton Evermann of Illinois boasted, "Scarcely does an eagle come into our State now and get away alive." Oscar Baynard reported in 1916 that in Florida, "I have known of several instances where the farmer has waited until the nest contained young, cut the tree and destroy[ed] the young and at that time [shot] the parents who are so solicitous for the young that they lose their usual caution."

Meanwhile, in Alaska, there was a bounty on the majestic birds from 1917 to 1954. During that period more than 128,000 were shot for fees ranging from fifty cents to two dollars per bird. Bounty hunters would kill dozens in a single day—this, our national symbol.

Considered vermin, birds of prey in general had long been persecuted. It was believed that they killed or spirited away chickens and other livestock, so they were shot on sight. Several unfounded and highly sensational stories (today we call them urban myths) made the rounds, telling of bald eagles carrying away toddlers. No one wants to see their baby snatched by a voracious bird.

By the 1940s and '50s, Florida became the one reliable place to still find nesting bald eagles in the Southeast, and that's where the serious study of the bird's breeding biology and migration habits began in earnest in 1938, although the principal researcher wasn't a career scientist. Charles Broley was a Canadian banker who became an expert birder around his native Ontario. In his later years he and his family began to spend their winters in the Tampa Bay region of Florida. With the support of Richard Pough, a National Audubon official, Broley started to inventory and band eaglets while they were still in their nest, no small feat since eagle nests are usually in trees 50 to 180 feet off the ground. The fifty-nine-year-old banker devised his own climbing gear and became comfortably proficient at ascending the tall pines that contained the great birds' nests. The more he climbed, the fitter he became. Once at the nest, Broley attached a numbered metal band around each eaglet's ankle. Traditionally, bald eagles have two young, and between 1939 and 1946 Broley banded a total of 814 of them in the nest before they fledged. Of these, 48 were later found dead. Their remains turned up in thirteen different states and four Canadian provinces, thus establishing for the first time that juvenile eagles travel a great distance in their early years. Like Jack Kerouac's hero in his 1957 novel, *On The Road,* juvenile eagles roam about, getting a good look at America, experiencing all it has to offer. But the 1950s were kinder to Kerouac than they were to eagles. America did not welcome them with open arms. Ninety percent of Broley's 48 recovered birds had been shot to death.

During this same period the banker-turned-birder observed that in Florida many of the tall pines preferred by the nesting birds were being cut for timber. Also, the popularity of owning property near the coast was pushing the nesting birds farther and farther inland, away from the waters where they hunted. Broley voiced his concern in an article he wrote for *Audubon* magazine in 1950. Eagle habitat in the Sunshine State was disappearing.

To make matters worse, Florida's eagle man soon became aware of another alarming trend. The mated eagle pairs that remained were producing fewer and fewer young. In 1946 he had banded 150 eaglets; by 1952 that number had dropped to 15. In 1955 the nests he monitored had an 84 percent failure rate, and just two years later the 43 active nests he watched produced only 7 young. In an *Audubon* article he penned in 1958, Broley concluded, "I am firmly convinced that about 80 percent of the Florida bald eagles are sterile." But why? Broley was the first to speculate that the use of organochlorine pesticides, most notably dichlorodiphenyltrichloroethane, or DDT for short, was somehow the cause. But he had no proof and didn't know how the chemical compound actually affected adult eagles.

In the late 1940s and 1950s, America was quite literally living in a fog. Swiss chemist Paul Müller had discovered that the synthetic compound DDT had tremendous insecticidal properties. It killed flies, mosquitoes, moths, and most other insects instantly upon contact. What a world this would be if all six-legged pests could be eliminated, what a boon to humankind. So the miracle of modern science was liberally sprayed across this country and abroad. At first agricultural areas and wetlands were targeted, but later it was used in urban locations. When Dutch elm disease—spread by bark beetles—and gypsy moths turned up in northern communities, DDT followed, and even though government biologists reported in 1946 that frequent use of DDT could kill small birds and fish, the spraying continued. It also didn't seem to matter that the insecticide killed beneficial insects: that was the price you paid to live in a pest-free world. Thousands of honeybee hives, important pollinators of crops, were destroyed, and in many American towns, robins, chickadees, and cardinals disappeared. It also didn't seem to matter that Dutch elm disease and gypsy moths continued to spread, although a few members of the scientific community began to take notice.

In Wisconsin ornithologist Joseph Hickey compared three local communities where elms had been repeatedly sprayed with DDT with three towns that had not. In 1959 he concluded that the three sprayed locations had suffered a 98 percent drop in robin populations. Meanwhile, in Great Britain, where organochlorine insecticides were also widely used, naturalist Derek Ratcliffe discovered that the peregrine falcon population was dramatically declining and that the ones remaining were failing to produce young. After a three-year survey, Ratcliffe concluded that the falcons were having trouble reproducing, not because of direct contact with the insecticides but because of secondary poisoning from eating prey tainted with the pesticide. What about the falcon population in this country? After Ratcliffe's findings were published, a survey of 133 peregrine sites from Georgia north to Nova Scotia did not turn up a single falcon fledgling. Clearly, more than just a few songbirds were being affected.

By 1963 it is believed that fewer that five hundred pairs of nesting bald eagles remained in the lower forty-eight states. Public awareness of the dire situation was ultimately awakened by the 1962 publication of *Silent Spring* by Rachel Carson. Perhaps the most influential environmental book ever written, Carson describes a quiet world without birdsong, all for the sake of eliminating a few insect pests. *Silent Spring* became a huge best seller.

It was Ratcliffe's study of peregrines in Great Britain that offered the first clues about how DDT might be affecting the bald eagles in this country. The English naturalist and his colleagues determined that the peregrine population crash was caused by "extraordinary reproductive failure" due to a buildup of toxins in the predators. DDT and other organochlorine pesticides bioaccumulated in the adult birds' bodies. The more tainted prey they ate, the greater the buildup.

A follow-up study conducted by Daniel Anderson looked at the eggshells of twenty-five different species, including bald eagles. He visited museums and private collectors weighing and measuring thirty-five thousand eggs collected from the late1800s (pre-DDT) to ones gathered in the late 1950s, after its widespread usage began. Anderson discovered that eggs laid after the introduction of DDT had shells that became progressively thinner—so thin, in fact, that they cracked rather easily. Simply the weight of an incubating parent would break the egg. At the U.S. Fish and Wildlife Service's Patuxent Wildlife Research Center in Maryland, a controlled study by toxicologists on American kestrels fed varying doses of DDT produced eggs with thin shells. (A control group of kestrels that were fed food not tainted with DDT produced normal eggs.) Additional studies on just bald eagle eggs indicated that reproductive failure occurred when toxin levels were as low as 3.6 parts per million. It was also determined that with bald eagles the actual structure and strength of the eggs were being altered. Scientists now know that shell thinning is caused by relatively low amounts of contaminants. The toxins prevent the calcium in a female eagle's bloodstream from entering the shell gland, where it crystallizes around the developing embryo. Some eggs had shells so thin you could see through them.

Despite the mounting evidence that the use of DDT was having a major impact on eagles, osprey, falcons, pelicans, and many other birds, it still took several years to get the pesticide usage stopped. The agrichemical industry is a powerful one. Its spokespersons argued that the compounds had no ill affect on humans and whatever problems it might cause was the price you paid to get rid of pests. In their opinion DDT was absolutely necessary for man's survival and health. Ultimately, the fate of the pesticide fell to the newly created Environmental Protection Agency (EPA) and its administrator, William Ruckelshaus. People concerned about the birds were labeled extremist do-gooders, while those supporting the chemical companies were called greedy capitalists; each group was the anathema of the other. On June 14, 1972, Ruckelshaus ended the domestic use of DDT. He cited the known impact it was having on a host of wildlife but also the unknown future effect it could possibly have on human beings. It could certainly accumulate in people as it had in birds of prey; both groups, after all, were at the top of the food chain.

Six years later, another beneficial measure happened. In 1978 all bald eagles living in the lower forty-eight states—the large eagle population in Alaska was never at risk—were given the full protection of the Endangered Species Act. As with the snail darter and gray bat, it became illegal to harm one.

After the banning of DDT, the eagle population began to recover in Florida. Charles Broley, who had banded hundreds of eaglets and was the first to document their rapid decline and champion their cause, did not live to see the turnaround. He died in 1959. The eagle's recovery was slow in the 1970s because it took time for the pesticide to be purged from the environment. However, the next decade saw a noticeable increase.

There are certain experiences in nature that leave indelible impressions. We hold them fresh and pristine in our memories, recalling them fondly for the rest of our lives. For me, one was created on November 15, 1987, in the Sunshine State not far from where Broley lived and began his eagle study in 1939. After the conference I attended ended in Tampa, I rented a car and drove south to J. N. "Ding" Darling National Wildlife Refuge in Sanibel on the Gulf Coast. Since I had grown up in the mountains, coastal environs were new to me. Florida's birds were different from the woodland varieties I was so familiar with in the Smokies. Not only were they large, but they also stood relatively still while admirers gawked and tripped over themselves, relishing their beauty. At Ding Darling I found white ibis, Louisiana tricolored heron, American anhinga, roseate spoonbill, wood stork, common gallinule, and greater yellowlegs—all new to me.

After a night in a local campground, I stirred early to drive back to the airport. Along the way I stopped by Oscar Scherer State Park south of Sarasota, hoping to see a few more new birds. Behind the ranger at the front desk, a photo of a blue and gray jay caught my eye. It was one I had never seen. "It's a scrub jay," answered the ranger. "It used to be a very prominent bird around here, but with all the development, it's rapidly on the decline." Like so many things in the natural world that find themselves squarely positioned between the "then" and "now," the Florida version of the scrub jay was drifting toward the past tense, now listed as an endangered species. "It's getting harder to find one. I don't see one that often myself," added the uniformed officer.

Along the eastern boundary of the park was a railroad track that separated the public land from private farm country. Given this railroad embankment as the best place to look for the disappearing jay, I proceeded there. Still bleary-eyed and sore from my night in a sleeping bag, I headed toward scrub country, clutching my binoculars and 7-Eleven "Big Gulp" coffee with equal intensity, listening for anything that sounded jaylike.

Jays are noisy and quarrelsome. They're great mimics and exhibit a high degree of intelligence. They possess a variety of notes and calls, some borrowed from other species of birds. In fact, the name of the subfamily in which they belong, *Garrulinae,* comes from the Latin word "garrio," meaning "to prattle." And prattle they do. Their calls are piercing, even raucous, and one soon presented itself. The ebullient passerine, a vocal member of the magpie and crow family, obviously wanted to be heard. Locating the railroad track, I followed the excited monologue to its source. There in the highest point of a tree to the right was a crestless, blue and brownish-gray jay. As the morning sun fell across its right shoulder, it began to preen—a dramatic pause between recitations. Its ritual was performed purely for me to see, or at least that's how such moments feel. The sun was beginning to climb in the sky; morning's newness was melting away. A gentle breeze flirted with me as I sat down between the rails on the wooden ties to watch the jay's forenoon routine. Its tone was fussy, even harsh; it seemed to have something on its mind, like a concerned citizen at the lectern of a town meeting.

Perhaps I was reading more into it than was really there, casting an anthropomorphic cloak over the scene, but we humans seek out the allegorical. As freethinkers lost in this world, having to fend for ourselves, we long for the hidden meaning as if secret messages have been inscribed somewhere for us to find. It's part of our nature; call it wanderlust. Like Eugene Gant, the troubled central character in Thomas Wolfe's novel *Look Homeward, Angel,* we look behind "every stone, every leaf and every unfound door," searching for answers to questions only we can pose.

For a time, there on the railroad track, I wondered about another Florida bird, the dusky seaside sparrow. It was once endangered—that is, until its decline became permanent. They were officially declared extinct in November 1990. Today the sparrow is only a memory. Can an individual bird sense its species is almost gone? Does it hear the death rattle? Feel the loneliness? I ruminated. Was this why the scrub jay sounded so harsh? The solo bird took a long time to straighten and clean each individual feather, pausing to vocalize now and again. After all, it was being watched, and I had come over four hundred miles to see the show. After a time that somehow seemed timeless, suspended in the ether of my life, the jay abruptly ended the show and flew away to attend to other business at hand.

Alone with the morning sunshine, I was left sitting in the middle of a state I did not know, like a man with no home, untethered to anything other than the planet itself, like Kerouac's Sal Paradise on the road. To paraphrase him: "The golden land lay ahead . . . where all kinds of unforeseen events wait lurking to surprise you and make you glad you're alive to see." At that moment I could have walked away from the rented car and all I had known, followed the scrub jay's leave, and found answers to my questions—and with that perhaps even freedom. Progressively, however, as my senses widened, some hawk activity nearby caught my attention, breaking my reverie. "Should I investigate or return to my life in the civilized world?" This is a question that most people lost in a natural moment often ask themselves. For me, at that instant, the mechanized world could wait, at least for a few more precious moments.

Another hundred yards down the track toward the north, a hawk was making itself known, obviously disturbed. Red-shouldered hawks are highly vocal. I stood, turned, and had not made three dozen steps toward the ruckus when a tall stand of pines to my left erupted with life. An adult bald eagle bobbed up and down, unfurling its seven-foot wingspan prior to takeoff. I knew instantly that the bird had been watching me, lost in my vagabond dream. My heart raced as the majestic bird of prey took flight and swooped down over the track, dipping low not fifty feet in front of me. It climbed and sailed off to my right, and since the railroad bed was raised, for a time we were virtually eye to eye.

I watched this country's symbol—talons free of arrows or snakes or olive branches—as it flew to the east and out of sight. Anytime a moment like this unfolds, the world slows; it's forever etched in your life's memories. I had never seen a bald eagle in the wild, and here it was in the southern state of its last stand and in some ways, because of the dedicated work of Charles Broley, where it also began its noted comeback.

To Native Americans, perhaps no other animal was as highly revered as the eagle. It was viewed by many as being a direct messenger from the Great Spirit. The Cherokee called the bird *awa'hili* and held eagle feathers sacrosanct, and although both species were revered, it was the black and white tail feathers of juvenile golden eagles that were most coveted. It was taboo to harm one, except for certain individuals who were designated by the tribe as eagle killers, and their methods were known only to themselves. By 1890 the eastern band of Cherokee centered in North Carolina only had one official eagle killer left. When feathers were needed for an eagle dance, the chosen one went to the mountains to hunt a sacrificial bird. His sojourn was steeped in ceremony, highly ritualized prayer, and fasting that could last for days. If an eagle was killed, the hunter stood over the body begging forgiveness, and if vengeance were sought, he proclaimed that it was not a Cherokee but a Spaniard that had done the deed. (The bitter memory of de Soto's corn-stealing conquistadors endured.) Once the eagle killer returned from the mountain, no special attention was paid to him or his deed, for his tribesmen didn't want to draw focus to their group. The eagle killer simply said, "A snowbird has died," and went about his business. The village knew the message behind his words, and four days later, warriors were dispatched to the mountain to retrieve the feathers, which were wrapped in a deerskin. Returning to the village, the warriors hung the holy feathers in a special round hut or "feather house" near the dance ground. Only great warriors or those well versed in the extreme sacredness of the dance were allowed to wear the feathers, for eagles were not killed irreverently and their power could not be abused.

In Tennessee golden eagles were historically found in the mountains of the eastern part of the state and bald eagles in the western part along the Mississippi River and Reelfoot Lake and farther east at Land Between the Lakes (LBL). John J. Audubon himself first reported two bald eagle nests in November 1820 in what is today Dyer and Lake counties, while in 1895 S. N. Rhoads detailed a secondhand report of nesting at Reelfoot Lake. In Decatur County there's a site called Eagle Nest Island in the Tennessee River that suggests that eagles also nested closer to the middle of the state. All of these accounts were historical, for in Tennessee, as in the rest of the country, eagle populations had declined, and even though 530,000 acres of large reservoirs—prime eagle habitat— had been created, primarily by TVA, nesting eagles completely disappeared from the state in the 1960s and '70s. There were no known successful bald eagle nests here between 1961 and 1983, a span of twenty-two years. With the banning of DDT in 1972 and protection afforded by the Endangered Species Act, bald eagles began to return, but they needed a little help.

Peter Nye pioneered the reintroduction technique known as "hacking" in New York State. Nye and his assistants raised young eaglets obtained from Alaska, where eagles were still common. This is no small task. No other North American bird grows as rapidly as a bald eagle. Young eaglets can gain six ounces of body weight per day, growing from a hatching weight of just over two ounces to over ten pounds in twelve weeks. At about eight weeks of age, the artificially raised young eagles were placed into faux nests called "hack towers," essentially large wooden boxes with bars across the front. Nye and his group hacked two eagles in 1976 that returned seven years later to successfully nest less than one hundred miles from their hacking site.

An active reintroduction hacking program began in Tennessee in 1980 with the Tennessee Wildlife Resources Agency, Tennessee Valley Authority, and Tennessee Conservation League working together on the project. The following year, young eagles were released at Land Between the Lakes in West Tennessee's Stewart County and at Reelfoot Lake. In 1983 a mated pair of unknown origin successfully nested and raised one eaglet at Cross Creek National Wildlife Refuge near

Dover, also in Stewart County, and an eagle hacked at LBL successfully nested at a second location at Cross Creek the following year. Bald eagles were returning to Tennessee.

Celebrating its sixteenth year in 2006, Wilderness Wildlife Week (WWW) in Pigeon Forge is a nine-day event that sees nature and wildlife experts from all over the country come together to conduct a series of programs and activities open to the public. In essence, it's a festival of nature and environmental education. Created by professional photographer and author Ken Jenkins, WWW is an award-winning event of national repute. "There's nothing like it in the country," says Louise Zepp, editor of the *Tennessee Conservationist* magazine. Jenkins and his wife Vicki own Beneath the Smoke, a nature-company and gallery in Gatlinburg, both are champions of the environment and both are still very active in WWW.

At the event I spoke with Bob Hatcher, who retired as TWRA's Nongame and Endangered Wildlife Coordinator in 2001. Hatcher was the driving force behind eagle reintroduction in the state and still remains active in the wildlife community, serving as a consultant to the American Eagle Foundation (AEF). He keeps track of all the nesting and numbers, answering all the e-mail inquires received by AEF. "Tennessee wasn't the first to hack young bald eagles," related Hatcher, "but it's now reintroduced more than any other state." As a man who had dedicated a large portion of his career to the eagles' recovery, he spoke with great pride about their successful return. Between 1980 and 2004, three hundred eaglets were hacked at seven locations in Tennessee. Three of these—Chickamauga, South Holston, and Douglas lakes—are in East Tennessee. Douglas Lake, south of Dandridge, has led the way. AEF hacked sixty-nine bald eagles at the TVA reservoir between 1992 and 2003, and the program continues today. In 1994, bald eagles were down-listed in Tennessee, moving from the endangered list to the threatened, and in 2000 they were moved again, now regarded as "in need of management" but no longer considered to be either endangered or threatened in the state. Clearly the national symbol's regional comeback is well underway. (An endangered species can either be listed on the state level or federal level or both.)

The American Eagle Foundation is a not-for-profit organization founded in 1985. Located in Pigeon Forge, its mission is three-fold: the restoration of eagles in the wild, the rehabilitation of injured eagles and other birds of prey, and environmental education designed to raise awareness of raptors among the general public. It's affiliated and partially funded by Dollywood, a Pigeon Forge theme park named for its co-owner and Sevier County native Dolly Parton. Dollywood's Eagle Mountain Sanctuary, a one-million-square-foot outdoor aviary, opened in 1991. Each year the "Bird of Prey" presentations at the site entertain thousands of visitors. AEF receives no governmental funding. In addition to the support it receives from Dollywood, it raises money through a variety of avenues: donations, memberships, and merchandizing, plus the fees earned by the foundation's most famous alumnus, Challenger, the bald eagle that's often seen flying over Super Bowls and other high-profile events. On those occasions, AEF president and founder Al Cecere serves as the celebrated raptor's handler. Challenger also often travels with its own medical acolyte, Dr. Michael Jones, a bird of prey expert from the University of Tennessee College of Veterinary Medicine.

It was late December, an unseasonably windy and warm day, when I visited AEF with Ijams staff members Pam Petko-Seus and Kelley Dodd and director Paul James, who had worked out our tour with AEF Operations Manager Kay Morrison. The new facility, located on twelve wooded, hilly acres of crumbling red clay belonging to Dollywood, is at the end of a one-lane gravel road that crawls up the East Tennessee hollow. Without a posted sign like so many other such roadways in the Smoky Mountain foothills, few would suspect that the unglamorous, gated path leads to such a lofty purpose. The complex of new, cocoa-brown buildings, plain and austere, also hides the facility's altruistic aspirations. Pete McManus, the curator of birds, led our tour. We rendezvoused with him as he burst through a door with a spectacular golden eagle on his gloved arm. It was my first up-close encounter, literally eyeball to eyeball, with the resplendent golden, amber, and tawny bird of the western mountains. Its inherent intensity stopped us in our tracks. Deftly handling the bird that was decidedly more than a handful, McManus was on his way to tether the winged warrior outside in a paddock for some preening in the morning sun.

After the great raptor was secure, McManus ushered us into a long, barnlike building. Inside we discovered its layout was like a livery stable with a long central hallway, flanked on both sides with over twenty individual enclosures side by side, much like the stalls of a horse barn, but its livestock was not hoofed but feathered. For the next several marvelous minutes, we were led from stall to stall and introduced to the most fantastic array of non-releasable birds of prey, each with sad tales of why they were there and not wild and free-flying. AEF had taken them in to rehabilitate but each had proven to be non-releasable because of its injury or imprinting, a term used to define a bird that has become too people-friendly. Wild animals, to be truly wild, should never be people-dependent because they lose their ability to fend for themselves. They'll seek handouts from total strangers, and most humans don't understand such behavior.

Inside the great barn, we were shown black and turkey vultures, Harris hawk, barred owl, peregrine falcon, caracara, barn owls, red-tailed, and Cooper's hawks, kestrel, and, if that weren't enough, eagle after eagle. It seemed that as we progressed up and down the hallway, each bird became larger and more intensely august. Finally we came to a stall with a gold star on its wooden door. It was there that McManus brought out Challenger, AEF's superstar. I think we collectively held our breath and stared at the imperial creature with giddy disbelief. We humbly looked at each other as though we were meeting royalty—as, indeed, we were.

Next we were led to a second long, brown, barnlike building, this one guarded by a blond mountain of a dog on a chain. It sniffed each of us as we strolled past its post and climbed an outside stairway to a second-floor central hallway. Here we were urged to be quiet, for inside this rustic building was where captive non-releasable mated pairs reproduce and raise what are totally healthy young, impressionable chicks that are kept sequestered from people and one day released to the world at hack towers. Small one-way glass-and-mirror windows covered with hinged wooded doors allowed us a peek inside at the raised platforms, where the captive pairs were already beginning to assemble crude stick nests. After all, it was late in the calendar year, and nesting season would soon begin. The center's staff covertly supplies food and sticks to each pair residing in their two-story, open-air, netted rooms as big as some condos. The building contained five such enclosures, and the last held the most surprising occupants of all: a pair of mated Andean condors. AEF was just beginning to use the same techniques perfected with eagles to captive-breed and raise the massive South American birds with wingspans of up to ten feet. Their work with bald and golden eagles has proven to be so successful that they are turning their attention to other endangered raptors.

In addition to captive breeding at AEF and zoos around the country, eggs or eaglets have also been removed from locations where populations are doing well. Many come from Alaska. Each year AEF raises several young birds that are hacked into proper habitat. Bald and even golden eagles are released at Douglas Lake only a few miles away from Pigeon Forge. These birds fledge and imprint on East Tennessee, returning to the valley they know as home after a few years of wandering. It's generally believed that the survival rate of hacked eagles is 55 percent the first year and 90 percent each succeeding year. For any bird of prey, the first winter is the hardest.

Imagine you're a young bald eagle, almost full grown at about thirteen weeks old, with a wingspan of close to eighty inches. You're full of life; yet, you've never flown. You were hatched by captive parents, a mated pair that because of their injuries will spend the rest of their lives inside an enclosure, their wild days over. But as for you, you're perfectly healthy.

Now you find yourself and a nest mate in an isolated room, solid plywood and particleboard on three sides, but one side, the front, is screened and faces a quiet finger of a lake. Your artificial nest sits atop a wooden platform, roughly twenty feet above the ground. You really never see or hear people, but instead are comforted by the sights and sounds of the natural world that surrounds your lofty perch. You've been in your temporary quarters for several weeks; food magically appears—like manna from heaven—through a slot in the back; and as the days have progressed, you've grown stronger and restless, unbearably restless. You flap your newly feathered wings and hop up and down, at times hovering slightly above the floor. In a word, your time has come. The wide world awaits. It's time for you to fledge—fly for the first time.

The hack tower operated by AEF on Douglas Lake is huge, much bigger than I expected. It's the size of a school bus, divided into four large rooms that sit atop ten wooden poles on a forested ridge that overlooks an isolated cove of the TVA reservoir near Dandridge. For many bald eagles the tower is their portal to freedom, the site of their entry into the winged life—that is, absolute freedom. Eagles that are raised in captivity and then released into the wild are taken to the private tower to fledge.

It was a warm morning in July when Paul James, Chris Burkhart, and I drove to Jefferson County to watch two juvenile bald eagles, hatched at the Birmingham Zoo, make their first flight. The temperatures the week before had topped out near one hundred degrees. Along with several other people, we were the guests of AEF president Al Cecere. The AEF hack tower is the only one in the state and one of only a very few in operation in the country.

Bald eagles are usually old enough and strong enough to fly by the time they've reached three months of age. The young birds are brought to the tower and spend the last five or six weeks of their nestling life—safe and surreptitiously fed—inside one of the four large rooms at the top of the elevated installation. They're visited daily; their growth and progress is quietly monitored. "When eaglets start jumping around, flapping their wings, hopping up to the highest perches, we know it's time to let them go," said Cecere.

"We really provide a service," he added, for not only is the tower used for eaglets raised at AEF's facility in Pigeon Forge, but it's also the release site for captive-bred eagles from other places like zoos. This was the second release of the summer. Two eagles raised by AEF had been released the week before. On this morning Cecere served as host to the group of about twenty-five people, including AEF part-time volunteer Pam Carey, who had flown from New Hampshire, and Martha Flory from Gatlinburg. It was a balancing act: Cecere made sure that the guests were comfortable and fully informed of what was about to happen, but he was also mindful of the juvenile eagles' needs. This meant keeping the people out of sight and quiet. "We want it to be a peaceful morning for the birds to leave," he related—a purely natural moment without any unnecessary stress.

With us were freelance photographer Craig Cutler from New York City, who was there to cover the event for *Audubon* magazine, and entertainer James Rogers, a member of AEF's board of directors for many years. "How many people can say they were there to watch two eagles take their first flight," commented Rogers. Everyone was aware of this distinction and tingled with anticipation.

An online "Name the Eaglet" contest selected each bird's name. The two eaglets released that morning had been christened "Dolly" and "Louis"; the female was named in honor of AEF's patron saint, Dolly Parton. After each was fitted with small radio telemetry devices and identification tags, the assembled group of eagle fans was divided and quietly ushered into place. Some were positioned in folding chairs behind the tower; their view was the same as the eagles. We took our places with several others hidden in the media blind, in front of and below the tower. As we looked up into the elevated room, we could see the eagle pair running back and forth behind the screen. Perhaps they sensed something was about to happen. The mesh front of their enclosure is really a gate that slides up. From behind, five area children—Laura, Gretchen, Ray Anne, Garrett, and Blake—were given the honor of pulling the heavy rope that lifted the portal.

It can take eaglets up to two hours to leave the safety of their nest, but most leave much sooner. "I believe these are going to bolt immediately," predicted AEF's Larry Morrison; they seemed far too lively not to fly as soon as the opportunity presented itself. "Don't look away or reach for a stick of gum," Cecere reminded us. When the eagles fly, it happens quickly, and they'll be gone, out of sight before you know it. And, indeed, as soon as the gate was raised, Dolly and Louis hopped out on a ledge in front of their artificial nest. One flew in an instant, testing its wings fully for the first time. The other looked around as if to savor the moment or work up the necessary courage. Fifteen seconds passed, and then it was off to follow its nest mate, for it certainly didn't want to be left alone.

"What usually happens," said Morrison, who has tracked many eaglets on their maiden voyage, is that "they only fly a short distance their first flight. They'll land in a tree near each other and spend the rest of the day and night just looking around, taking it all in." The great wide world is almost too much to comprehend immediately. They go from a box that's roughly eight feet square to wide-open country and spacious vistas. Around sunrise the next morning, they'll make their second flight, and this one will last a lot longer, for now they are free-flying eagles eager to test the limits of their newfound ability.

"It just gives you chills, to be here and see it happen," said eagle watcher Ginny Moorer. It's a sight you never forget. I nodded quietly, knowing that eagles had a way of giving you such moments.

Today, the end result of Tennessee's twenty-five years of eagle reintroduction can readily be seen. Once hacked into an area, eagles imprint on the site and generally return to within seventy-five miles of the location about five years later, when they've reach sexual maturity and it's time for them to nest on their own. In recent years active eagle nests have appeared on Watts Bar, Tellico, Norris, Cherokee, Douglas, and Ft. Loudoun lakes. Most bald eagles build their aeries at the edge of large tracts of forests near water. They mate for life and may use the same refurbished nest for several years. Egg laying in Tennessee occurs in February and early March.

It was a damp morning in early spring when Paul James and I met Linda Claussen at Seven Islands Wildlife Refuge, located at Kelly Bend on the French Broad River in east Knox County. Heavy rains had fallen through the night, but the clouds were beginning to break. As we walked down Kelly Lane towards the river, the vociferous yearnings of thousands of chorus frogs could be heard singing from the soppy floodplain along the river. Spring was definitely here. At one point we watched a male American kestrel hovering above the alluvial floodplain. We were above the silent hunter, looking down on his pursuits, an angle one rarely attains. The refuge itself was the brainchild of Linda's husband, Pete. In the late 1990s he formed the Seven Islands Foundation (SIF), a privately owned land conservancy, and began to set aside property to be protected and restored to a variety of natural habitats. Most of the acreage had recently been fescue pasture maintained for grazing livestock and hay production. "The vision of SIF," writes refuge manager Wayne Schacher, "is to increase habitat diversity to the benefit of native botanical and zoological communities." Twenty-seven habitat types have been identified in the ecological assessment. It's a patchwork. The majority of the refuge, around 325 acres, is in a variety of stages of succession. "Most of the alluvial bottoms and rolling uplands," continues Schacher, "were within this category of succession." That means the environs are rapidly changing, no longer being forced into servitude.

What strikes the casual visitor to Seven Islands is the overall lay of the land, for the narrow roadway opens up to a dramatic sylvan panorama with the Great Smokies off in the distance. It's a excellent place to view the valley. When you park at the entrance and walk into the site, you have little idea of the grandeur that awaits you because it's revealed slowly as you stroll down the lane. To the northeast, behind you, the rolling hills, some wooded and some recently pastured, melt down to a broad expanse of bottomland—old southern soil deposited in the flats along the river. Kelly Bend is a long, pudgy finger that points southeast toward Union Valley, while Bays Mountain comes to an abrupt end across the river opposite the bend.

The name of the refuge comes from the several islands located on the western flank of the reserve. There are four large ones that split the river into two channels and several smaller ones, steamboat-sized or less, depending on the shifting shorelines. During the low-flow months of summer, you can practically wade from island to island, as indeed I have. Like any such place, the smaller landforms refuse to commit themselves to any definite shape. Yet, such is the nature of an island, and a cluster of several only adds to the capriciousness. But this is not to say that the islands are not established, for the towering sycamores that grow from them keep their hearts deeply anchored and are most assuredly substantial.

It was perhaps this viability or the pastoral remoteness of the location itself that attracted the refuge's newest residents, for Linda, Paul, and I had only walked about ten minutes down the paved rural roadway when we spotted the first white head, and although we were at least three hundred yards away, its form was unmistakable. There, perched on a bare sycamore branch forty or fifty feet above the swirling water sat an adult bald eagle. It was looking upstream over the same rich bottomland that lay supine below us. Surveying its territory, the regal raptor was not alone, for behind it, high in another sycamore, was a classic stick nest as big as a household stove, except that it was conical like a funnel. On the nest a second eagle was hunkered down, incubating. The succession that was sweeping across the site was not limited to grasses and trees. Much to my companions' surprise, I whooped loudly, full of an eight-year-old's zeal. Seventeen years after I saw my first eagle in Florida, I had finally seen an eagle on its aerie, and to view one so close to my own nest was a thrill unparalleled. As the crow flies, Seven Islands is slightly less than twelve miles northeast of my Chapman Ridge home—practically my backyard. The nascent refuge had proven the wisdom of Hollywood's *Field of Dreams* adage: "If you build it, they will come."

As we watched from our equally lofty vantage point, the first eagle took flight and circled over the island to disappear to the west, downstream. A short time later, it reappeared and adroitly maneuvered through the tree's uppermost branches to land on the nest and deliver a midmorning meal to its mate. For a brief time they were together exchanging eagle pleasantries, and again the sovereign hunter took flight to disappear downstream. It is certainly possible, and highly likely, that the pair of eagles we watched were hacked at Douglas Lake by the AEF, since Seven Islands is just a short distance downstream. Our trio discussed this very possibility and smiled at its implication.

The pair of Seven Islands eagles raised two fledglings, and as far as anyone knows, it's the first successful bald eagle nesting in the history of Knox County.

At the March 2005 meeting of KTOS, Knoxville's bird club, state ornithologist Michael Roedel was asked: "Are there any Tennessee birds once on the decline that are making a comeback?" Without hesitation he answered, "Bald eagles are coming back with great enthusiasm. In 2004, there were over fifty successful nests." Early reports for 2006 indicated that even more nesting was underway. To close out its evening report on Thursday, May 4, 2006, *ABC World News Tonight* anchor Elizabeth Vargas announced that Vermont had a bald eagle nest with eggs in it, making it the last of the lower forty-eight contiguous states to have the national symbol return as a nesting bird. It was one of those warm and fuzzy good-news stories placed at the end of the broadcast to brighten a day of otherwise somber events. Everyone could feel good about what the banning of DDT and the Endangered Species Act had accomplished. As the report detailed, forty years ago there were only 417 bald eagle nests in the country, but today there are over 7,000—so many, in fact, that individual birds were fighting over choice nesting sites. The species will soon be federally down-listed, no longer considered threatened. Once again, the majestic raptor is flourishing, free to survey the countryside as lord and master. As John Burroughs wrote in 1904:

> He draws great lines across the sky; he sees the forest like a carpet beneath him; he sees the hills and valleys as folds and wrinkles in a many colored tapestry; he sees the river as a silver belt connecting remote horizons. We climb mountain-peaks to get a glimpse of the spectacle that is hourly spread out beneath him. Dignity, elevation, repose, are his. I would have my thoughts take as wide a sweep. I would be as far removed from the petty cares and turmoils of the noisy and blustering world.

No better description of freedom has ever been penned. I'm sure Kerouac would have agreed. And I saw it first along a railroad track that November morning and have known it ever since. That great bird had witnessed my intrusion and had judged me harmless, for indeed, I certainly was that: just a wanderer in the middle of a life going from the known to the unknown in a seemingly pathless woods. I could easily argue that that long-ago moment on the road had changed my life forever, for I picked up a pen and, holding it firmly, have been writing ever since.

Eagles have a sort of play. They carry a large stick up and down a river playing keep-away from one another. Every so often a second eagle will grab the stick and snatch it free, or the baton-bearer may drop it, only to dive at breakneck speed to catch it before it hits the water. They'll play this game back and forth like kids with a ball, wild and free.

Only on rare occasions do we get to look into the heart of absolute splendor and know its naked truth—that nature is dynamic and resilient, a swirl of starts and stops and tenacious rebirths and, by all means, as fluid and swift and everchanging as the river that flows past my Tennessee Valley home.

Should you ask where Nawadaha
Found these songs so wild and wayward,
Found these legends and traditions,
I should answer, I should tell you,
"In the bird's-nests of the forest,
In the lodges of the beaver,
In the hoof-prints of the bison,
In the eyry of the eagle!
"All the wild-fowl sang them to him,
In the moorlands and the fen-lands,
In the melancholy marshes;
Chetowaik, the plover, sang them,
Mahn, the loon, the wild goose, Wawa,
The blue heron, the Shuh-shuh-gah,
And the grouse, the Mushkodasa!" . . .

Ye who love a nation's legends,
Love the ballads of a people,
That like voices from afar off
Call to us to pause and listen,
Speak in tones so plain and childlike,
Scarcely can the ear distinguish
Whether they are sung or spoken;—
Listen to this Indian Legend,
To this Song of Hiawatha!

Henry Wadsworth Longfellow
The Song of Hiawatha, 1855

Sources

An asterisk (*) next to an entry indicates that it can be found online at *Making of America,* Cornell Univ. Online Digital Library: http://library8.library.cornell.edu/moa/.

Preface

*Lacy, R. "The Land of the Cherokee." *United States Magazine and Democratic Review* 28, no. 154 (April 1851): 325–26.

Olsenius, Christine. "The Southeast: Biodiversity Center of North America." In *Return of the Natives.* Nashville, TN: Southeast Watershed Forum, 2004. See p. 2.

Rakes, Pat. E-mail to author, February 20, 2006.

Carolina Chickadee

Bonter, David N. and Wesley M. Hochachka. "Declines of Chickadee and Corvids: Possible Impacts of West Nile Virus." In *American Birds: The 103rd Christmas Bird Count, 2002–2003.* Ivyland, PA: Audubon, 2003. See pp. 23–25.

Conniff, Richard. "The Discover Interview: Edward O. Wilson." *Discover* 27, no. 6 (June 2006): 61.

Freeberg, Todd M., and Jeffrey R. Lucas. "Receivers Respond Differently to Chick-a-dee Calls Varying in Note Composition in Carolina Chickadees, *Poecile carolinensis.*" *Animal Behavior* 63 (2002): 837–45.

Freinkel, Susan. "If All the Trees Fall in the Forest . . ." *Discover* 23, no.12 (Dec. 2002): 68.

Kleeman, Elise. "Biologists Crack Code of Chickadee Song." *Discover* 26, no. 10 (Oct. 2005): 12.

Nicholson, Charles P. *Atlas of the Breeding Birds of Tennessee.* Knoxville: Univ. of Tennessee Press, 1997. See pp. 217–21.

Pollock, Judy. "Study Finds Chickadees Gone in Large Areas." E-mail report, Oct. 30, 2002, to Troy Ettel, Tennessee State Ornithologist, forwarded to author. Pollock is the bird conservation project manager for Audubon–Chicago Region.

Pyle, Robert Michael. *Wintergreen: Listening to the Land's Heart.* Boston: Houghton Mifflin Company, 1986. See p. 274.

Thoreau, Henry David. *Thoreau on Birds.* Boston: Beacon Press, 1993. See pp. 418–23.

Sibley, David Allen. *The Sibley Guide to Birds.* New York: National Audubon Society. Alfred A. Knopf, 2000. See pp. 374–77.

Smith, Susan M. *The Black-capped Chickadee.* Wild Bird Guides. Mechanicsburg, PA: Stackpole Books, 1997. See p. 34.

———. *The Black-capped Chickadee: Behavioral Ecology and Natural History.* Ithaca, NY: Comstock Publishers Association, 1991.

"West Nile Virus: Background; Virus History and Distribution." Centers for Disease Control and Prevention, Division of Vector-Borne Infectious Diseases, Web site: http://www.cdc.gov/ncidod/dvbid/westnile/background.htm.

"West Nile Virus." *National Biological Information Infrastructure: Wildlife Disease Information Node.* Web site developed and maintained by the U.S. Geological Survey's National Wildlife Health Center: http://westnilevirus.nbii.gov/.

"West Nile Virus Decimates Black-capped Chickadees." *Chicago Wilderness Magazine,* Winter 2003. Available online at http://www.chicagowildernessmag.org/issues/winter2003/news/westnile.html.

Yakutchik, Maryalice. "Plight of the Vanishing Songbirds." *Defenders,* Spring 2003. Available online at Defenders of Wildlife Web site: http://www.defenders.org/defendersmag/issues/spring03/plightsongbird.html.

River Cane

Bartram, William. *Travels of William Bartram.* Ed. Mark Van Doren. New York: Dover, 1928. See p. 198.

Duggan, Betty J., and Brett H. Riggs. *Studies in Cherokee Basketry.* Knoxville: Univ. of Tennessee Publications Center, 1991. See p. 21.

Hanley, Wayne. *Natural History in America.* New York: Quadrangle/The New York Times Book Co., 1977. See p. 130.

Hoig, Stanley W. *The Cherokees and Their Chiefs: In the Wake of Empire.* Fayetteville: Univ. of Arkansas Press, 1998. See p. 167.

Jahoda, Gloria. *The Trail of Tears: The Story of the American Indian Removals, 1813–1855.* New York: Wings Books, 1975. See pp. 232–37.

King, Duane H., and Jefferson Chapman. *Official Guidebook to the Sequoyah Birthplace Museum.* Vonore, TN: Sequoyah Birthplace Museum, 1988. See p. 44.

*King, Edward. "Southern Mountain Rambles." *Scribner's Monthly* 8, no. 1 (May 1874): 7.

*M.A.H. "Historical Traditions of Tennessee." *American Whig Review* 15, no. 87 (March 1852): 237, 246.

Beaver

"The Beaver and Other Pelts." Available online at McGill Univ. Library and Digital Collections Web site: http://digital.library.mcgill.ca/nwc/history/01.htm.

Billinghurst, Jane. *Grey Owl: The Many Faces of Archie Belaney.* New York: Kodansha International, 1999. See p. 72.

Cranford, Marcella. Conversation with author, Oct, 1, 2005.

Grey Owl, *Pilgrims of the Wild.* New York: Scribner, 1971. See pp. xiv, 42, 48.

Hoig, Stanley W. *The Cherokees and Their Chiefs: In the Wake of Empire.* Fayetteville: Univ. of Arkansas Press, 1998. See p. 167.

Jahoda, Gloria. *The Trail of Tears.* New York: Wing Books, 1975. See p. 232.

Lawson, John. *A New Voyage to Carolina; Containing the Exact Description and Natural History of That Country; Together with the Present State Thereof. And A Journal of a Thousand Miles, Travel'd Thro' Several Nations of Indians. Giving a Particular Account of their Customs, Manners, etc.* London, 1709. See p. 120. Available online at Research Laboratories of Archaeology, Univ. of North Carolina at Chapel Hill, Web site: http://rla.unc.edu/Archives/accounts/Lawson/Lawson.html.

Linzey, Alicia V., and Donald W. Linzey. *Mammals of the Great Smoky Mountains National Park.* Knoxville: Univ. of Tennessee Press, 1971. See p. 32.

Longfellow, Henry Wadsworth. *The Song of Hiawatha.* Boston: Houghton Mifflin Company, 1901. See p. 37.

Minser, William G. E-mail to author, Oct. 6, 2005.

American Toad

*Bolles, John A. "Toads." *Harper's New Monthly Magazine* 35, no. 209 (Oct. 1867): 633–38.

Dahl, T. E. "Wetlands: Losses in the United States, 1780's to 1980's." Available online at U.S. Department of the Interior, U.S. Geological Survey, Web site (last updated Mar. 29, 2004): http://www.npwrc.usgs.gov/resource/wetlands/wetloss/wetloss.htm.

Holland, Jennifer S. "Farewell to Frogs?" *National Geographic* 209, no. 1 (Jan. 2006): n.p. (front matter).

Houlahan, Jeff E., C. Scott Findlay, Benedikt R. Schmidt, Andrea H. Meyer and Sergius L. Kuzmin. "Quantitative evidence for global amphibian population declines." *Nature* 404 (Apr. 13, 2000): 752–53.

LaClaire, Linda. "Amphibians in Peril: Resource Management in the Southeast." In *Aquatic Fauna in Peril: The Southeastern Perspective.* Ed. George W. Benz and David E. Collins. Decatur, GA: Lenz Design & Communications, 1997. See pp. 307–33.

Mitchell, John G. "Our Disappearing Wetlands." *National Geographic* 182, no. 4 (Oct. 1992): 3–45.

Morgan, Kenneth L. and Thomas H. Roberts. *An Assessment of Wetland Mitigation in Tennessee.* Nashville: Tennessee Dept. of Environment and Conservation,

Environmental Policy Office, 1999. Available online at http://www.aswm.org/
science/mitigation/morgan99.pdf.

"Population Clocks." U.S. Census Bureau Web site: http://www.census.gov/main/www/
popclock.html.

Royte, Elizabeth. "Transsexual Frogs." *Discover* 24, no. 2 (Feb. 2003): 46–53.

——. "20 Things You Didn't Know About Garbage." *Discover* 27, no. 6 (June 2006): 22.

Thoreau, Henry David. *The Writings of Henry David Thoreau.* Ed. Bradford Torrey. Boston:
Houghton Mifflin. The Riverside Press, 1906. See vol. 5, p. 453, and vol. 8, p. 289.

"Worldwide Amphibian Declines." *Amphibiaweb:* http://amphibiaweb.org/declines/
declines.html.

Freshwater Mussels

Anderson, Margaret, and Robert Marlowe, eds. *Clinton: An Identity Rediscovered.*
Clinton, TN: Clinton Courier-News, 1985. See p. 67.

Clayton, Lawrence, Vernon James Knight, Jr., and Edward C. Moore, eds. *The De Soto
Chronicles: The Expedition of Hernando de Soto to North America in 1539–
1543.* Tuscaloosa: Univ. of Alabama Press, 1993.

Conrad, Joseph. *Heart of Darkness.* New York: St. Martin's Press. 1989. See p. 41.

Hudson, Joyce Rockwood. *Looking for De Soto: A Search through the South for the
Spaniard's Trail.* Athens: Univ. of Georgia Press, 1993. See p. xiv.

Kollar, Robert, and Kelly Leiter. *The Tennessee Valley: A Photographic Portrait.* Lexington: Univ. Press of Kentucky, 1998. See p. 141.

Kunz, George Frederick, and Charles H. Stevenson. *The Book of the Pearl.* New York:
The Century Company, 1908.

Mair, Rachel. Interviewed by author at Virginia Tech, Blacksburg, VA, Mar. 21, 2005.

Parmalee, Paul W., and Arthur E. Bogan. *The Freshwater Mussels of Tennessee.*
Knoxville: Univ. of Tennessee Press, 1998.

Southern Appalachian Biodiversity Project. "Critical Habitat Proposed for Eleven
Mussel Species." *Wild Mountain Times,* May–June 2003: 1.

Tennessee Historical Markers. Eighth Edition. Nashville: Tennessee Historical
Commission, 1996. See p. 131.

Wilson, E. O. *The Diversity of Life.* New York: W.W. Norton, 1992. See p. 182.

Whip-poor-will

Allen, Juanita. "Courtship Behavior of Whip-poor-wills." *The Migrant* 17, no. 2 (June
1946): 28–29.

Bent, Arthur Cleveland. *Life Histories of North America Cuckoos, Goatsuckers, Hummingbirds and Their Allies.* Part 1. New York: Dover Publications. 1964. See p. 176.

*Burroughs, John. "April." *Scribner's Monthly* 13, no. 6 (April 1877): 799.

Burt, William. *Rare and Elusive Birds of North America.* New York: Universe Publishing, 2001. See p. 124.

Chapman, Jefferson. Conversation with author, Oct. 6, 2005.

Emerson, Ralph Waldo. "The Poet." *Essays: Second Series.* In *The Works of Ralph Waldo Emerson.* New York: Tudor Publishing Company, 1941. See p. 256.

*Guernsey, A. H. "Thomas Jefferson and His Family." *Harper's New Monthly* 43, no. 255 (Aug. 1871): 374.

Line, Les. "Silence of the Songbirds." *National Geographic* 183, no. 6 (June 1993): 68–90.

*Munger, Charles A. "Four American Birds." *Putnam's Monthly* 13, no. 18 (June 1869): 729–30.

Nichols, T. Edward. "The Case of the Disappearing Warbler." *National Wildlife* 44, no. 3 (April/May 2006): 22–26.

Robinson, Scott K. "The Case of the Missing Songbirds." *Consequences* 3, no. 1 (1997). Available online at U.S. Global Change Research Information Office Web site: http://www.gcrio.org/CONSEQUENCES/vol3no1/songbirds.html.

"When Population Growth Comes Home to Roost." National Audubon Society Web site: http://www.audubon.org/campaign/population_habitat/poproost.html.

Periodical Cicadas

Andrews, E. A. "Periodical Cicadas in Baltimore, MD." *Scientific Monthly* 12, no. 4 (April 1921): 310–20.

Dykeman, Wilma. *Tennessee: A Bicentennial History.* New York: W. W. Norton, 1975. See p. 41.

Hale, Frank A. *Insects: Periodical Cicadas.* Information sheet SP341-F. Knoxville: Univ. of Tennessee Agricultural Extension Service, 2004 (rev. 2006).

Jacot de Boinod, Adam. "Global Wording." *Smithsonian* 36, no. 12 (Mar. 2006): 112.

Myres, J. G. *Insect Singers. A Natural History of the Cicadas.* London: George Routledge and Sons, 1929. See pp. 22–40.

Ostfeld, Richard S., and Felicia Keesing. "Ecology: Enhanced; Oh the Locusts Sang, Then They Dropped Dead." *Science* 306 (Nov. 26, 2004): 1488–89.

"Seventeen Year Locusts Appear in Battle Array." *Knoxville Journal and Tribune,* May 18, 1919.

"Sgt. York, His Mother, Sister and Bride in Mountain Home." *Knoxville Journal and Tribune,* June 8, 1919.

Simmons, Morgan. "Cicada Mania." *Knoxville News Sentinel,* May 24, 2004.

Smith, Luke. "Old Broods of the Periodical Cicada." *Insect Life* 4, no. 3 (Nov. 1891): 141.

Thoreau, Henry David. *The Natural History Essays.* Salt Lake City: Peregrine Smith Books, 1980. See p. 5.

Webster, F. M. "An Early Occurrence of the Periodical Cicada." *Insect Life* 2, no. 5 (Nov. 1889): 161.

Yang, Louie. H. "Periodical Cicadas as Resource Pulses in North American Forests." *Science* 306 (Nov. 26, 2004): 1565–67.

Gray Bat

Ackerman, Diane. *The Moon by Whale Light.* New York: Random House, 1991. See p. 33.

Allen, Glover Morrill. *Bats.* New York: Dover Publications, 1939.

"Endangered Species Recovery Team Reports Gains and Losses." *Bats* 6, no. 2 (Summer 1988): 11.

*Fawcett, William Lyman. "A Tour in the Dark." *Atlantic Monthly* 20, no. 122 (Dec. 1867): 671.

*"A Good Word for the Bats." *Manufacturer and Builder* 3, no. 7 (July 1871): 161.

"Gray Bat: *Myotis grisescens.*" Species account. U.S. Fish and Wildlife Service, Division of Endangered Species, Web site: http://www.fws.gov/endangered/i/a/saa4l. html.

*Gray, F. M. "A Trip to the Wyandotte Cave." *The Galaxy* 5, no. 6 (June 1868): 749.

Harvey, Michael J., J. Scott Altenbach, and Troy L. Best. *Bats of the United States.* Asheville, NC: Arkansas Game and Fish Commission and U.S. Fish and Wildlife Service, 1999.

Lawson, John. *A New Voyage to Carolina; Containing the Exact Description and Natural History of That Country; Together with the Present State Thereof. And A Journal of a Thousand Miles, Travel'd Thro' Several Nations of Indians. Giving a Particular Account of their Customs, Manners, etc.* London, 1709. See p. 125. Available online at Research Laboratories of Archaeology, Univ. of North Carolina at Chapel Hill, Web site: http://rla.unc.edu/Archives/accounts/Lawson/ Lawson.html.

Locke, Robert. "The Gray Bat's Survival." *Bats* 20, no. 2 (Summer/Fall 2002): 4–9.

Mitchell, Wilma A. *Species Profile: Gray Bat (Myotis grisescens) on Military Installations in the Southeastern United States.* Technical Report SERDP-98-6. Washington, DC: U.S. Army Corps of Engineers, 1998.

"Reasons for Decline." U.S. Fish and Wildlife Service, Division of Endangered Species, Bats, Web site: http://www.fws.gov/endangered/bats/threats.htm.

Shakespeare, William. *Macbeth.* In *The Oxford Shakespeare: The Complete Works.* 2nd Edition. Oxford: Clarendon Press, 2005. See p. 984.

*Sheldon, George. "Forty Years of Frontier Life in the Pocomtuck Valley." *New England Magazine* 4, no. 3 (Mar. 1886): 247.

Tuttle, Merlin. E-mail to author, July 29, 2004.

———. "Endangered Gray Bat Benefits from Protection." *Bat* 4, no. 4 (Dec. 1986): 1–3.

———. "Joint Effort Saves Vital Bat Cave." *Bats* 2, no. 4 (Dec. 1985): 3–4.

Passionflower

Akhondzadeh S., H. R. Naghavi, M. Vazirian, et al. "Passionflower in the Treatment of Generalized Anxiety: A Pilot Double-Blind Randomized Controlled Trail with Oxazepam." *Alternative Medicine Review* 6, no. 6 (Dec. 2001): 617.

Banks, W. H. "Ethnobotany of the Cherokee Indians." M.S. thesis, Univ. of Tennessee, 1953. See p. 89.

Coffey, Timothy. *The History and Folklore of North American Wildflowers.* New York: Houghton Mifflin Company, 1993.

Ehrlich, Gretel. *John Muir: Nature's Visionary.* Washington, DC: National Geographic Society, 2000. See p. 62.

Els, David, ed. *The National Gardening Association Dictionary of Horticulture.* New York: Penguin Books, 1994. See p. 594.

Fisher, Alex A, Patrick J. Purcell, David G. Le Couteur. "Toxicity of Passiflora incarnata L." *Journal of Toxicology: Clinical Toxicology* 38, no. 1 (Jan. 2000): 63.

Fausz, J. Frederick. "Pocahontas (Matoaka)." *Encyclopedia of North American Indians.* Available online at Houghton Mifflin Web site: http://college.hmco.com/ history/readerscomp/naind/html/na_029700_pocahontas.htm.

*King, Edward. "The Great South." *Scribner's Monthly* 7, no. 5 (Mar, 1874): 528.

King, Frankie. E-mail to author, June 26, 2003. King is the Tennessee state librarian.

Muir, John. *A Thousand-Mile Walk to the Gulf.* San Francisco: Sierra Club Book, 1991. 18–23.

Perry, Myra Jean. "Food Use of 'Wild' Plants by Cherokee Indians." M.S. thesis, Univ. of Tennessee, 1975. See p. 50.

"School Children to Vote on State Flower." *Nashville Banner,* Jan. 26, 1919.

Smith, John. "Of such things which are naturally in Virginia, and how the[y] use them." from John Smith's *Generall Historie of Virginia.* Available online at Virginia Commonwealth Univ. Web site: www.vcu.edu/engweb/eng385/jsmith.html.

———. "The Travels of Captaine John Smith in Two Volumes: The Generall Historie of Virginia, New England & The Summer Isles." London, 1624. Available online at *WebRoots.org: Nonprofit Library for Genealogy & History-Related Research:* http://www.webroots.org/library/usahist/ghov1-00.html.

Darters

Abbey, Edward. *Down the River.* New York: Penguin Books, 1991. See p. 48.

Ayres, Drummond. "Controversy Over 3-Inch Fish Stalls the Mighty T.V.A." *New York Times,* Mar. 14, 1977.

Beazley, Ernie, and John Means. "Senate Again Blocks Tellico Dam." *Knoxville Journal,* July 18, 1979.

Brewer, Carson. "TVA—Saint or Sinner? Environmental Record of Agency is Impressive." *Knoxville News Sentinel,* Feb. 24, 1974.

———. "TVA—Saint or Sinner? Fight Over Tellico Dam Has Raged Since 1965." *Knoxville News Sentinel,* Feb. 13, 1974.

Carter, Luther J. "Lessons from the Snail Darter Saga." *Journal Science* 203, no. 4382 (Feb. 23, 1979): 730.

Etnier, David A. and Wayne C. Starnes. *The Fishes of Tennessee.* Knoxville: Univ. of
   Tennessee Press, 1993.

"Foes of Tellico Dam Press Carter To Veto Bill OK'd in Senate." *Knoxville News Sentinel,*
   Sept. 11, 1979.

Rakes, Patrick, and J. R. Shute. Conversation with author. Aug. 29, 2005.

Reid, Clark. "House Approves Tellico Dam Go-Ahead." *Knoxville News Sentinel,*
   June 19, 1979.

Starnes, Wayne C. "The Ecology and Life History of the Endangered Snail Darter,
   Percina (Imostoma) Tanasi Etnier." Ph.D. diss., Univ. of Tennessee, 1977.

"Tellico Triumph: Defeat of the Snail Darter." *Time Magazine,* Oct, 8, 1979, 105.

Thompson, Jim, and Cynthia Brooks. *Tellico Dam and the Snail Darter.* Knoxville:
   Spectrum Communications, 1991.

Venable, Sam. Conversation with author, Aug. 1, 2005.

———. "Huh?" *Knoxville News Sentinel,* Oct. 13, 1974.

———. "Snail Darter is Endangered: 'New' Fish Could Stop Tellico Dam." *Knoxville News
   Sentinel,* Oct. 27, 1974.

Wheeler, Marcey. E-mail to author, June 18, 2005.

Wheeler, William Bruce, and Michael J. McDonald. *TVA and the Tellico Dam, 1936–
   1979.* Knoxville: Univ. of Tennessee Press, 1986. See p. 189.

Pawpaw

Glick, Barry. "Pawpaws: Tropical Trees for the Temperate Zone." *Plants & Garden News*
   12, no. 3 (Fall 1997, Brooklyn Botanic Garden website. (www.bbg.org/gar2/
   topics/wildflower/1997fa_pawpaws.html).

———. "Pawpaws—A Tropical Tree for the Temperate Zone." Brooklyn Botanic Garden
   Web site: http://www.bbg.org/gar2/topics/wildflower/1997fa_pawpaws.html.

"Jefferson's Confidential Letter to Congress." A transcription of the original letter,
   Jan. 18, 1803. Monticello: The Home of Thomas Jefferson Web site: http://
   monticello.org/jefferson/lewisandclark/congress_letter.html.

Lawson, John. *A New Voyage to Carolina; Containing the Exact Description and Natural History of That Country; Together with the Present State Thereof. And A
   Journal of a Thousand Miles, Travel'd Thro' Several Nations of Indians. Giving
   a Particular Account of their Customs, Manners, etc.* London, 1709. See pp. iv,
   105. Available online at Research Laboratories of Archaeology, Univ. of North
   Carolina at Chapel Hill, Web site: http://rla.unc.edu/Archives/accounts/Lawson/
   Lawson.html.

Lembke, Janet. *Shake Them 'Simmons Down.* New York: Lyons & Burford, 1996.
   See p. 146.

"Lewis and Clark: The Journey Ends." *Smithsonian* 36, no. 9 (Dec. 2005): 32–33.

Moulton, Gary E. ed. *The Journals of the Lewis and Clark Expedition.* 13 vols. Lincoln: Univ. of Nebraska Press, 1993–2001. See vol. 8, *Clark's Journal,* pp. 361, 365; vol. 9, *Ordway's Journal,* p. 365; vol. 10, *Glass's Journal,* p. 279.

———. *The Lewis and Clark Journals: An American Epic of Discovery; The Abridgment of the Definitive Nebraska Edition.* Lincoln: University of Nebraska Press, 2003.

"'Ocian in View! O! The Joy': Lewis and Clark; 200 Years Ago This Month." *Smithsonian* 36, no. 8 (Nov. 2005): 22.

Pickering, Charles. *Chronological History of Plants.* Boston: Little, Brown, 1879. See p. 880.

Riley, James Whitcomb. *The Complete Poetical Works of James Whitcomb Riley.* New York: Grosset & Dunlap, 1937. See p. 522.

Opossum

Araiza, A.E. "Arizona Roadkill: Huge Toll on Park-Area Highways." *Arizona Daily Star* (Tucson), May 16, 2005.

*"The Contributor's Club." *Atlantic Monthly* 73, no. 437 (March 1894): 427–28.

Eastman, Charles R. "Early Portrayals of the Opossum." *American Naturalist* 49, no. 586 (Oct. 1915): 585–594. Available online at *JSTOR: The Scholarly Journal Archive:* http://www.jstor.org/.

Fox, Douglas S. "Pouch or No Pouch. That is the Question." *Discover* 25, no. 7 (July 2004): 68–75.

Lawson, John. *A New Voyage to Carolina; Containing the Exact Description and Natural History of That Country; Together with the Present State Thereof. And A Journal of a Thousand Miles, Travel'd Thro' Several Nations of Indians. Giving a Particular Account of their Customs, Manners, etc.* London, 1709. See pp. 120–21. Available online at Research Laboratories of Archaeology, Univ. of North Carolina at Chapel Hill, Web site: http://rla.unc.edu/Archives/accounts/Lawson/Lawson.html.

*Lossing, Benson J. "Early Secessionists." *Harper's New Monthly* 24, no. 142 (Mar. 1862): 515.

Hoig, Stanley W. *The Cherokees and Their Chiefs: In the Wake of Empire.* Fayetteville: Univ. of Arkansas Press, 1998. See p. 72.

Nickens, T. Edward. "A Strange, Wondrous Beast of Our Backyards." *National Wildlife* 41, no. 1 (Dec.–Jan. 2003): 18–19.

Parrish, Susan Scott. "The Female Opossum and the Nature of the New World." *William and Mary Quarterly,* 3rd ser., 54, no. 3 (July 1997): 475–514. Available online at *JSTOR: The Scholarly Journal Archive:* http://www.jstor.org.

Smith, John. *A Map of Virginia: With a Description of the Countrey, the Commodities, People, Government and Religion.* Oxford, 1612. See p. 93. Available online at *American Journeys: Early Accounts of American Exploration and Settlement;*

A Digital Library and Learning Center, Web site developed by Wisconsin Historical Society. See document no. AJ-075: http://www.americanjourneys. org/aj-075/index.asp.

Wild Turkey

"About the NWTF." National Wild Turkey Federation Web site: http://www.nwtf.org/ about_us.

Bartram, William. *Travels of William Bartram.* Ed. Mark Van Doren. New York: Dover Publications, 1928. See pp. 39, 89, 90.

Bent, Arthur Cleveland. *Bent's Life Histories of North American Birds.* New York: Harper & Brothers, 1960.

Bradford, William. "From *History of Plymouth Plantation,* c. 1650." *Internet Modern History Sourcebook,* Web site sponsored by Fordham Univ.: http://www. fordham.edu/Halsall/mod/1650bradford.html.

"Mid-Winter, Christmas Bird Counts." *The Migrant* 17–28 (Dec. issues, 1946–57).

Dickson, James G. "Return of Wild Turkeys." In *Our Living Resources: A Report to the Nation on the Distribution, Abundance, and Health of U.S. Plants, Animals, and Ecosystems,* Web site developed by U.S. Dept. of the Interior, National Biological Service: http://biology.usgs.gov/s+t/noframe/b028.htm.

Espinoza, Mauricio. "Talking Turkey: Myth and Truth about the All-American Bird." Nov. 26, 2002. Online article at Ohio State Univ. Web site: http://extension.osu. edu/~news/story.php?id=2347.

Heath, Dwight, ed. *A Journal of the Pilgrims at Plymouth: Mourt's Relation, A Relation or Journal of the English Plantation settled at Plymouth in New England, by certain English adventurers both merchants and others.* New York: Corinth Books, 1963. See p. 82.

*Hennepin, Father. "Early American Travels." *United States Democratic Review* 5, no. 16. (Apr. 1839): 382.

Hodge, Bob. "Turkey Boom Over?" *Knoxville News Sentinel,* Apr. 30, 2006.

Isaacson, Walter. *Benjamin Franklin: An American Life.* New York: Simon & Schuster, 2003.

Lewis, James C. "The Status of Wild Turkeys in Tennessee." *The Migrant* 33, no. 4. (Dec. 1962): 61.

Lewis, M. N. Thomas, and Madeline Kneberg. *Hiwassee Island: An Archaeological Account of Four Tennessee Indian Peoples.* Knoxville: Univ. of Tennessee Press, 1946.

Morton, Thomas, of Merrymount. *New English Canaan.* Ed. Jack Dempsey. Scituate, MA: Digital Scanning, Inc, 2000. See page 64.

Rasles, Father Père Sébastien. Letter dated October 12, 1723. From "The Jesuit Relations and Allied Documents: Travels and Explorations of the Jesuit Mission-

aries in New France, 1610–1791." Transcribed by Jon Zychowski, Parkland
College. Available online at http://virtual.parkland.edu/lstelle1/len/Illini%20eth
nohistory%20project/rasles.htm.

Ross, Jack Winfield. "Tennessee Wildlife on the Comeback Trail." *Tennessee
Conservationist,* Oct. 1993, 24–28.

Savage, Henry, Jr., and Elizabeth Savage. *André and François André Michaux.*
Charlottesville: Univ. Press of Virginia, 1986.

Schorger, A. W. *The Wild Turkey: Its History and Domestication.* Norman: Univ. of
Oklahoma Press, 1966.

Wetmore, Alexander. "The Turkeys, Grouse, Quail, and Pigeons." In *The Book of Birds.*
Vol. 1. Washington: National Geographic Society, 1932. See p. 219.

Williams, Lovett E. *Wild Turkey Country.* Minnetonka, WI: NorthWord Press, 1991.

Wilson, Alexander, and Charles Lucian Bonaparte. "The Wild Turkey." Excerpt from *The
American Ornithology. The Migrant* 16, no. 2 (June 1945): 18–19.

Osage Orange

*Barnard, Charles. "Silk Culture at Home." *The Century* 28, no. 3 (July 1884): 475.

"The Battle of Franklin." The Carter House Web site: http://www.carter-house.org/
TheBattle.htm.

Catton, Bruce. *Never Call Retreat.* New York: Washington Square Press, 1965. See
pp. 390–91.

Chisholm, Colin. "Undaunted Botany." *Sierra* 87, no. 3 (May–June, 2002). Available
online at Sierra Club Web site: http://www.sierraclub.org/sierra/200205/
botany.asp.

Dougherty, Steve. "Havens; . . . And Bulldozing It." *New York Times,* Apr. 30, 2004.

Gleick, James. *Chaos: Making a New Science.* New York: Penguin Books, 1987. See p. 23.

Goodheart, Adam. "Civil War Battlefields: Saving the Landscapes of America's
Deadliest War." *National Geographic* 207, no. 4 (Apr. 2005): 62–85.

Horn, Stanley F. *The Army of Tennessee.* Norman: Univ. of Oklahoma Press, 1941.

*J.T.D. "Osage Orange Hedges and Mulching Potatoes with Straw." *Scientific American*
11, no. 20 (Nov. 12, 1864): 310.

*Lodge, William C. "Among the Peaches." *Harper's* 41, no. 244 (Sept. 1870): 514.

Logsdon, David R. *Eyewitnesses at the Battle of Franklin.* Nashville: Kettle Mills Press,
1996. See pp. 46–47.

McDonough, James Lee, and Thomas L. Connelly. *Five Tragic Hours: The Battle of
Franklin.* Knoxville: Univ. of Tennessee Press, 1983. See pp. 145, 156–57.

*"Osage Orange Fences." *Scientific American* 13, no. 30 (Apr. 3, 1858): 238.

"The South." *The William Wing Loring World Wide Web Site:* http://loring.atomicmartinis.
com/south.htm.

Sources

*"The Osage Orange for Hedges." *Scientific American* 9, no. 32 (Apr. 22, 1854): 254.

Stoeckeler, Joseph H., and Ross A. Williams. "Windbreaks and Shelterbelts." *Yearbook of Agriculture 1949*. Washington: United States Department of Agriculture/U.S. Government Printing Office, 1949.

"Tennessee Champion Trees." Tennessee Department of Agriculture, *Tennessee.gov* Web site: http://www.state.tn.us/agriculture/forestry/champions/.

Eastern Sycamore

"Alan Shepard –Golf Out of This World." *Pasture Golf* Web site: http://www.pasturegolf. com/archive/shepard.htm.

*Barry, J. S. "Old Trees." *Atlantic Monthly* 34, no. 206 (Dec. 1874): 683.

De Wall, Frans. *Good Natured*. Cambridge, MA: Harvard Univ. Press, 1996. See p. 41.

Ganier, Albert F. "The Wild Life Met by Tennessee's First Settlers." *The Migrant* 44, no. 1 (Sept. 1973): 65.

Harris, Marjorie. *Botanica North America*. New York: HarperCollins, 2003.

*King, Edward. "The Great South." *Scribner's Monthly* 7, no. 5 (Mar. 1874): 527–28.

Lawson, John. *A New Voyage to Carolina; Containing the Exact Description and Natural History of That Country; Together with the Present State Thereof. And A Journal of a Thousand Miles, Travel'd Thro' Several Nations of Indians. Giving a Particular Account of their Customs, Manners, etc.* London, 1709. See p. 142. Available online at Research Laboratories of Archaeology, Univ. of North Carolina at Chapel Hill, Web site: http://rla.unc.edu/Archives/accounts/Lawson/Lawson.html.

McKinley, Daniel. "A Review of the Carolina Parakeet in Tennessee." *The Migrant* 50, no. 1 (March 1979): 1.

Nicholson, Charles P. *Atlas of the Breeding Birds of Tennessee*. Knoxville: Univ. of Tennessee Press, 1997. See pp. 11–12, 41–42.

Parmalee, Paul. Conversation with author, Dec. 8, 2005.

Peattie, Donald Culross. *A Natural History of Trees of Eastern and Central North America*. Boston: Houghton Mifflin, 1948.

Petrides, George A. *Eastern Trees*. Peterson Field Guide. Boston: Houghton Mifflin, 1988. See p. 123.

Phillips, Tony. "In Search of Moon Trees." *Science @ NASA* Web site: http://science.nasa.gov/headlines/y2002/13aug_moontrees.htm.

Snyder, Noel F. R., and Keith Russell. "Carolina Parakeet (*Conuropsis carolinensis*)." In *The Birds of North America*. No. 667. Ed. A. Pool and F. Gill. Philadelphia: Birds of North America, Inc., 2002. Available at *The Birds of North America Online*: http://bna.birds.cornell.edu/BNA/account/Carolina_Parakeet/.

Wilson, Alexander. "Carolina Parakeet." Excerpt from *Wilson's American Ornithology with notes by Jardines* (1840), available online at Virginia Commonwealth University Web site: http://www.vcu.edu/engweb/eng385/parrakeettxt. htm#parakeet.

Bald Eagle

Beans, Bruce E. *Eagle's Plume: The Struggle to Preserve the Life and Haunts of America's Bald Eagle.* New York: Scribner, 1996. See pp. 57, 72–103.

Breining, Greg. *Return of the Eagle: How America Saved its National Symbol.* Guilford, CT: Globe Pequot Press, 1994. See p. 43.

*Burroughs, John. "Glimpses of Wild Life about My Cabin." *Century Popular Quarterly* 58, no. 4 (Aug. 1899): 511.

Cokinos, Christopher. *Hope is the Thing with Feathers.* New York: Jeremy P. Tarcher/ Putnam, 2000. P. 336.

Hatcher, Robert M. E-mail to author, July 21, 2004.

———. "Encounters of a Tennessee-Hacked Bald Eagle." *The Migrant* 64, no. 2 (1993): 32.

———. "Nesting Bald Eagles in Tennessee: 1965–1990." *The Migrant* 61, no. 4 (1990): 89–90.

Hoff, Ron. "The 2002 Christmas Bird Count." *The Migrant* 74, no. 2 (June 2003): 36–38.

Kerouac, Jack. *On the Road.* New York: Viking Penguin, 1997.

Longfellow, Henry Wordsworth. *The Song of Hiawatha.* Boston: Houghton Mifflin, 1901. See pp. 13–15.

Mooney, James. *History, Myths, and Sacred Formulas of the Cherokees.* Asheville, NC: Historical Images/Bright Mountain Books, 1992. See pp. 280–83.

Nicholson, Charles P. *Atlas of the Breeding Birds of Tennessee.* Univ. of Tennessee Press. Knoxville, TN. 1997. See pp. 100–101.

Roedel, Michael and Bob Hatcher. *Bald Facts about Bald Eagles.* TWRA fact sheet. January 2005.

Schacher, Wayne H. "Seven Islands Wildlife Refuge: The Vision and Concept." *through the biKNOXulars* (KTOS newsletter), Aug. 2004, 3.

———. "Seven Islands Wildlife Refuge: The Early Successional Habitats Present." *through the biKNOXulars* (KTOS newsletter), Oct. 2004, 3.

Index

Natural Histories was designed and typeset on a Macintosh computer system using InDesign software. The body text is set in 9.5/13.5 Warnock Pro and display type is set in Zapfino and ITC Stone Sans. This book was designed and typeset by Kelly Gray, and manufactured by Thomson-Shore, Inc.